THE GLOBAL MANAGEMENT SERIES

The Essentials of Digital Marketing

Kathryn Waite and Rodrigo Perez-Vega

 Goodfellow Publishers Ltd

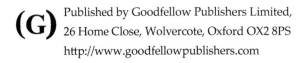

Published by Goodfellow Publishers Limited,
26 Home Close, Wolvercote, Oxford OX2 8PS
http://www.goodfellowpublishers.com

Published 2018

British Library Cataloguing in Publication Data: a catalogue record for this title is available from the British Library.

Library of Congress Catalog Card Number: on file.

ISBN: 978-1-911396-00-0

This book is part of the Global Management series

ISSN: 2514-7862

Copyright © Kathryn Waite and Rodrigo Perez-Vega, 2018

 Design and typesetting by P.K. McBride, www.macbride.org.uk

Cover design by Cylinder

Printed by Baker & Taylor, www.baker-taylor.com

Contents

Acknowledgements

We position this book as an essential introduction to digital marketing activity. The rapid rate of change associated with digital technology makes writing a comprehensive book about digital marketing practically impossible! Emerging areas as we write are wearable tech, the internet of things and the use of virtual reality. The current book contains topics that form the basis of our teaching and research and which offer insight into established areas of digital marketing practice. We owe thanks to the guest lecturers and students on the undergraduate and postgraduate Digital Marketing courses that we teach, who inspire, inform and challenge us. Special recognition is given to Sam Weston for the invaluable technical insight into search marketing and to Sally North at Goodfellow Publishers for inspiring and guiding the writing process.

KW & RPV

Dedication

To my husband Martin, who puts up with me spending more time with my computer than with him, and to my Mum, Dad and sister, Helen. Thank you! KW

To Arturo and Maud, who bring so much happiness to my life, and to my parents, for all their love and support. Thank you.

RPV

Preface

Digital technology has transformed marketing practice, resulting in a need to update practical marketing skills, to gain knowledge of specialist terms and to gain understanding of new patterns of consumer behaviour (Wymbs 2011). Exact digital marketing terms are still being determined which can lead to inconsistency and confusion. For clarity, this book uses the terminology set out in Table A.

Table A: Digital Marketing Terminology

Term	Description	Examples
Device	The technology used to access the internet	PC, Tablet or Phone, Game console
Platform	The generic form	Web 1.0 (websites), Web 2.0 (Social Media), Video on demand, Mobile Messaging etc.
Provider	Company which owns the channel or vehicle	Facebook, Twitter, Alphabet (Google), Yahoo , Amazon, Microsoft, etoc
Channel	The communication or transaction channel	LinkedIn, Facebook, Instagram, Twitter, Youtube, Google+, Flickr, Tumblr Word Press, Instagram, Whatsapp, retailer website, etc
Website or page	The location denoted by an URL or other identifier of the brand	e.g. the Heriot Watt Website, the Heriot Watt Facebook page, the textbook page on Amazon, the Hotel review page on Tripadvisor, etc.

This book is designed to give the reader a 'place to start' in addressing the challenges and opportunities of the digital marketspace. The featured topics provide an overview of essential concepts and techniques that comprise digital marketing; each chapter combines academic theory with digital marketing techniques to deliver a robust understanding of this exciting new area. This approach will help students transition to being marketing practitioners and supply practitioners with frameworks for digital brand management. The content assumes some familiarity with marketing concepts gained by work experience or in preceding education. Useful introductory reading is found in the following Global Management Series publications:

- Bell, G. and Taheri, B. (2017) *Marketing Communications, An Advertising, Promotion and Branding Perspective,* Goodfellow Oxford.
- Mckay, G., Hopkinson, P. and Lai Hong, N. (2018), *Fundamentals of Marketing,* Goodfellow Oxford.

Book contents and layout

Chapter 1: The Digital Marketing Mix. At the core of the marketing discipline are the processes of segmentation, targeting and positioning (STP) that inform the design of the marketing mix. The reduction of marketing tactics to the 4Ps (or 5Ps or 7Ps) is criticised as being too simplistic, but this long-standing framework has proven its worth in acting as a checklist of techniques. The Internet provides access to information and products regardless of time of day or place of transaction. Digital marketing activity needs to ensure that the brand engages meaningfully with current and future customers in order to meet their needs across all digital channels, platforms and devices. The purpose of this chapter is to act not only as a reminder of STP and the marketing mix elements but also to introduce you to how developments in digital technology provide new opportunities and challenges for marketing academics and practitioners.

A suite of three chapters: **2: Digital Technology Adoption**; **3: Customer Experience Design** and **4: Digital Service Quality** focus upon the digital market-space and behaviours linked to digital product and place. Digital technology adoption applies to the continued use of a device, platform channel or website process. Chapter 2 explains the processes of innovation adoption, continuance and discontinuance using the established theories of technology acceptance, the diffusion of innovation, and uses and gratifications theory to identify the key influences upon consumer decision making.

Customer Experience Design (CXD) has the goal of providing consumers with personalised and memorable engagement. Each point of contact between brand and consumer provides a customer experience and the number of contact points has exploded with the advent of digital channels, platforms and devices. Chapter 3 introduces the concept of the customer journey and draws theories and processes from psychology and design.

One strategy open to digital marketers is to ensure repeat custom through offering a quality e-service that delivers customer satisfaction. Chapter 4 explains the concept of digital service quality with reference to theories of expectation disconfirmation and the SERVQUAL measurement process (Parasuraman et al., 1988). Increasing competition in the market-space means that it is important to ensure that customers make judgements of e-service quality and satisfaction when using a digital channel. Digital marketing managers need to make careful choices regarding which features to include in the channel design in order to control implementation costs.

This chapter explains how system quality, information quality, transaction quality and community quality should be managed.

Engagement is a concept applied to digital marketing and chapters **5: Online Consumer Engagement, 6: Crowdsourcing and Crowdfunding** and **7: Digital Content Planning** focus upon this concept. Online consumer engagement (OCE) refers to online interactive experiences between consumers and the brand, and/or other consumers. There are many benefits associated with an engaged consumer, including opportunities to co-create value, products, and ideas. However, brands may not have complete control of how and when consumer engagement occurs (e.g. in blogs and forums that are not controlled by the brand). In Chapter 5, it argued that an understanding of social influence principles (and in particular the application of social impact theory in different digital contexts) can be a productive tool to harness engagement across digital environments.

Chapter 6 discusses the new concepts of crowdsourcing and crowdfunding. Crowdsourcing is practice of "taking a job traditionally performed by a designated agent (usually an employee) and outsourcing it to an undefined, generally large group of people in the form of an open call" (Saxton et al., 2013: 3). Crowdfunding is "an open call, mostly through the Internet, for the provision of financial resources" (Belleflamme et al., 2014:4). Whilst there are several benefits of these approaches, there are also risks of poor output quality and questions about the ethics of replacing paid employment with crowdsourced labour. This chapter focuses upon the benefits and challenges and provides an account of the processes and mechanisms that digital marketers can use to manage these activities.

Chapter 7 examines how the diversification of communication models in digital media gives marketers a wide range of media channels from which to choose when creating and disseminating content. In general terms, these channels can be classified as owned, paid, and earned media. Once the media channels are selected, designing digital content to reach marketing objectives requires a good understanding of the effects of different types of content, messages, and sources of content, as these will have an impact on the consumer and its perception of the brand. This chapter examines how a transmedia and integrated approach to digital content can magnify impact and facilitate brand positioning.

The following three chapters focus upon the evaluation of digital marketing activity. Organisations use metrics and analytics to continuously improve their digital content in order to better serve customer needs, maintain functionality and remain competitive. It is tempting to use the terms metrics and analytics interchangeably as if they have the same meaning but they are two distinct concepts.

Chapter 8: Metrics and Analytics explains the difference between metrics and analytics and shows how this information can be applied to generate understanding of the digital customer life cycle as well as key marketing to develop customer insight, assess campaign effectiveness and calculate return on investment.

Chapter 9: Website Analytics explains that digital marketers need to understand how to measure website performance and link these outcomes to marketing activity at each stage of the digital customer lifecycle. Conversion goals are important as they help an organisation achieve its overall marketing aim, for example to make a sale or to encourage interaction with particular content. This chapter introduces a range of metrics and analytics that are available at each stage towards conversion.

Chapter 10: Social Media Analytics shows how social media metrics and analytics assess the influence of social media activities on the relationship between the brand and the consumer. Social media platforms provide a range of real-time data that shows the level of brand involvement, interaction, intimacy and the degree of influence of brand advocates. In order to track the performance of a social media marketing campaign digital marketers need to select the analytics that are appropriate for the digital strategy. This chapter introduces the considerations of channel performance and attribution of influence and also considers issues of ethics and legality to ensure that the brand reputation is protected.

The final two chapters focus upon digital marketing practice: **11: The Digital Marketing Skills Gap** and **12: Developing an Online Profile.** Many students who are interested in a career in digital marketing may be discouraged from pursuing jobs in this sector because of the often incorrect assumption that a deep technical knowledge is needed to succeed as a digital marketer. However, there are many roles in this field that are suitable for those with skills in management, marketing, and creative arts. Chapter 11 examines the digital marketing skills gap and uses the Digital Marketer Model (Royle and Laing, 2014) to show that digital marketing roles can be placed on a spectrum with technical skills at one extreme and with marketing management skills at the other extreme.

Chapter 12 suggest that like brand, an individual can strategically select and highlight those attributes that will advance them towards their goals.

Personal branding can differentiate an individual within a competitive job market. The availability, low-costs and ease of use of a range of online tools enable individuals to effectively communicate across a range of digital channels. This chapter outlines key considerations when publishing a blog and developing an online professional network on LinkedIn. It shows how a strategic selection of content is needed to develop a compelling narrative and connect with the audience.

Digital marketing is a fast-moving and evolving professional discipline and we both feel fortunate to be researching and teaching in this exciting field of knowledge. We hope that this book communicates our enthusiasm for this subject and inspires you to pursue this topic further.

Kathryn and Rodrigo

References

Belleflamme, P., Lambert, T. and Schwienbacher, A. (2014), Crowdfunding: tapping the right crowd, *Journal of Business Venturing,* **29**(5), 585-609.

Parasuraman, A., Zeithaml, V.A. and Berry, L.L. (1988), SERVQUAL: A multiple-item scale for measuring consumer perceptions of service quality. *Journal of Retailing,* **64**(1), 12-40.

Royle, J. and Laing, A. (2014), The digital marketing skills gap: developing a digital marketer model for the communication industries, *International Journal of Information Management*, 34(2), 65-73.

Saxton, G.D., Oh, O. and Kishore, R. (2013), Rules of crowdsourcing: models, issues, and systems of control, *Information Systems Management*, **30**(1), 2-20.

Wymbs, C. (2011), Digital Marketing: The time for a new "academic major" has arrived, *Journal of Marketing Education*, **33**(1), 93-106.

1 Digital Marketing Mix

Welcome to the world of digital marketing! The development of the Internet can be traced from 1991 when the creation of Hypertext mark-up language enabled the sharing of documents over the World Wide Web (Chaffey et al., 2009). Early use of the Internet required not only technical expertise but also access to computer hardware and software (Breitenbach and Van Doren, 1998). However, developments in software, the launch of the Netscape browser and the rise in the number of households with personal computers all contributed to an expansion of personal and commercial use which is continuing today (Chaffey et al., 2009). Indeed, with 4G and mobile phone access the Internet has become "potentially available to all." (Wyatt et al., 2002:25). In this chapter we examine how marketing practices have been translated to the digital medium, beginning with a discussion of market segmentation and the marketing mix.

Market segmentation

Having a mass marketing strategy – where one product and marketing plan fits all – is no longer a prominent view in marketing academia and practice. Even commodity products, such as salt or water, are targeted to meet the needs of different market segments. Market segmentation is the process of identifying "homogenous subsets of the mass market by clustering (grouping) customers on a set of variables" (Kara and Kaynak, 1997). In general terms, there are two ways in which marketers can segment their market:

- **A-priori** segmentation where the classification variables are set from the beginning, and then buyers are put into a group based on those variables. An example of this would be a mobile phone manufacturer who decides to divide the market into two segments by gender (male and female) and then designs a marketing mix that is gender specific

- **Post hoc** segmentation, where the marketer uses research to cluster individuals into distinct groups, based on similarity in response scores to a combination of criteria that can include behavioural, psychological, demographic and geographic variables (Wind, 1978). In contrast to a-priori the criteria by which groups will be divided is not deductively imposed on the groups but inductively generated. If the mobile phone manufacturer selected this approach they could identify market segments based on attitude towards technology, location and extent of phone use.

The market segment that a marketer decides to focus on is known as the *target audience*. One company can have several target audiences. For examples, a cereal company such as Kellogg's have target audiences based on age (kids and adults), and also target markets based on psychographic variables such as lifestyle (people on a diet, people looking for high fibre breakfast, people craving for a tasty breakfast). A particular market segment of interest to digital marketers are Millennials, a generational cohort that were born between 1981 and 1997. Millennials have grown up being familiar with and using digital technology (Taken Smith, 2012). In addition to segmenting Millennials a-priori according to age, researchers have undertaken post-hoc segmentation to further separate individuals into distinct target markets. For example, Tanyel et al. (2013) examine attitudes to internet advertising amongst Millennials. Marketers use the insight gained from segmentation to position their product in the marketplace using an appropriate formulation of the marketing mix.

Positioning

Positioning is the way a target audience perceives a product or service in relation to its competitors. The judgement will be based on previous experience and signals given by the marketing mix components. After conducting a strategic marketing analysis, a brand can choose to assume a particular position within a marketplace. Baines et al. (2011) identify four key market positions

- **Market leader** – when taking this position the brand communicates that: it sets standards; it continually innovates and claims the largest market share. In the design and execution of its marketing mix it will indicate that it clearly excels on key consumer decision-making criteria. An example of a market leader would be the Apple i-phone.

- **Market challenger** – when taking this position the brand seeks to beat the market leader in one or more areas of key performance in order to gain market supremacy. The emphasis will be placed on being better than the market leader in particularly important areas. The market challenger signals that it aims to be the market leader of the future through its selection of important areas. An example of a market challenger would be the Google phone.

- **Market follower** – when taking this position the brand accepts that it will have a lower market share but that it can maintain and defend this position by learning from the market leader in the field. A market follower copies the successes and avoids the mistakes of the market leader, this is called a me-too approach. An example of a market follower would be an LG phone.

- **Market nicher** – when taking this position the brand seeks to be recognised as a specialist in a clearly delimited area. The purpose is that by meeting the needs of a small subset of the total market the brand can take a position that is defendable and profitable. An example of a market nicher would be the Zanco Fly – a phone that is made entirely of plastic and undetectable by scanning devices.

To position a product successfully within the market, an appropriate formulation of the marketing mix is required. The marketing mix has changed in response to the technological changes of the last two decades, thus it is important to consider each element of the digital marketing mix.

Marketing mix elements

The marketing mix is a prominent model within marketing education, and it is widely used among practitioners. Developed in the late 60s by Borden (1964) and then refined to its most popular stage (the 4Ps) by Jerome McCarthy (1964), it provides a framework that is easy to understand and apply. The four elements of the marketing mix are: Product, Place, Price and Promotion (Table 1.1).

Table 1.1: - The 4Ps of the marketing mix

Element of the marketing mix	Definition
Product	This element refers to the characteristics of the offering from the company to the consumer. A product has both core (the product itself) and augmented (guarantees, extra services) features.
Place	Place relates to the distribution channels in which the product or service is sold. It's about having the right product at the right place, at the right time.
Price	The financial value that companies expect customers will pay for the services and products being offered.
Promotion	All the promotional activities that make consumers aware, and entices them to buy the product or service above the competitors. Within this element, there is also the promotional mix which includes: advertising, sales promotion, personal selling, public relations, and direct marketing.

The marketing mix has been both praised and criticised by academics since its introduction in the 60s (Constantinides, 2006). Those in favour of it argue that it provides a memorable and practical framework for marketing decision making, and one that forces marketers to consider the parameters they have control of, and which influence the consumer buying process and decision making (Kotler, 2003). However, some of the limitations identified in this model are:

■ the inward-looking approach that it takes, focusing mainly on what the company can deliver and change, and

■ it does not sufficiently acknowledge the role of the customer and his or her needs.

More contemporary views of marketing focus on building relationships with customers, and look at the co-creation of value by both the company and the consumer (Vargo et al., 2008).

An extended version of the marketing mix was developed to include three extra elements in the context of services. These added elements are: Process, People, and Physical Evidence. In the following sections, we examine the 4Ps of the marketing mix and apply these to the digital context. We will see that despite the several limitations of the marketing mix model, it provides a useful digital marketing framework.

Product

In marketing, a product is defined as the item that a company offers to its customers. A product has core and augmented features. Core features relate to the characteristic of a product itself. If we take an example of a smartphone, core features would be the screen size, battery life, and colours in which a customer can purchase the product. Augmented features are physical and non-physical attributes that are part of the product and that add value to it in the mind of customers. The use of digital technology can help companies add augmented features to a product to increase customer value and competitiveness. For example, augmented features of a product sold offline can take the form of online customer service on the company's website or videos explaining how to make full use of the newly purchased products. Many e-commerce websites provide added features, such as ratings and reviews that can help customers with their purchase decision and can be seen as augmented features as compared to buying it on a website that doesn't show these.

Digital products refers to goods and services that can be accessed through digital tools. Hui and Chau (2002) classify digital products based on two dimensions: product category and product characteristic. Hui and Chau (2002) suggest three broad categories:

- **Tools and utilities**, which are digital products that allow users to accomplish a specific goal or task; e.g. mainly software such as Microsoft Word or Illustrator.

- **Content-based** digital products, where the value of the product is embedded in the information that is being provided; e.g. newspapers, video sites.

- **Online services**, which provide access to useful resources over the internet; e.g. Google Search.

The main differentiator between online services and tools and utilities are that customers cannot actually 'purchase' the online service.

Product characteristics are qualities that are intrinsic to the digital product. Typically these are features that are 'born' with the product. Three broad categories are identified:

- **Delivery mode**, which relates to the delivery mechanisms of the product (i.e. either the full product is delivered at one time, or continuously over a period of time).

■ **Granularity** refers to the degree of divisibility of the product. For example, some digital products can be easily divisible, which provide several business model opportunities for a company owning that digital product. An obvious example of this would be digital music, which can be sold as a unit (i.e. a song) as a bundle of songs, or as a subscription.

■ **Trialability** refers to the level in which the customer can preview a subset of the full product or use the product for a limited period of time.

Another important distinction between physical and digital products is the perceived value that people attach to each of them. There is evidence suggesting that people are willing to pay more for physical goods than for equivalent digital goods like films or books (Atasoy and Morewedge, 2017). Therefore, marketers need to consider these implications on their pricing strategy, especially when marketing products that deliver a similar benefit online and offline.

Place

Place in the digital context is defined as the different channels from which information and digital goods can be accessed. Whereas in an offline context, the focus of place is on making sure that the right product is at the right place at the right time; in online environments, place focuses on four areas: transaction place, customisation place, storage place and delivery place (Figure 1.1)

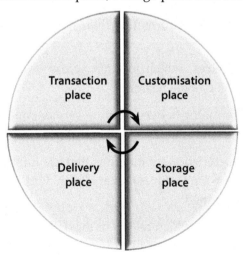

Figure 1.1: Four areas of digital place

Important aspects to consider when thinking of place online are the attitudes and behaviours of users in different locations, as these might vary significantly and brands need to be able to adapt to these changes if they want to be succesful. A good example of a company that learned to adapt to change is Souq.com, an e-commerce platform created in 2005 that is headquartered in Dubai, UAE. For those unfamiliar with the platform, Souq is known as the Amazon of the Middle East, and just like Amazon it sells a wide variety of products online. The Middle East, and in particular Dubai, is a true melting pot, with 75% of the population in the Emirate being foreign-born. As such, people living there bring with them their own customs regarding payment for products and services.

While in certain regions like in North America and Western Europe the volume of non-cash transactions are among the highest in the world, other regions in Latin America, Central Europe, Middle East and Africa (CEMEA) as well as some emerging areas in Asia prefer cash payments (World Payment Report, 2015). Thus companies operating in more cash-intensive regions, and wanting to operate e-commerce websites, need to take this into consideration. Souq's directors did just that when thinking on the transactional elements of the website, and allowed users to order products and to pay for them cash in hand when they received them. So in this particular case, the transaction place occurs both at the website and continues into the delivery place, once the product has arrived safely to its keen owner.

■ Transaction place

Transaction places can be classified depending on the focus and ownership of the site, which can range from seller-controlled sites at one end, to buyer controlled sites at the other end (Table 1.2, page 8).

■ Customisation place

In addition, activities other than purchase occur within the online place. Digital technology means that the core and augmented features can be customised at a greater level of detail at the place of purchase. Examples of customisation include allowing the customer to configure certain features, request certain design features such as the colour or personalise the product with a message. Customisation occurs online rather than in-store. For example, it is hard for a smartphone producer to offer a great level of customisation at each of the stores that they own, as it would require a significant amount of investment in each store, and additional staffing. In digital environments, customisation

Table 1.2: Types of transactional places

Type of transaction place	Examples
Seller-controlled	These sites are usually owned by the supplier company. Examples of these can be: dell.com, BA.com
Seller-oriented	These sites are controlled by third parties but represent the seller. This means that they do not provide a full range of options to the buyer, but those options that the sellers choose to show. Examples of this type of site is Opodo.com , a site that represents a selection of airlines.
Neutral sites	These sites are independent intermediaries that enable price and product comparison, and the purchase is fulfilled on the target site. An example can be Google Search, which features products from third parties in their results. The user is then directed to the third-party website to make the purchase. This service has recently become under scrutiny by the EU, as European regulators believe that Google favours results from it owns search engine over others (Boffey, 2017).
Buyer-oriented	These sites are controlled by third parties but have the buyer's interest in mind. An example of this type of website would be moneysupermarket.com which provides a comparison of different providers in a broad range of services (e.g. banking, insurance, energy).
Buyer-controlled sites	These sites usually are used for procurement purposes, which are common in the B2B and public sectors. Sites like contractsfinder. service.gov.uk are controlled by the buyers (i.e. councils, hospitals).

request from customers can be centralised to the manufacturer, yet made available to anyone buying the product online. Companies like Apple allow customers to customise their products when they purchase online. Similar strategies are also seen in the fashion industry where products such as shoes or jewellery can be customised when purchased online.

Storage place

Digital environments also led to the creation of digital-stored products and services (Gayer and Shy, 2003). Examples of digital-stored products are computer software, digitised media like songs, video and books. Digital services, on the other hand, can be purely digital or a combination of online and offline elements. For example, Chinese company Ofo, which allows users to book bicycles in many locations in Asia and Europe, would be a good example of a digital service that combines online (i.e. the app where you book the bicycle) and offline (i.e. the bicycle itself) elements.

■ Delivery place

In online environments the transaction place and the delivery place are not necessarily the same. For example, imagine that you're running out of note-pads for your digital marketing class, and that you go to Amazon to order a couple. The transaction place would be Amazon's website, however, since this is a tangible product the delivery place won't be the website itself (or your computer), instead the company will make the delivery to the customer's designated address. Therefore, from a marketing perspective, place is not limited to having a functional transactional website that can accept different payments methods, and that customers feel confident buying from, but also a marketer needs to consider how the delivery experience can improve (or harm) that company's image if the experience is not satisfactory.

Price

Price is defined as the monetary value that consumers pay for a digital product. The digital environment facilitates the use of new dynamic pricing models, indeed traditional ways of allocating price have been "turned on their head" (Chaffey and Smith, 2013). We identify four pricing options that are facilitated when selling digital products: purchase, rental or subscription, freemium, and pay-per-use.

- **Purchase** is the most straightforward pricing option, but also the one that bears the higher risk for piracy of digital goods. Many software services started selling their digital products this way, however, sufficient security measures are needed to reduce piracy and copyright infringement. In the early 2000s peer-to-peer platforms like Napster, that allowed users to exchange purchased music files among other peers were under pressure to close down due to copyright infringement (The Guardian, 2000). Similar piracy issues was not uncommon for other types of software such as Microsoft Office. This is one of the reasons why today many of the companies selling digital products have now adopted other pricing options such as subscription based or freemium.

- **Rental** or **subscription-based** pricing requires users to subscribe to access the service or digital product. This is a common pricing model used for music (e.g. Spotify) or image banks (e.g. iStock Photo) where users pay a monthly subscription fee, and this usually gives them unlimited access to the product or services. Many software companies, including Microsoft and Adobe, have now adopted this type of pricing option. In some cases, a longer subscription period (yearly vs. monthly subscriptions) leads to lower prices for the user for this time commitment to the service.

■ A **freemium** pricing model is where users get access for free to basic features of a digital product, and they can access for a fee or subscription premium features of the same product. Many digital companies make this pricing model sustainable by changing the revenue model. Advertising usually supports free version, whilst users' fees support the premium version.

■ Finally, **pay-per-use** pricing only charges users for the times they use the service. This is intrinsically related to the granularity of certain digital products that can be bundled into different formats. An example of this would be image banks like iStock. They offer both subscriptions and pay-per-use access to their pictures, and each has different pricing as they convey different benefits to the user. On the one hand, pay-per-use allows for full flexibility regarding use, but at a premium in pricing. Purchasing ten images on a pay-per-use basis from their service would cost £90, whereas a subscription that would allow a user to download 10 images monthly costs £25.

In addition, access to the Internet allows customers easy price comparison, leading to greater price transparency. For instance, in countries like the UK, where smartphone penetration is high (80.3%) according to eMarketer (2016), a large proportion of users can access the Internet while they are in physical stores to compare the price of the products that they want to buy. A study from Columbia Business School conducted in the US, Canada and the UK found that 52% of users regularly check prices using their mobile and 50% of users read info and reviews while in the store (Quint et al., 2013). These figures suggest that access to prices from different retailers both online and offline would lead to price reduction and standardisation. However, evidence regarding click-through-rates (CTRs) based on the position in search results also suggests that users don't spend too much time looking and comparing prices beyond the first page. In fact, some studies find that 76.6% of traffic goes to the first five results, and this percentage increases up to 95% for the top 10 results in search engines (Petrescu, 2014). This highlights the importance of being well ranked in search engine result pages (SERPs).

Exercise 1.1

It is not uncommon to see different pricing models even within the same industry. A good example of this would be online counselling, where different competitors have chosen to differentiate based on their pricing models. Conduct a web search of the main providers of online counselling and map out the different pricing strategies that they follow.

Promotion

Promotion is defined as the element in the mix that looks to communicate with the target audience to generate awareness and increase sales. The promotional mix includes advertising, sales promotion, personal selling, public relations and direct marketing. Digital channels can be classified into three major categories: owned, earned and paid media channels (Fill, 2009).

Table 1.3: Media types and digital platforms

Media type	Examples of digital platforms
Owned media: digital channels that the brand owns and can control.	Company website Company blog Facebook Fan page Organisation's Twitter account
Paid media: brand paying to appear on third-party websites.	Display ads (banners) in third party websites Sponsored posts in third party blogs
Earned media: brand mentioned on third-party websites without payment involved.	Non-paid mentions in third party websites Mentions in social media (Facebook, Twitter, blogs). User reviews

■ Owned media

Owned media are the channels that the company owns and has full control over. In the digital context, the most obvious example would be the company's website. However, the proliferation of channels in particular social media results in businesses 'owning' other social channels, such as a Facebook Page or a Twitter account. This trend of extending owned channels is becoming the norm among both large and small organisations. According to eMarketer (2014) 88% of Fortune 500 companies were already using at least one type of social media website. The level of control in this type of platform is higher than with any other, yet owned media is sometimes considered to be less credible as it can be biased towards the organisation (Chu and Kim, 2011). Marketers also need to consider the implications of being present in several owned media platforms. Presence in each of the platforms has implications in terms of financial and human resources. Therefore marketers should take a strategic approach to the proliferation of owned media and its alignment with their marketing objectives.

■ Paid media

Paid media or advertising, refers to media activity that is generated on other websites because the brand paid for it. A common example would be a paid ad being display in a user's newsfeed on Facebook, or a blogger writing about a brand because he or she received a payment or a free sample. There is a proliferation of paid advertising channels in which companies can be present. These can be classified broadly into search and display advertising. Search engine marketing refers to the ads that appear when a user is looking for something in search engines. The company bids for certain keywords and compete with other companies that also want to advertise when the user searches that particular keyword.

■ Earned media

Earned media refers to the mentions of the brand or company that were not paid for by the organisation, but that can be found online. Examples of earned media can be a blogger writing an unpaid review of their experience with a certain product or a film, or someone posting something about a product in their Facebook profile. Evidence suggests that consumer-generated content such as online reviews (a type of earned media) can affect sales (Chevalier and Mayzlin, 2006). Earned media is perceived as being commercially unbiased and more trustworthy compared to other forms of media, as it considered to be outside the direct control of the organisation and is frequently based on a direct experience with the product or service in question. However, the lack of direct control means that earned media is not always positive,and can contain criticism of the brand. Therefore, understanding why people talk about brands online is important for marketers as it can help them devise strategies to foster positive earned media.

Earned media is described as electronic word-of-mouth (eWOM). The concept of electronic word-of-mouth finds its roots in its offline cousin, word-of-mouth (WOM) communication. Jalilvand et al. (2011) define WOM as the advice or recommendation that is given from an unpaid source, usually a consumer, to another consumer. This kind of communication occurs both offline and online between friends, acquaintances and thanks to digital technologies, between strangers over the Internet. When this type of communication takes place in online environments, it is known as electronic word-of-mouth. Hennig-Thurau et al. (2003:39) define eWOM as "any positive and negative statements made by potential, actual, or former customers about a product or company, which is provided to a multitude of people and institutions via the Internet". Several academics view this type of communication as more persuasive than any other marketing communication tool (Allsop et al., 2007; Cheung et al., 2008; Trusov et al., 2008). eWOM is one of the most effective forms of marketing communications, and there is an extensive body of literature around this behaviour.

■ Characteristics of eWOM

There are some similarities and differences between WOM and eWOM. Both forms of communication share Buttle's (1998) five characteristics of word-of-mouth communication. These characteristics are valence, focus, timing, solicitation and intervention (Figure 1.2).

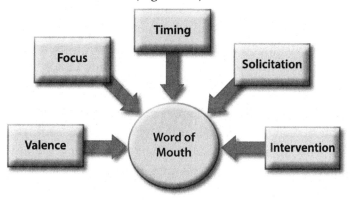

Figure 1.2: Characteristics of word-of-mouth. Adapted from Buttle, 1998

Valence refers to the extent to which the message transmitted by the sender is positive or negative. In the context of online reviews, there is evidence that suggests negative reviews can positively affect awareness of certain products and increase purchase likelihood under certain circumstances (Berger et al., 2010).

Focus refers to the target of those eWOM communications. Buttle (1998) identifies six different targets that can be the focus of the communications effort. These are: (1) customer-oriented, (2) supplier/alliance, (3) referral, (4) recruitment, (5) influencer, and (6) internal.

Exercise 1.2: The job of my dreams

Look at the online reviews of a company where you have worked before, or where you would like to apply to once you finish your degree. Visit Glassdoor.com and look at the online reviews already available.

What is the incidence of positive vs. negative eWOM? How trustworthy does this information seem to you? Why does it feel this way? How does this affect your intentions to apply to this company in the future? Have they changed or remained the same?

Timing refers to when the message is received: pre- or post-purchase. When the message is received before purchase, it has a significant effect on the judgements of the product (Lim and Chung, 2011). In addition, there is evidence that eWOM can alter the perception of evaluation attributes after usage (Lim and Chung, 2011). Online environments allow for both synchronous and asynchronous interactions. For example, synchronous interaction occurs when you're having a live conversation with a friend on Whatsapp about a restaurant. The same conversation occurring over a thread of emails would be an example of asynchronous interactions. Depending on the platform configuration, consumers can be exposed to eWOM from other consumers prior, during and after their purchase. Many travel sites include reviews from other customers that stayed at the same accommodation so that the prospective customers can look at them and take a more informed choice.

Solicitation refers to the process by which users receive word of mouth. Users may be passive recipients, i.e. they listen as a friend tells them of the benefits of using an i-phone; or they may be active seekers, i.e. they ask their friend who has an i-phone about their experiences. When WOM is solicited, it is more influential, as the person receiving the information has recognised a need state and will be focused upon processing that information. Individuals will habitually share their brand or product experiences as part of social interaction. There are a range of motivations for sharing WOM (Table 1.4). For example, consumers might actively share their experience with a product for reasons such as self-involvement. Consumers may speak negatively about the products. Research has found that this helps consumers cope with a bad experience, as it reduces the level of anxiety experienced if it is shared with others or with the brand (Sundaram et al., 1998). Some customers may seek revenge against a brand as a result of a negative experience, and will actively generate comments to damage the image of the brand.

Table 1.4: Motivations for the generation of positive and negative eWOM

Valence	Motivation	Description
Positive eWOM	Altruism	Consumers want to help other consumers to make satisfying purchase decisions.
	Product-involvement	Consumers' use of the product/service is highly important and speaking about it helps vent those positive feelings.
	Self-enhancement	Consumers share their experiences to enhance their image among other by projecting themselves as intelligent shoppers.
	Helping the company	Similar to altruism, only that in this case the consumer wants to help the company because of the positive experience that they had with it.
Negative eWOM	Altruism	Consumers want to help other consumers by preventing other consumers experiencing the same problems that they had encountered.
	Anxiety reduction	Consumers want to share their negative experience with others to reduce their anger, anxiety and frustration.
	Vengeance	Consumers express their negative experiences publicly to retaliate against the company associated with that experience.
	Advice seeking	Consumers share their negative experience with the intention to get some advice on how to resolve their problems.

Adapted from: Sundaram et al. (1998)

However unsolicited word of mouth also shapes decision-making and forms a part of the information landscape. Some social media websites (e.g. Facebook Check-ins, Sponsored Stories, Instagram picture postings) push unsolicited eWOM messages to their users. In this matter, there is already some evidence from online advertising that additional exposure to brand names and logos contributes to increasing the probability of purchase of the product/service, since it creates familiarity to it and it also helps to raise awareness (Mitchell and Valenzuela, 2005).

Intervention refers to the strategies that brands adopt to manage WOM. Digital platforms make it easier for companies to adopt a proactive approach to encouraging and rewarding positive word of mouth behaviours. WOM strategies might include providing online tools to enable customers to post reviews, rewarding customers who frequently post reviews of their experiences and sending direct communication to invite customers to generate reviews. Intervention is an important aspect that brands need to take into consideration, especially when consumers generate negative WOM. Research suggest that consumers perceive brands to be more trustworthy and caring to their customers when they respond to negative WOM communication (Sparks et al., 2016). Other factors that also can help the perception of the brand, even when negative WOM exists, is the tone of voice used by the brand and the response time. Using a human voice rather than a more corporate one, and responding to messages at a reasonable time frame (i.e. within 24 hours) produce favourable inferences about the brand in the mind of consumers (Sparks et al., 2016).

In terms of the differences between WOM and eWOM, Tham et al. (2013) argue that in the case of electronic word of mouth the source-receiver relationship usually is non-existent, as you would normally not know the person writing an online review. There is also a wider variety of channels and presentation of contents in which eWOM can take form. eWOM can be displayed in written forms, or as podcast or a YouTube video.

Viral marketing is another strategy used by marketers to stimulate and capitalise on word of mouth (WOM) behaviours (Hinz et al., 2011:55). There are several advantages to viral campaigns, the content is a form of eWOM peer-to-peer recommendation, and this can give the message credibility (Dobele et al., 2007:292). Viral campaigns are considered to be cost-effective and able to reach niche consumer groups and so address the problem of audience fragmentation (Dobele et al., 2005). However, a negative characteristic of viral campaigns is the lack of control over the reach of content, the speed of message spread and also over the message itself. Viral campaigns can be a stimulus for user generated content (UGC) and as such the message can be changed from the one that was originally intended.

Summary

When the marketing mix is applied to the digital environment there are new opportunities and challenges for marketing academics and practitioners. Digital products have different characteristics than physical ones, which in turn affect other elements of the marketing mix such as pricing and distribution. New pricing models have emerged, with subscription based products as well as freemium models of payment being common pricing models. The Internet also empowers consumers, by allowing them to compare prices in real time when browsing physical shops, however there are limitations to the level of transparency in an environment where most views and clicks are limited to the first page in search results. Place in online environments has several dimensions, from different types of transaction places, to hybrid situations where customisation of a product or service occurs online, and then the delivery happens offline. Finally, when thinking of promotion in digital environments, it is crucial to acknowledge the difference between earn, paid and owned media, as each type of media poses its own challenges for marketers online.

Exemplar paper

Constantinides, E. (2006), The marketing mix revisited: towards the 21st century marketing, *Journal of Marketing Management*, **22**(3-4), 407-438.

> This paper assesses the current standing of the 4Ps Marketing Mix framework as the dominant marketing management paradigm and identifies market developments, environmental changes, and trends, as well as changing academic attitudes likely to affect the future of the Mix as theoretical concept and also the favourite management tool of marketing practitioners. The paper also identifies some of the limitations of this model.

Additional Reading

Dubosson-Torbay, M., Osterwalder, A. and Pigneur, Y., (2002), E-business model design, classification, and measurements, *Thunderbird International Business Review*, **44**(1), 5-23.

Hanna, R., Rohm, A. and Crittenden, V. L. (2011), We're all connected: The power of the social media ecosystem, *Business Horizons*, **54**(3), 265-273.

Lovett, M. J. and Staelin, R. (2016), The role of paid, earned, and owned media in building entertainment brands: Reminding, informing, and enhancing enjoyment, *Marketing Science*, **35**(1), 142-157.

References

Allsop, D.T., Bassett, B.R. and Hoskins, J.A. (2007), Word-of-mouth research: principles and applications, *Journal of Advertising Research,* **47** (4), 398-411.

Atasoy, O. and Morewedge, C.K. (2017), Digital goods are valued less than physical goods, *Journal of Consumer Research*, https://doi.org/10.1093/jcr/ucx102, [Accessed 14th October 2017]

Baines, P., Fill, C. and Page, K. (2011), *Marketing*, Oxford University Press, Oxford.

Berger, J., Sorensen, A.T. and Rasmussen, S.J., (2010), Positive effects of negative publicity: When negative reviews increase sales, *Marketing Science*, 29(5), 815–827.

Boffey, D. (2017), Google fined record €2.4bn by EU over search engine results, The Guardian, https://www.theguardian.com/business/2017/jun/27/google-braces-for-record-breaking-1bn-fine-from-eu, [Accessed 30th June 2017].

Borden, N. H. (1964), The concept of the marketing mix, *Journal of Advertising Research*, **4**(2), 2-7.

Breitenbach, C.S. and Van Doren, D.C. (1998), Value-added marketing in the digital domain: enhancing the utility of the Internet, *Journal of Consumer Marketing*, **15**(6), 558-575.

Buttle, F.A., (1998), Word of mouth: Understanding and managing referral marketing, *Journal of Strategic Marketing*, **6** (3), 241–254.

Chaffey, D. and Smith, P. R. (2013), *eMarketing eXcellence: Planning and Optimizing your Digital Marketing*, Routledge, Abingdon.

Chaffey, D., Ellis-Chadwick, F., Mayer, R. and Johnston, K. (2009), *Internet Marketing: Strategy, Implementation and Practice*, Pearson Education, Harlow.

Cheung, C.M.K., Lee, M.K.O. and Rabjohn, N. (2008), The impact of electronic word-of-mouth: the adoption of online opinions in online customer communities, *Internet Research*, **18** (3), 229–247.

Chevalier, J.A. and Mayzlin, D. (2006), The effect of word of mouth on sales: online book reviews. *Journal of Marketing Research*, **43**(3), 345–354.

Chu, S.C. and Kim, Y. (2011), Determinants of consumer engagement in electronic word-of-mouth (eWOM) in social networking sites, *International Journal of Advertising*, **30**(1), 47-75.

Constantinides, E., (2006), The marketing mix revisited: towards the 21st century marketing. *Journal of Marketing Management*, **22**(3-4), 407–438.

Dobele, A., Toleman, D. and Beverland, M. (2005) Controlled infection! Spreading the brand message through viral marketing, *Business Horizons*, **48**(2), 143-149.

Dobele, A., Lindgreen, A., Beverland, M., Vanhamme, J. and Van Wijk, R. (2007), Why pass on viral messages? because they connect emotionally, *Business Horizons*, **50**(4), 291-304.

eMarketer (2014), Social Marketing 2015: The Key to ROI Will Come from Within, https://www.emarketer.com/Article/Social-Marketing-2015-Key-ROI-Will-Come-Within/1011305, [Accessed 20th July 2017].

eMarketer (2016), Mobile Trends That Will Reshape the UK in 2017, https://www.emarketer.com/Article/Mobile-Trends-That-Will-Reshape-UK-2017/1014901, [Accessed 21st July 2017].

Fill, C. (2009), *Marketing Communications: Interactivity, Communities and Content.* Pearson Education, Harlow.

Gayer, A. and Shy, O. (2003), Internet and peer-to-peer distributions in markets for digital products. *Economics Letters,* **81**(2), 197–203.

Hennig-Thurau, T., Walsh, G. and Walsh, G. (2003) Electronic word-of-mouth: motives for and consequences of reading customer articulations on the Internet, *International Journal of Electronic Commerce,* **8**(2),51-74.

Hinz, O., Skiera, B., Barrot, C. and Becker, J.U. (2011), Seeding strategies for viral marketing: an empirical comparison, *Journal of Marketing,* **75**(6), 55-71.

Hui, K.L. and Chau, P.Y.K. (2002), Classifying digital products, *Communications of the ACM,* **45**(6), 73–79.

Jalilvand, M.R., Esfahani, S.S. and Samiei, N. (2011), Electronic word-of-mouth: Challenges and opportunities, *Procedia Computer Science,* **3**, 42–46.

Kara, A. and Kaynak, E., (1997), Markets of a single customer: Exploiting conceptual developments in market segmentation, *European Journal of Marketing,* **31**(11/12), 873–895.

Kotler, P. (2003), *Marketing Management,* 11th ed. Prentice Hall, Upper Saddle River, NJ

Lim, B.C. and Chung, C.M. (2011), The impact of word-of-mouth communication on attribute evaluation, *Journal of Business Research,* **64**(1), 18-23.

McCarthy, E. J. (1964), *Basic Marketing,* Richard D. Irwin, Illinois.

Mitchell, A. and Valenzuela, A. (2005), How banner ads affect brand choice without click-through, in Haugtvedt, C.P., Machletit, M. and Yalch, R. (eds), *Online Consumer Psychology: Understanding and Influencing Consumer Behavior in the Virtual World,* Taylor and Francis Ltd, 125-142

Petrescu, P. (2014), Google Organic Click-Through Rates in 2014, https://moz.com/blog/google-organic-click-through-rates-in-2014 [Accessed 21st July 2017].

Quint, M., Rogers, D. and Ferguson, R. (2013), *Showrooming and the Rise of the Mobile-Assisted Shopper,* Columbia Business School, Center on Global Brand Leadership, Columbia.

Sparks, B. A., So, K. K. F. and Bradley, G. L. (2016), Responding to negative online reviews: the effects of hotel responses on customer inferences of trust and concern, *Tourism Management,* **53** (April), 74-85.

Sundaram, D.S., Mitra, K. and Webster, C. (1998) Word-of-mouth communications: a motivational analysis, *Advances in Consumer Research,* **25**, 527–531.

Taken Smith, K. (2012), Longitudinal study of digital marketing strategies targeting millennials, *Journal of Consumer Marketing,* **29**(2), 86-92.

Tanyel, F., Stuart, E.W. and Griffin, J. (2013), Have 'Millennials' embraced digital advertising as they have embraced digital media? *Journal of Promotion Management*, **19**(5), 652-673.

The Guardian (2000), Napster Loses Net Music Copyright Case, The Guardian, https://www.theguardian.com/technology/2000/jul/27/copyright.news [Accessed 21st July 2017].

Tham, A., Croy, G. and Mair, J. (2013) Social media in destination choice: distinctive electronic word-of-mouth dimensions, *Journal of Travel and Tourism Marketing*, **30**(1-2), 144-155.

Trusov, M., Bucklin, R.E. and Pauwels, K. (2008), Effects of word-of-mouth versus traditional marketing: Findings from an internet social networking site, Robert H. Smith School Research Paper No. RHS 6–65.

Vargo, S.L., Maglio, P.P. and Akaka, M.A. (2008), On value and value co-creation: a service systems and service logic perspective, *European Management Journal*, **26** (3), 145–152.

Wind, Y. (1978), Issues and advances in segmentation research, *Journal of Marketing Research*, **15**(3), 317-337

World Payment Report (2015) Non-Cash Payments. https://www. worldpaymentsreport.com/reports/noncash#non-cash-transactionsglobally--regionally [Accessed 20th July 2017].

Wyatt, S., Thomas, G. and Terranova, T., (2002), They came, they surfed, they went back to the beach: conceptualizing use and non-use of the Internet in Woolgar, S. (ed), *Virtual Society?: Technology, Cyberbole, Reality*, Oxford University Press, Oxford, pp. 23-40.

2 Digital Technology Adoption

Digital technology may apply to the device, channel or process (Yoo et al., 2010). For example, a digital technology adoption might relate to a new device (i.e. a new digital phone); a new platform (i.e. the adoption of Web 2.0 over Web 1); a new channel (i.e. the adoption of Snap Chat over Facebook) or a new process (i.e. the process of sharing information using Cloud technology). In our daily lives we may be offered an array of digital innovations that we use for the first or second time; or we use so frequently that we barely notice. Equally, we may reject a digital technology as it no longer meets our needs or because we feel guilty about the amount time we 'waste' through its use.

Innovation is characterised as occurring in three stages of (1) invention, (2) innovation and (3) diffusion (Dosi, 1988). Invention is the formation of the new idea or process that may have economic value; innovation is where the invention is refined so it is becomes usable; and diffusion is the spread of the innovation so that it is accepted, adopted and continually used (King et al., 1994). Not every innovation is successful, with the failure rate being estimated as being as high as 90% (Fisher, 2014). Digital marketers need to predict and understand user reactions to digital technology in order to plan marketing campaigns that encourage consumers to accept and adopt innovations. In this chapter we examine the process of digital technology adoption.

The innovation adoption process

There are five stages in the innovation adoption process (Figure 2.1) The first stage is becoming aware of the innovation, the second stage is acceptance where the individual mentally rehearses innovation use, the third stage may involve trialling the innovation and the fourth stage involves an adoption or rejection decision and in the final fifth stage either maintaining regularly patterns of use or discontinuing use. It is clear that adoption is not immediate but takes place over time. At each stage marketing has an important role to play in influencing the decision-making. Awareness and acceptance are shaped by marketing communications. Trial is influenced by promotional pricing strategies that "reward" the customer for any risks involved. Adoption depends on product availability and also product design. Finally continuance involves gathering and understanding customer insight in order to identify threats to discontinuance.

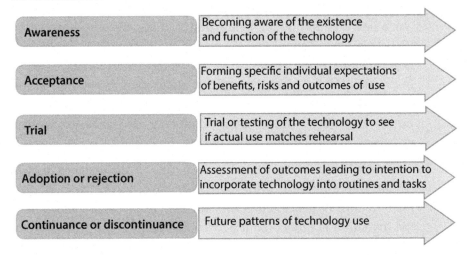

Awareness	Becoming aware of the existence and function of the technology
Acceptance	Forming specific individual expectations of benefits, risks and outcomes of use
Trial	Trial or testing of the technology to see if actual use matches rehearsal
Adoption or rejection	Assessment of outcomes leading to intention to incorporate technology into routines and tasks
Continuance or discontinuance	Future patterns of technology use

Figure 2.1: Innovation adoption process

Rogers (1995) proposes that a mandatory collective adoption decision will be more rapid than one that is individual and voluntary. It is common to consider whether adoption is voluntary, i.e. the individual chooses to use the innovation of their own free will, or whether it is mandatory. Mandatory and collective adoption are usually associated with the implementation of technology within the workspace. For example, insisting the employees manage their own holiday leave online compared to notifying their human resource department. The individual user adoption decision is usually voluntary.

Awareness

The role of innovation awareness was first proposed in the Diffusion of Innovation Theory (Rogers, 1995). At the awareness stage the individual becomes aware of the innovation's existence and gains some insight into how the technology works. Awareness can be gained either passively or actively. Passive awareness is gained through being in receipt of sales messages from reading marketing communications or meeting sales people. Active awareness is gained through the individual seeking for a solution to a problem they have identified. A key aspect in generating awareness is the individual's ability to observe others gaining advantage from an innovation which is considered a vicarious trial and thus facilitates rapid diffusion.

Rogers (1995) highlights that there is a complex relationship between innovation awareness and the formation of a need-state regarding that innovation. A need state is when a consumer's actual state differs from their ideal or desired state and may result in feelings of dissatisfaction and frustration which prompt action to resolve the difference (Solomon et al., 2011). In some situations a need state occurs and then the consumer will seek information about whether an innovation will provide a solution to a particular problem; in other situations knowledge of an innovation creates a need state.

For example, whilst most of us own a wristwatch, we might not all own a SMART watch such as the Apple watch, which connects to an iPhone to enable the use to answer calls, deliver notifications and run apps such as fitness and health trackers. Whilst some individuals might have already felt the need to combine various devices into one easy to access interface, others might have only experienced a need state when they viewed celebrities such as Kanye West, Beyonce and Anna Wintour, the editor of *Vogue* magazine, wearing their limited edition Apple watches (Price, 2015). Rogers (1995) argues that if an innovation has high observability then it will be adopted. In other words, if the results from using the innovation are easily observed and the benefits are easily communicated to others, then users will be more motivated to adopt. As we can see in the case of the Apple watch, one way for digital marketers to generate high observability is to use public relations tools such as celebrity endorsement, to draw attention to a particular digital innovation.

Exercise 2.1

Think about the innovations of which you are currently aware (this might be a device, a channel or a process). Note down whether you need each innovation.

Did this need state arise from you identifying a problem or from you observing others use the innovation?

Acceptance

There is an important distinction between *adopting* a technological innovation and *accepting* a technological innovation (Renaud and van Biljon 2008). Technology adoption occurs when the consumer makes full use of the technology, when they will replace the technology if it became broken, and would feel 'lost' or 'excluded' without access to the technology. For example, a UK survey found that almost 45% of 11-18 year olds check their mobile phones after they have gone to bed, with a tenth saying that they would feel stressed about missing out if they did not have access to a mobile phone (Sellgren 2016). In contrast, technology acceptance is an attitude towards technology, which if positive will result in adoption and if negative will not result in adoption. A core theory that seeks to predict acceptance is the Technology Acceptance Model (TAM) (Davis, 1989).

TAM seeks to predict individual acceptance of information technology by identifying attitudinal influences on use intentions. TAM focuses on measuring attitudes in two key areas:

1 **Perceived usefulness**, defined as the "user's subjective probability that using a specific application system will increase his or her job performance" and;

2 **Perceived ease of use**, defined as "the degree to which the user expects the target system to be free of effort" Davis (1989:985).

TAM theorises that a user's intention to adopt a technology is determined by the extent to which there is a positive belief that the technology will be useful in achieving a specific task and where using the technology will be free from effort.

TAM enables researchers to measure individual response to a digital technology in order to predict intention to use an innovation. There are various published scales of measurement and Davis' model is considered easy to understand and simple to apply (Legris et al., 2003). There is research evidence that TAM has explanatory power and is able to account for over 40 percent of the differences between individual intentions to use technology (Venkatesh and Davis, 2000), which is a good power of explanation for social science research (Eisend, 2015). However, there is also criticism of the model. One criticism of TAM is that it was primarily developed within an organisational context and it is designed to predict adoption after a brief period of interaction with a technology in the workplace, for example after a training session or pre-purchase trial of the technology (Davis, 1989). Thus it is not applicable to individual use situations, where the technology is voluntarily used and there might not be any training or support.

A second criticism is the failure to account for the influence of prior consumer experience upon perceived ease of use. This means that inexperienced consumers value "perceived ease of use" more than "perceived usefulness" (Castaneda et al., 2007) but that as consumer experience develops there is greater value placed upon "perceived usefulness". Therefore if digital marketers were trying to assess the acceptance of a particular technology amongst a target market segment, they would need to ensure that they were also measuring levels of users' prior technology use in order to account for this phenomenon.

A third criticism is that technology acceptance varies according to whether the task being undertaken is intrinsic or extrinsic to the technology. "Perceived ease of use" is more important for intrinsic tasks "where the [technology] itself provides the primary "ends" i.e. the product or service" (Gefen and Straub, 2000:3). An example is Facebook where the channel itself provides the connection service. In contrast, "perceived usefulness" is more important for extrinsic tasks where using the technology is "the means to achieving the primary product or service... [and] is the interface through which one accomplishes a goal" (ibid:3). An example is a website used to purchase clothing, i.e. the primary goal is clothing purchase and the website is the means to achieving this. For digital marketers this means that it is important to assess consumers' attitudes towards a technology for a range of intrinsic and extrinsic tasks for which it might be used.

A concept that can help us in researching the differing use of technology according task, is Task Technology Fit (TTF) which is defined as the degree to which technology assists an individual in performing a range of tasks (Goodhue and Thompson, 1995). TTF captures consumer anticipations of the fit between technology features and task requirements and is an important influence upon pre-use attitudes and post-use evaluation (Goodhue and Thompson 1995).

Trial

Before adoption, Rogers proposes that an individual will wish to trial an innovation to assess the risks and benefits. Trialability is the extent to which an innovation "can be experimented with on a limited basis (Rogers 1995:16). An innovation that can be tried easily will have a more rapid rate of adoption (Davis, 1989; Venkatesh et al., 2003). Trial can take place through using divisible elements of the overall innovation (Waite, 2009) and "innovations that can be divided for trial are generally adopted more rapidly" (Rogers 1995:171). A divisible element is an aspect of the complete innovation that can be accessed on a probationary basis.

In the context of online banking adoption, Waite and Harrison (2002) discuss how online information search acts as a divisible element by which to assess bank web site functionality. Information search demonstrates the convenience and efficiency of the bank website (Webster and Ahuja, 2006) and the credibility of the information provided on a web site is important in establishing trust in the provider of a product or a service and thus is used as an attribute in assessing risk (Fogg et al., 2001). Ramaswami et al. (2000) find that consumers who use the Internet for information search have a greater tendency to use it for transactions, and argue that obtaining information is a low-risk way to gain experience of the Internet.

Exercise 2.2

Think of how you have adopted a digital technology.

Can you identify how you began use through trial? What were the divisible elements that you used to assess the digital technology? Look at Table 2.3, and identify how the divisible elements helped you to manage risk.

The degree to which trialability is valued differs between different digital technologies. Research into social media adoption by Zolkepli and Kamarulzaman (2015) conducted amongst Malaysian Internet users questions the importance of trialability for social media innovations since focus group participants argued that "social media is free and trial is not possible in this form" (p. 206). When examining app adoption, Roma and Dominici,

(2016:15) argue that in the app market trialability is key to establishing app value since "consumers generally pay a higher price if given the opportunity to test the product before buying... and that developers often release a free trial version associated with the paid version of their apps". This variability is consistent with other research has demonstrated that trialability does not always predict an individual's adoption decision (Agarwal and Prasad, 1998; Tornatzky and Klein 1982).

Adoption

Adoption is defined as "a decision to make full use of an innovation as the best course of action available" (Rogers, 1995:171). According to the Difffusion of Innovation theory there are five innovation attributes that facilitate adoption (Table 2.1), and of these attributes we have already discussed trialability and observability in the preceding sections. Research has demonstrated that *'relative advantage'* is the best predictor of adoption and continued use (Agarwal and Prasad, 1998; Karahanna et al., 1999; Moore and Benbasat, 1991). However, results also show that relative advantage and *'compatibility'* are closely related concepts and that this may inflate the importance of relative advantage (Moore and Benbasat, 1991).

Table 2.1: Attributes that facilitate adoption. Adapted from Rogers (1995:212-244)

Innovation attribute	Definition
Relative advantage	The degree to which the innovation is perceived as being better than the idea it supersedes.
Compatibility	The degree to which the innovation is perceived as consistent with existing values, past experience and the needs of potential adopters.
Complexity	The degree to which an innovation is perceived as relatively difficult to understand and use.
Trialability	The degree to which an innovation may be experimented with on a limited basis.
Observability	The degree to which the results of an innovation are visible to others.

Relative advantage is determined by the adoption context and will vary according to the digital technology under examination. This means that the digital marketer needs to identify which forms of relative advantage are offered by the technology that they are marketing, through either conducting primary research or searching the published literature. Table 2.2 provides some examples of relative advantage that is found in research into different digital technologies. Thinking back to technology acceptance we can see a clear link to perceived usefulness, however relative advantage is framed in comparison to an alternative technology rather than the degree to which the technology helps achieves a particular end result.

Table 2.2: Examples of relative advantage

Digital innovation	Relative advantage	Source
Mobile shopping apps	Time convenience Interactivity	Kang et al (2015)
Social media	Synchronisation across devices Geographically unlimited Control over network	Zolkepli and Kamarulzaman (2015)
Augmented reality	Time convenience Effort reduction	tom Dieck and Jung (2015)
E-government services	Information gathering efficiency Interaction efficiency Increased control	Carter and Belanger (2005)

Compatibility is an encompassing concept that captures the individual's enduring value systems, accumulated knowledge and present need. Researchers have included within the term *value system* various different influences including cultural values (Cho and Kim, 2001), societal norms (Taylor and Todd, 1995), daily routines and habits (Tornatzky and Klein, 1982) and consumer lifestyle (Kleijnen et al., 2004). Kleijnen et al. (2009: 346) note that "any behaviour that is contrary to group norms, or societal and family values creates a barrier" to adoption. For example, spending too much time using a mobile phone or playing online games.

Researchers have also extended the idea of compatibility to consider the extent to which the perceived image of the innovation is compatible with the consumer's self-image perceptions (Ram and Sheth, 1989). Accumulated knowledge comprises the familiar mental tools or frameworks that the individual uses to assess innovation, since any innovation has to be assessed against a known standard (Rogers, 1995). For example, a consumer contemplating using Twitter might draw on frameworks accumulated through their use of Facebook. Finally, compatibility relates to the extent to which the innovation resolves the need state which was the driver of innovation awareness.

Complexity shows similarity with the concept of 'ease of use', however complexity is considered as existing relative to alternative innovation.

Complexity also includes not only difficulty in use but also in understand-ability. The cognitive effort required to overcome the complexity of a tech-nology innovation can be considered a 'cost' of adoption (Hourahine and Howard, 2004). Whilst technology becomes easier to use there are different levels of complexity and options in both device, software and provider options (van Dijk and Hacker, 2003). Indeed, complexity is found to be an important determinant of mobile phone adoption in a study by Turnbull et al. (2000), who find that in sectors characterised by rapid technological change consumers become confused and thus it is important for digital marketers to design marketing strategy and tactics that take this into account.

Rejection

Uncertainty and risk are considered important influences upon adoption. Rogers (1995) suggests that any decision to adopt an innovation involves a degree of risk. Given its importance, perceived risk is used in consumer-based studies as a significant influence upon adoption. The more knowledgeable a consumer becomes about a product or service, the more they understand the risks to which they are exposed and thus perceptions of risk are lowered. There are six specific types of consumer risk (Table 2.3).

Table 2.3: Defining the components of perceived risk. Source: Pires et al. (2004).

Risk component	Definition
Financial risk	The likelihood of suffering a financial loss due to hidden costs, maintenance costs or lack of warranty in the case of faults.
Performance risk	The chances of the technology failing to meet the performance requirements sought by the user
Physical risk	The probability of the technology causing harm or injury
Psychological risk	The chances of a specific technology being inconsistent with the self-image of the consumer
Social risk	The likelihood of technology use resulting in others thinking of the consumer less favourably
Convenience risk	The probability of the technology resulting in lost time in terms of delay in use, problems in configuration and repair/downtime
Overall risk	The likelihood that the technology will result in general dissatisfaction

If we consider web site functionality, there are several attributes that may increase risk perceptions. For example, a web site may be slow to download, information may be difficult to locate, graphics may be insufficient and information may not be relevant or may be dated. Web site providers may also introduce 'Privacy risk' through requiring a consumer to register an interest and supply personal details before being able to view information. In addition web site users may be required to actively input information into the system before receiving more detailed information in return. Thus 'Performance' in the case of web site failure and 'Security risk' in the case of third party interception might also be perceived.

Individuals have different attitudes towards risk, some individuals are risk-seeking and others are risk-averse (Mitchell, 1999). Attitudes to risk are considered to determine the point in time that individuals will adopt. Drawing upon risk attitudes, amongst other influences, Rogers (1995) proposes that individuals can be classified into five discrete adopter categories (Figure 2.2).

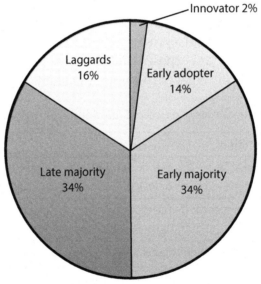

Figure 2.2: Adopters categories. Adapted from Rogers (1995)

Those first to adopt, namely innovators and early adopters, tend to be risk-seeking and enjoy new experiences. Those later to adopt, such as the early majority, are less tolerant of risk with the late majority needing some assurance that the product is tried and tested before committing themselves to adoption. The final group, the laggards, are very tradition-bound and are suspicious of change and will not adopt an innovation unless there is evidence that it has been fully adopted elsewhere.

Digital marketers need to remember that within any consumer group there will be those who will reject innovation due to risk concerns. It is important to design a marketing mix that communicate the benefits of technology adoption, educates the consumer about the safety features or protocols that off-set any risk and also rewards the consumer for trial, either through reduced pricing or exclusive offers. One of the key elements for early adopters is that promotional materials need to show specifically what the product can do for the individual, and to connect with a lifestyle that values efficiency (Adage, 2010).

Technology continuance

Technology continuance is the final stage of adoption, when there is revaluation of the earlier adoption decision, and a further decision whether to continue or discontinue use (Rogers 1995). Whilst there has been a focus upon theories to explain the necessary requirements of an innovation for it to gain acceptance, it is important to remember that patterns of technology use can change over time, with the intensity of use fluctuating and sometimes use discontinuing. Technology continuance occurs when technology use "transcends conscious behaviour and becomes part of normal routine activity" (Bhattacherjee, 2001:353). Whilst gaining first-time use is important, it is technology continuance that ensures that the innovation is viable in the long term. Digital product success factors, such as market share and revenue, depend upon the ability both to gain new users and to retain them as continued users (Bhattacherjee 2001).

In 2016, *The Information* reported that personal or 'original' sharing on Facebook had declined by 21% (Efrati, 2016). It was claimed that this was a result of the growth of the social network, so that it no longer was an intimate place but rather had become an impersonal and professional space (Fortune, 2016). Patterns of use have changed from posting personal status updates, to sharing professional content and also content published elsewhere on public websites such as news sites. One explanation is that Facebook has been in operation since 2004 and that the longer people are using it the greater the number of friends they acquire. This results in what is termed "context collapse" (Frier, 2016), which is where people feel their updates are not relevant or appropriate for all their connections. The result is that there is a change in behaviour, with people seeking channels that give access to smaller audiences, such as Snapchat or Instagram.

It is important to understand why some individuals gain from using technology, in order to ensure that the relative advantage gained initially continues after adoption. Uses and gratifications theory (UGT) is an approach to understanding why and how individuals consume certain media and why this use changes over time and between individuals (Katz and Blumler, 1974). UGT assumes that individuals are not passive but active choosers of media and discusses how consumers deliberately choose and integrate into their lives media that will satisfy given needs such as: to enhance knowledge; relaxation; social interactions/companionship; diversion, or escape. UGT was developed at a time when people were concerned about people watching too much TV or consuming certain images. UGT differed from earlier theories that asked what the media did to an individual? UGT asked what does the individual do with the media? Which needs are met by watching television?

The introduction of the Internet and online media consumption led to UGT being revived as an approach to understanding media choice. Brands were interested in what made people consume digital content. Initially researchers sought to understand whether digital media were being used to satisfy the same needs that had been satisfied using traditional media. However several researchers developed measurement scales that are specific to digital technologies. For example, Smock et al. (2011) develop items that relate to Facebook motivations, including expressive information sharing, social interaction, relaxing entertainment and professional advancement, and Lee et al. (2010) develop items related to mobile game playing that include information discovery, entertainment, socialisation and relationship maintenance. These scales can be used in surveys to gain insight into what keeps consumers using a particular digital innovation.

Technology discontinuance

Technology discontinuance is when the individual decides to stop using a website or an app and does not return to using it. It is incorrect to assume that the reasons for discontinuance of digital technology are the mirror image of adoption intentions; the influencing factors that determine continuance and discontinuance are very different (Bhattacherjee, 2001). Turel (2015:2) emphasises that discontinuance decisions "whilst related, are not the simply the opposite poles of the same concept". Some of the reasons given for discontinuance include that the technology wastes time, is a distraction from other more important tasks, and that it is becoming a barrier between forming relationships with others. These feelings might arise after periods of intensive technology use where the consumer feels that they are becoming addicted to use of the technology. In particular, addiction has been associated with the intensive use of computer games (Charlton and Danforth, 2007) and social media (Woollaston, 2013). Research into discontinuance shows that guilt feelings increase the intention to quit, but that guilt feelings are cancelled out by the strength of the habit and the feelings of satisfaction associated with use (Turel, 2015).

In order to stop people from discontinuing using a technology, digital marketers need to increase habit and satisfaction with the technology. Satisfaction can be increased by revising the product and pricing elements of the market mix to including intrinsically rewarding features that meet or exceed consumer expectation. Habit can be increased by making it easy to train on many features of an application and incentivising frequent and feature-based use through financial or status reward (Limayem et al., 2007). However, over-driving continuance behaviours might result in greater feelings of guilt and stronger intentions to quit. In order to ensure continuance, a marketing mix might contain place elements that make it difficult to deactivate or remove a user profile from a site, or promotion elements that feature an e-mail campaign to remind and encourage repeated use after a period of inactivity.

Summary

Digital technology developments mean that digital marketers need to understand the reasons why consumers choose to adopt or reject, continue or discontinue technology use. A digital innovation might be a new device, a new platform or a new process. The challenge might be to launch a new innovation or to persuade those who are late adopters to begin using an established digital innovation. This chapter has provided details of what happens at each stage of the adoption decision and has drawn on established theories of Technology Acceptance, the Diffusion of Innovation and Uses and Gratifications Theory to identify the key influences upon consumer decision making.

Exemplar paper

Curran, J.M. and Meuter, M.L., (2005), Self-service technology adoption: comparing three technologies, *Journal of Services Marketing*, **19**(2), 103-113.

The paper tests a conceptual model of technology adoption across three different technologies in order to explore differences in consumer attitudes. The results show that the adoption decision for each technology is subject to different influences. The research provides support for the argument that the introduction of new technology involves taking into account the variations in consumer attitude when planning marketing activity.

■ Additional reading

Rauniar, R., Rawski, G., Yang, J., and Johnson, B. (2014). Technology acceptance model (TAM) and social media usage: an empirical study on Facebook, *Journal of Enterprise Information Management*, **27**(1), 6-30.

Venkatesh, V., Morris, M.G., Davis, G.B. and Davis, F.D. (2003), User acceptance of information technology: toward a unified view, *MIS Quarterly*, **27**(3),425-478.

Waite, K. and Harrison, T. (2015), Online banking adoption: we should know better 20 years on. *Journal of Financial Services Marketing*, **20**(4), 258-272.

References

Adage (2010) Shiny New Things: White Paper, http://adage.com/images/bin/pdf/ shiny_new_things.pdf. [Accessed 15th March 2016].

Agarwal, R., and Prasad, J. (1998). A conceptual and operational definition of personal innovativeness in the domain of information technology, *Information Systems Research*, **9**(2), 204–215

Bhattacherjee, A. (2001), Understanding Information systems continuance: an expectation-confirmation model, *MIS Quarterly*, **25**(3), 351-370.

Carter, L. and Bélanger, F. (2005), The utilization of e-government services: citizen trust, innovation and acceptance factors, *Information Systems Journal*, **15**(1), 5-25.

Castañeda, J.A., Muñoz-Leiva, F. and Luque, T. (2007), Web Acceptance Model (WAM): Moderating effects of user experience, *Information and Management*, **44**(4), 384-396.

Charlton, J.P. and Danforth, I.D. (2007), Distinguishing addiction and high engagement in the context of online game playing, *Computers in Human Behavior*, **23**(3),1531-1548.

Cho, I. and Kim, Y. (2001), Critical factors for assimilation of object-orientated programming languages, *Journal of Management Information Systems*, **18**(3), 125–156.

Davis, F. D. (1989). Perceived usefulness, perceived ease of use, and user acceptance of information technology. *MIS Quarterly*, **13**(3), 319–340.

Dosi, G. (1988), The nature of the innovative process, in G. Dosi et al., *Technical Change and Economic Theory*, Pinter Publishers, New York, 221-238.

Efrati, A. (2016), Facebook Struggles to Stop Decline in Original Sharing, The information, 7th April, https://www.theinformation.com/facebook-struggles-to-stop-decline-in-original-sharing [Accessed 28th October 2016]

Eisend, M. (2015), Have we progressed marketing knowledge? a meta-meta-analysis of effect sizes in marketing research, *Journal of Marketing*, **79**(3), 23-40.

Fisher, A. (2014), Why Most Innovations are Great Big Failures", *Forbes Magazine*, October 7th, http://fortune.com/2014/10/07/innovation-failure/ [Accessed 28th October 2016]

Fogg, B.J., Marshall, J., Laraki, O., Osipovich, A., Varma, C., Fang, N., Paul, J., Rangnekar, A., Shon, J., Swani, P. and Treinen, M. (2001), What makes web sites credible? a report on a large quantitative study, In *Proceedings of the SIGCHI Conference on Human factors in Computing Systems*, (61-68).

Fortune (2016), Facebook users are sharing fewer personal updates and it's a big problem, http://fortune.com/2016/04/07/facebook-sharing-decline/ [Accessed 28th Ocober 2016].

Frier, S. (2016), Facebook wants you to post more about yourself, Bloomberg Technology, https://www.bloomberg.com/news/articles/2016-04-07/facebook-said-to-face-decline-in-people-posting-personal-content [Accessed 28th October 2016]

Gefen, D. and Straub, D.W. (1997), Gender differences in the perception and use of e-mail: an extension to the technology acceptance model, *MIS Quarterly*, **21**(4), 389-400.

Goodhue, D.L. and Thompson, R.L. (1995), Task-technology fit and individual performance, *MIS Quarterly*, 213-236.

Hourahine, B. and Howard, M. (2004), Money on the Move: opportunities for financial service providers in the 'third space', *Journal of Financial Services Marketing*, **9**(1), 57–67.

Kang, J.Y.M., Mun, J.M. and Johnson, K.K. (2015), In-store mobile usage: downloading and usage intention toward mobile location-based retail apps, *Computers in Human Behavior*, **44** (May), 210-217.

Karahanna, E., Straub, D.W. and Chervany, N.L. (1999) Information Technology adoption across time: a cross-sectional comparison of pre-adoption and post-adoption beliefs, *MIS Quarterly*, **23**(2), 183-213.

Katz, E. and Blumler, J.G. (1974), *The Uses of Mass Communications: Current Perspectives on Gratifications Research*, Sage Publications.

King, J.L., Gurbaxani, V., Kraemer, K.L., McFarlan, F.W., Raman, K.S. and Yap, C.S. (1994), Institutional factors in information technology innovation, *Information Systems Research*, **5**(2), 139-169.

Kleijnen, M. H. P., de Ruyter, K. and Wetzels, M. G. M. (2004), Consumer adoption of wireless services: Discovering the rules, while playing the game, *Journal of Interactive Marketing*, **18**(2), 51–61.

Kleijnen, M., Lee, N. and Wetzels, M. (2009), An exploration of consumer resistance to innovation and its antecedents, *Journal of Economic Psychology*, **30**(3), 344-357.

Lee, C.S., Goh, D.H., Chua, A., and Ang, R.P., (2010), Indagator: Investigating perceived gratifications of an application that blends mobile content sharing with gameplay, *Journal of the American Society for Information Science and Technology*, **61**(6), 1244-1257.

Legris, P., Ingham, J. and Collerette, P. (2003), Why do people use Information Technology? A critical review of the technology acceptance model, *Information and Management*, **40**(3), 191-204.

Limayem, M., Hirt, S.G. and Cheung, C.M. (2007), How habit limits the predictive power of intention: the case of information systems continuance, *MIS Quarterly*, **31**(4), 705-737.

Mitchell, V.W. (1999), Consumer perceived risk: Conceptualisations and models, *European Journal of Marketing*, **33**(1/2), 163-195.

Moore, G.C. and Benbasat, I. (1991), Development of an instrument to measure the perceptions of adopting an information technology innovation, *Information Systems Research*, **2**(3), 192-222.

Pires, G., Stanton, J. and Eckford, A., (2004), Influences on the perceived risk of purchasing online, *Journal of Consumer Behaviour*, **4**(2), 118-131.

Price, R. (2015), Beyonce Has Been Spotted Wearing an Ultra-Exclusive Luxury Apple Watch that Isn't for Sale, *Business Insider UK*, http://uk.businessinsider.com/beyonce-apple-watch-edition-link-bracelet-gold-karl-lagerfeld-2015-4, [Accessed 5th January 2017].

Ram, S., and Sheth, J. N. (1989), Consumer resistance to innovations: the marketing problem and its solutions, *Journal of Consumer Marketing*, **6**(2), 5–14

Ramaswami, S.N., Strader, T.J. and Brett, K. (2000), Determinants of on-line channel use for purchasing financial products, *International Journal of Electronic Commerce*, **5**(2), 95-118.

Renaud, K. and Van Biljon, J. (2008), Predicting technology acceptance and adoption by the elderly: a qualitative study, in Proceedings of the 2008 annual research conference of the South African Institute of Computer Scientists and Information Technologists on IT research in developing countries: riding the wave of technology, 210-219.

Rogers E. M. (1995), *Diffusion of Innovations*, Wiley, New York.

Roma, P. and Dominici, G. (2016), Understanding the price drivers of successful apps in the mobile app market, *International Journal of Electronic Marketing and Retailing*, **7**(2), 159-185.

Sellgren, K. (2016), Teenagers Checking Mobile Phones in the Night, http://www.bbc.co.uk/news/education-37562259, [Accessed 4th April 2017]

Solomon, M.R., Marshall, G.W. and Stuart, E.W. (2011), *Marketing: Real People Real Choices*, 7th Edition. Prentice Hall.

Smock, A.D., Ellison, N.B., Lampe, C. and Wohn, D.Y. (2011), Facebook as a toolkit: a uses and gratification approach to unbundling feature use, *Computers in Human Behavior*, **27**(6), 2322-2329.

Taylor, S. and Todd, P. (1995), Decomposition and crossover effects in the Theory of Planned Behavior: A study of consumer adoption intentions, *International Journal of Research in Marketing*, **12**(2), 137–155

tom Dieck, M.C. and Jung, T. (2015), A theoretical model of mobile augmented reality acceptance in urban heritage tourism, *Current Issues in Tourism*, 1-21.

Tornatzky, L. G. and Klein, K. J. (1982). Innovation characteristics and innovation adoption-implementation: A meta-analysis of findings. *IEEE Transactions on Engineering Management*, **29**(1), 28–45.

Turel, O. (2015), Quitting the use of a habituated hedonic information system: a theoretical model and empirical examination of Facebook users, *European Journal of Information Systems*, **24**(4), 431-446.

Turnbull, P.W., Leek, S. and Ying, G. (2000) Customer confusion: the mobile phone market, *Journal of Marketing Management*, **16**(1-3), 143-163.

van Dijk, J. and Hacker, K. (2003), The digital divide as a complex and dynamic phenomenon, *The Information Society*, **19**(4), 315-326.

Venkatesh, V. and Davis, F.D. (2000), A theoretical extension of the technology acceptance model: four longitudinal field studies, *Management Science*, 46(2), 186-204.

2

Venkatesh, V., Morris, M.G., Davis, G.B. and Davis, F.D. (2003), User acceptance of information technology: toward a unified view, *MIS Quarterly*, **27**(3), 425-478.

Waite, K. and Harrison, T., (2002), Consumer expectations of online information provided by bank websites, *Journal of Financial Services Marketing*, **6**(4), 309-322.

Waite, K.M. (2009) Exploration of normative and predictive expectations of bank web site features: a tale of two task scenarios. https://www.era.lib.ed.ac.uk/handle/1842/4299 [Accessed 14th February 2017]

Webster, J. and Ahuja, J.S. (2006), Enhancing the design of web navigation systems: the influence of user disorientation on engagement and performance, *MIS Quarterly*, **30**(3), 661-678.

Woollaston, V. (2013), Facebook users are committing 'virtual identity suicide' in droves and quitting the site over privacy and addiction fears, *Daily Mail*. http://www.dailymail.co.uk/sciencetech/article-2423713/Facebook-users-committing-virtual-identity-suicide-quitting-site-droves-privacy-addiction-fears.html [Accessed 20th February 2017].

Yoo, Y., Henfridsson, O. and Lyytinen, K. (2010), Research commentary—the new organizing logic of digital innovation: an agenda for information systems research, *Information Systems Research*, **21**(4), 724-735.

Zolkepli, I.A. and Kamarulzaman, Y. (2015), Social media adoption: the role of media needs and innovation characteristics, *Computers in Human Behavior*, 43, 189-209.

3 Customer Experience Design

The term *'experience economy'* is used to identify goods that consumers purchase to give them an immersive and memorable experience (Pine and Gilmore, 2011). In an increasingly competitive marketplace the ability of an organisation to create a positive customer experience can deliver competitive advantage (Gentile et al., 2007). For example, Uber drivers provide complimentary water and sweets to passengers in order to differentiate the customer experiences when using their taxi from others. Customer experience design (CXD) has the goal of providing consumers with personalised and memorable engagement. CXD has typically been applied by the leisure industry but is now being extended to other industry sectors, notably retail (Pine and Gilmore, 1998). Each point of contact between brand and consumer provides a customer experience, and the number of contact points has exploded with the advent of digital channels, platforms and devices (Lemon and Verhoef, 2016:69). As a result, two specialist areas of digital marketing activity have emerged which focus on integrating digital and offline marketing activity: **experiential marketing**, which designs and delivers customer experiences; and **omni-channel marketing**, which integrates online and offline experience into a consistent whole.

The customer experience

The customer experience is defined as "the internal and subjective response customers have to any direct or indirect contact with a company" (Meyer and Schwager, 2007:2). A customer experience is "holistic in nature and involves the customer's cognitive, affective, emotional, social and physical response" (Verhoef et al., 2009:32). Experiences vary according to whether the customer is active or passive, and whether they are mentally absorbed or physically immersed; these four characteristics facilitate the development of four realms of experience (Figure 3.1) (Pine and Gilmore, 1998). Experiential marketing is an approach that directly seeks to create a specific emotional attachment to a brand and in particular aims to make the customer feel part of the brand (Luo et al., 2011).

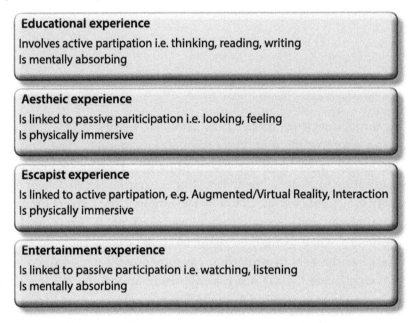

Educational experience
Involves active partipation i.e. thinking, reading, writing
Is mentally absorbing

Aestheic experience
Is linked to passive pariticipation i.e. looking, feeling
Is physically immersive

Escapist experience
Is linked to active partipation, e.g. Augmented/Virtual Reality, Interaction
Is physically immersive

Entertainment experience
Is linked to passive participation i.e. watching, listening
Is mentally absorbing

Figure 3.1: Realms of experience. Adapted from Pine and Gilmore (1998)

Experience design (XD) decisions relate to how two or more of these realms can be combined, with the richest experiences combining all four realms (Pine and Gilmore, 1998). For example, the travel industry use of VR enables companies to provide detailed information on available services, entertain customers through a novel presentation of information and also get active participation through physical immersion. However, consumers have more choice over the direction of the story as they move through virtual reality since they are free to explore, this means that advertisers lose control over the message elements and the content has to be more nuanced, detailed and anticipatory of a wide range of reactions (Greenwald, 2017).

Research how different brands have used VR in their advertising and consider how they have combined the four realms of experience in the finished advert. For example watch the video of the BMW Breakfast of Champions campaign https://vimeo.com/185515456

Touchpoints

3

A customer experience is delivered at each interaction or touchpoint with the brand; these interactions are also known as moments of truth (Stein and Ramaseshan 2016). There are three touchpoint categories (Meyer and Schwager, 2007; Forlizzi and Battarbee, 2004) (Figure 3.2):

1 Direct or active contact when the customer seeks out the brand, e.g. going to a brand website;

2 Indirect or passive contact when the brand seeks out the customer, e.g. through an e-mail campaign; and

3 Interactive contact or co-experience is where there is exchange between the brand and the customer or between customers, e.g. on social media.

Touchpoints are both digital and non-digital, e.g. a call centre. Customers will move between touchpoints, with experiences at one touchpoint informing and influencing subsequent points of contact. Each touchpoint presents the marketer with an opportunity to influence the customer (Stein and Ramaseshan, 2016). However, the dynamic pinball-like movement of customers between touchpoints and the different nature of each touchpoint means that the organisation does not have complete control over how the customer experience is shaped (Stein and Ramaseshan, 2016). For example, interactive touchpoints such as Facebook pages add a social dimension to customer experience over which the brand has limited control (Verhoef et al., 2009).

A psychological theory that is helpful in understanding customer interaction with touchpoints is the Stimulus-Organism-Response theory (S-O-R) (Mehrabian and Russell, 1974). S-O-R theory states that stimuli (S) are processed by an organism (O), and which, in turn, influence behavioural responses (R) by approaching or avoiding the stimuli. In experience design, each touchpoint contains stimuli that are processed by the customer, who then responds (Stein and Ramaseshan, 2016). In a retail setting, consumer approach behaviour is conceptualised as the desire to remain in a store, and to explore its offerings, whilst avoidance is associated with a desire to terminate any engagement with a store or service (Bitner, 1992). In a digital setting, approach behaviour includes engagement measures, duration of visit and transaction (Dailey, 2004; Perez Vega et al., 2016) and avoidance behaviour including exit or rejection of the technology (Lee et al., 2011).

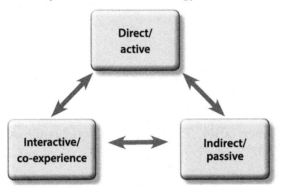

Figure 3.2: Touchpoint categories

Researchers have drawn on S-O-R Theory to develop the concept of a servicescape which classifies stimuli into those related to spatial layout, background ambient conditions and signs, symbols and artefacts that communicate directly to customers (Bitner, 1992); these stimuli are often referred to as *atmospherics* (Kotler 1973). This framework can be extended to formulate an e-servicescape that can be used to understand the range of stimuli present within the website touchpoint (Figure 3.3) (Waite and Rowley, 2014).

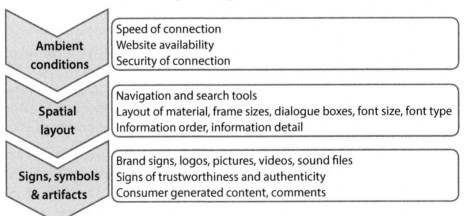

Figure 3.3: E-servicescape

Social network touchpoints will include the e-servicescape elements of the channel plus social stimuli. Servicescape research shows that social density, the number of individuals present, influences customer response (Tombs and

McColl-Kenndy, 2003). In addition the behaviour of fellow customers and the behaviour of frontline employees are also significant influences (Daunt and Harris, 2012).

Exercise 3.2

Visit the website of a brand and evaluate your response to the E-servicescape, consider which features make you want to 'approach' and which make you want to 'avoid'. Next visit the Facebook page of the same brand and consider, which social stimuli features influence your approach/avoidance behaviour.

Design thinking

Analysing how customers interact with multiple touchpoints is a major consideration. Marketing scholars have drawn from the engineering and design industries to develop analytical techniques (Wilson et al., 2008). Service blueprinting maps out customer interactions with the brand (Bitner et al., 2008) and incorporates process improvement and quality measurement techniques (Lemon and Verhoef., 2016). A criticism of this technique is that it is internally focussed, does not take into account developments in digital technology and is insufficiently customer-focussed (Lemon and Verhoef, 2016). A growing trend is towards *design thinking* (Rowe, 1987), which is characterised by focus on observation of actual use and being centred upon the user (Brown, 2009).

Figure 3.4 presents the three main steps to design thinking:

1 Inspiration which aims to generate a deep insight and define the problem from the user viewpoint.

2 Ideation where many different solutions are generated using divergent thinking to generate a wide range of possible solutions, e.g. such as might be achieved in a brainstorm or using crowdsourcing.

3 Implementation using convergent thinking to choose the best option. Implementation also involves sub-processes of designing a small prototype of the solution to test and feeding the results back to the inspiration phase.

Design thinking ensures that organisational actions remain focused upon the consumer at the inspiration stage, encourages fresh thinking at the ideation stage and tolerates failure and flexibility at the implementation stage (Schybergson, 2016).

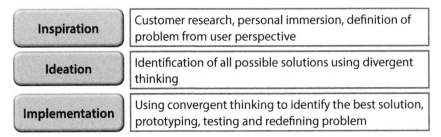

Inspiration	Customer research, personal immersion, definition of problem from user perspective
Ideation	Identification of all possible solutions using divergent thinking
Implementation	Using convergent thinking to identify the best solution, prototyping, testing and redefining problem

Figure 3.4: Three phases of design thinking

Companies need to be distinct and relevant in the digital marketplace, and the focus upon the customer experience has elevated the importance of design-based approaches (Consultancy.uk, 2016). Organisations are appointing to the new role of Chief Experience Officer whose responsibilities include determining where to invest resources, how to implement marketing strategy and how to measure and respond to campaign outcomes (Edelman and Singer, 2015; Kapko, 2017). Investment will be made into the most influential touchpoints and this may mean redirecting marketing budgets away from traditional mass media advertising. For example, 32% of respondents to the UK Institute of Practitioners in Advertising survey reported that they had increased their internet marketing budgets (Vizard, 2017).

Implementing CXD will mean selecting and combining elements such as visuals, audio, information content, interaction opportunities and message source to contribute to the user experience. Finally metrics will need to be selected to form a customer experience dashboard, which is a combination of metrics that provide continuous information on both perception-based (brand awareness, customer sentiment) and performance-based metrics (call centre completion rate, time to delivery). With an increase in digital marketing investment there is an increased focus upon digital marketing metrics and attribution.

The customer journey

The idea of touchpoints, where micro-decisions occur, has lead to the concept of the customer journey being applied to customer decision making. A customer journey is the sequence of steps that a customer goes through when interacting with a company offering (Norton and Pine, 2013). When making decisions customers use a combination of cognitive/utilitarian reasons and enjoyment seeking/hedonic reasons, with customer experiences being linked to the hedonic reasons (Holbrook and Hirschman, 1982). For example, a combination of utilitarian and hedonic reasoning is used when booking a train ticket to choose between train time and carriage class (standard or first class). Utilitarian reasoning will look at cost of the ticket, journey duration and arrival time, hedonic reasoning will look at the comfort and amenities offered by carriage class.

Previous work has applied a 5-stage or E model to consumer decision making, of 1) need recognition 2) information search 3) evaluation 4) purchase and 5) post-purchase evaluation (Engel et al., (1973). Practitioners refer to this process as the customer funnel. At the large end of the funnel, the customer considers a wide range of brands that is then reduced by comparison on price vs value until the consumer is considering only one brand to purchase. The 5-stage model's linearity and emphasis on utilitarian reasoning resulted in it being criticised for not taking into account the whole consumption experience, particularly the pleasurable and social aspects (Court et al., 2009).

A second limitation of the funnel idea is that it results in marketers pushing marketing information on price and product features at key points in order to ensure that their product is chosen. Research into customer decision making indicates that it has changed in response to digital communications (Court et al., 2009). Push communication does not account for the ways in which the digitally empowered consumer is able to use a range of digital and offline channels to gather information (Edelman and Singer, 2015). For example, the role of the physical retail outlet is important to meet customer needs to examine the product in action – as a result of visually inspecting the product up to 40% of customers will change their minds (Court et al., 2009). The majority of touch points used at the pre-purchase phase are those which are active or interactive, such as in-store interactions, internet reviews and word-of-mouth recommendations from friends and family, which are combined with recollections of past experiences (Court et al., 2009). Only a third of the touchpoints involve company-driven marketing (Court et al., 2009).

It is argued that consumer behaviour has changed so that the five stage model is now only three stages 1) pre-purchase, 2) purchase and 3) post-purchase (Court et al., 2009; Lemon and Verhoef, 2016). Table 3.1 summarises the differences and shows that the number of products under consideration at the outset vary. In the EKB model customers search exhaustively for information, constantly adding brands and products to their consideration set, which is a subset of brands that customers evaluate (Howard and Sheth, 1969). In contrast, in the revised model the number of brands added is limited and vary by industry, Court et al. (2009) find that customers shopping for personal computers only add an average of one brand to the initial-consideration set of 1.7. An explanation for this behavior is that customers are seeking to reduce cognitive demands caused by the accessibility and availability of information by considering only a limited set of brands at the outset based on their experience (Court et al., 2009).

Table 3.1: Comparison of EKB model and revised customer journey

EKB model	Customer activity
Need recognition	Customer experiences a need-state which requires purchase to resolve
Initial consideration	Consumer has large number of products under consideration
Active evaluation	Consumer compares each product on its key attributes and finally selects final product for purchase
Purchase	Purchase of single product
Post-purchase experience	Evaluation of product and decision to repurchase in future

Revised model	Customer activity
Pre-purchase	Customer begins with a small initial set of products based on previous experience and interaction with touchpoints Customer adds or subtracts products as a result of interaction with touchpoints
Purchase	Consumer may purchase single or multiple products for comparison
Post-purchase	Customers keep or return product, returns to information seeking, learns about process and product, uses/shares this information to inform future consumption

Source: Adapted from Court et al., 2009; Lemon and Verhoef, 2016

At post-purchase customers show either active or passive loyalty. Those who are actively loyal repurchase and give positive word of mouth whilst those who are passive only repurchase through inertia. Court et al. (2009) find that customers go online to conduct further research immediately after purchase, an action which was not considered when the funnel model was conceived. These factors mean that it is important for companies to generate positive word of mouth and invest in digital assets such as websites and social media sites. The trend towards internet shopping means that goods are inspected at post-purchase and then possibly returned. This changes the role of the retail touchpoint to that of a "concierge geared toward helping consumers, rather than focusing only on transactions and deliveries" (Brynjolfsson et al., 2013:24).

Omni-channel marketing

The concept of the customer journey has prompted a re-evaluation of earlier ideas regarding marketing channel strategy. Initially it was argued that a retailer should use multiple channels and specifically adopt digital channels to reduce costs, provide 24/7 opportunities to purchase and increase geographical spread (Deleersnyder et al., 2002). A customer would choose the appropriate channel and conduct their shopping activity solely within that channel. Multi-channel marketing focuses on the effectiveness of the retail function and develops marketing mixes that vary by channel (i.e. pricing) with each channel being managed separately within the firm (Verhoef 2012). However technological developments have resulted in a blurring of boundaries between the offline and online store (Brunjolfsson et al., 2013). As a result omni-channel marketing focuses on a wide range of channels that when combined deliver the brand experience. Each distribution channel is viewed as the place where goods can be purchased and where brand information is communicated (Verhoef et al., 2015). It is important to understand how consumers draw on the online and offline service environments to form impressions, make inferences and form transactional intentions.

Omni-channel marketing considers both the way in which goods are supplied and also the way in which customers shop for them. A key objective of omni-channel marketing is to create of a "seamless experience" that integrates the touchpoints within the customer journey (Rigby, 2011). Seamlessness means that the customer can move smoothly between channels and have a consistent experience. A seamless channel experience should provide a consumer with a sense of control, level of enjoyment and focus resulting in a state of flow (Csikszentmihalyi, 1977).

Flow is an enjoyable state that occurs when the individual is so immersed in an activity that they lose awareness of time and self (van Noort et al., 2012). Digital researchers propose that flow can be experienced when one is immersed in an online activity (Hoffman and Novak, 2009). As such flow can be considered as a positive consequence of providing a satisfactory omni-channel consumer experience. Flow positively influences internet shopping behaviour such as purchase intention and impulse buying (Hsu et al., 2012), improving the overall shopping experience (Wang and Hsiao, 2012). Digital marketing professionals are encouraged to develop websites that facilitate the experience of flow (Gao and Bai, 2014).

Poor experiences which disrupt the customer journey and prevent flow experiences are called *points of friction* or *pain points*. For example, Hasan (2016) examines how website design elements can cause or reduce feelings of irritation. He compares visual information and navigation design and finds that good navigation design reduces perceptions of irritation. Points of friction can occur when customers move between devices (i.e. from a PC to a mobile phone) and between platforms (from website to app). Omni-channel marketers need to ensure that content is provided that is optimised for the mobile device, that the website and app content are consistent and that location based information is used to full effect. For example, mobile phone penetration means that customers can make transactions independent of their home or office based computer when they are out of the home or work. Customers use mobile devices in store to *showroom*, i.e. to compare prices online and offline, and also to *webroom*, i.e. conduct research online before purchasing in store (Lemon and Verhoef, 2016). Brands can design a seamless customer experience by having wi-fi and tablets or even augmented reality in-store to assist pre-purchase information search and post-purchase product comparison (Poncin and Mimoun, 2014).

■ Benefits and challenges of omni-channel marketing

There are benefits from adopting an omni-channel approach particularly when it is coupled with data capture and management that allows an organisation to track the customer across all touchpoints. When interactive channels are integrated with mass communication channels, for example when customers use mobile devices to access content during television broadcasts, it is possible to track the impact of advertising and sports sponsorship (Verhoef et al., 2015). In addition there are operational benefits from integrating online and offline channels that allow customers to order online and either collect or return offline. Bell et al (2013:4) argue that an offline showroom "confers an awareness and brand benefits that drive incremental sales in the existing online channel". For example Amazon expanded into physical stores for its online grocery business in 2017 (Chafkin, 2017)

However, omni-channel marketing brings several challenges. Although, survey evidence shows that 72% of customers prefer an integrated marketing approach, businesses remain hesitant to drive cross-channel marketing (Brynjolfsson et al., 2013). When channels are used across the search and purchase process it is difficult for firms to control the customer journey (Verhoef et al., 2015). The aggregation of online and offline content have made the retail landscape more competitive and means that businesses have to be more transparent in their processes and honest in their information provision (Brynjolfsson et al., 2013). For example, customers can share reviews and photos to their social networks and potential customers on review websites which influences their decision making. Some restaurants banned food 'selfies' as they mean the food gets cold and destroys the restaurant atmosphere (Clay, 2014). There is also evidence that the difference between online and offline pricing has narrowed with aligned prices for clothing and electronics (Cavallo, 2017).

Omni-channel marketing capabilities

Edelman and Singer (2015) identify four key capabilities of omni-channel marketing: automation, proactive personalisation, contextual interaction and journey innovation.

■ Automation

Automation helps to streamline the customer omni-channel journey by using digital technology to automate manual processes or remove steps. Examples include:

- Providing QR codes for the consumer scan to gain access to video content, advice and reviews without the step of typing in an URL.
- Providing e-coupons or mobile tickets to remove the step of printing out documents.
- Using location based technology to automatically 'push' promotions to the consumer's mobile device after they have connected to a wi-fi system.
- Providing one touch ordering buttons to refill essentials, e.g. Amazon Dash.
- Providing apps to track delivery or provide information on stock availability in a local store.
- Providing voice-activated devices such as Alexa and SIRI that automatically enhance search capability by making recommendations.

■ Proactive personalisation

Proactive personalization uses information gathered either from past interactions or from consumer indicated preferences to not only automate functions but also customize these to match with the individual. Examples include:

- ■ Designing a personalised landing page for those who click-through e-mail links or scan a QR code.

- ■ Using a content management system to create online advertising to take into account geographical location and preference for certain products.

- ■ Remembering products that you have looked at previously on a website when you return.

■ Contextual interaction

Contextual interaction uses knowledge about the customer journey stage to influence their progress. Contextual interaction can be used to deepen customer engagement or stimulate purchase Examples include:

- ■ Enabling individuals to share and like content with others; in these situations the consumer experience is influenced by observing and being observed by others (Forlizzi and Battarbee, 2004).

- ■ Choosing an interface that shapes user experience by allowing or disallowing certain online actions (Forlizzi and Battarbee, 2004). For example, Facebook debated whether they should use a dislike button but instead elected to use a range of emoji.

- ■ Monitoring online word of mouth, analyzing content and responding with brand messages.

- ■ Using programmic advertising to place discounted offers for products that have been recently browsed.

- ■ Filtering messages in a social network so that only content that is congruent with the consumer's interests is shown.

■ Journey innovation

Journey innovation provides new and innovative experiences for the customer. This will involve experimenting with new technology. With the roll-out of high speed broadband, marketers have taken the opportunity to develop new technology to entertain and inform customers. For example:

- ■ Fashion retailers can use Shoogle-It which uses touch screen technology to approximate the movement of a fabric or augmented reality changing rooms that allow you to 'try on' garments (Cano et al., 2017).

- Grocers can use recipe apps that generate a shopping list and places an order at the retailer.
- Holiday destinations can use virtual reality applications to allow consumers to experience resort destinations or cruise ships.
- Museums and historic locations can use virtual reality to 'transport' visitors back to past times.

3

Summary

Customer experience design is a marketing approach that seeks to ensure that customers have a seamless journey across different channels when interacting with a brand. Digital marketers need to consider how to manage a variety of brand touchpoints to facilitate deeper customer engagement and support purchasing behaviour. This chapter shows how the theories and processes from psychology and design can help experience design management.

Exemplar paper

Lemon, K.N. and Verhoef, P.C. (2016), Understanding customer experience throughout the customer journey, *Journal of Marketing*, **80**, 69-96.

This paper contains a detailed examination of existing definitions and conceptualisations of the customer experience. The authors present an integrated view of the customer experience across the customer journey. They suggest that IT can be used to enhance the emotional components of the customer experience and provide several examples of brand activity in this area, including Disney and the Bank of Scotland.

■ Additional reading

Huang, Y.C., Backman, K.F., Backman, S.J. and Chang, L.L. (2016) Exploring the implications of virtual reality technology in tourism marketing: An integrated research framework. *International Journal of Tourism Research*, **18**(2), 116-128.

Homburg, C., Jozić, D. and Kuehnl, C. (2017) Customer experience management: toward implementing an evolving marketing concept. *Journal of the Academy of Marketing Science*, **45**(3), 377-401.

Tuten, T. and Solomon, M. (2015) *Social Media Marketing.* 2nd Ed. Sage Publications.

References

Bell, D.R., Gallino, S. and Moreno, A. (2013), Inventory showrooms and customer migration in omni-channel retail: the effect of product information. Available at SSRN 2370535. https://www.misrc.umn.edu/wise/2014_Papers/17.pdf [Accessed on 15th August 2017]

Bitner, M.J. (1992), Servicescapes: the impact of physical surroundings on customers and employees, *The Journal of Marketing*, **56**(2), 57-71.

Bitner, M.J., Ostrom, A.L. and Morgan, F.N. (2008), Service blueprinting: a practical technique for service innovation, *California Management Review*, **50**(3), 66-94.

Brown, T. (2009), *Change by Design: How Design Thinking Transforms Organizations and Inspires Innovation*, Harper Collins Publishers, London.

Brynjolfsson, E., Hu, Y.J. and Rahman, M.S. (2013), Competing in the age of omnichannel retailing, *MIT Sloan Management Review*, **54**(4), 23-29.

Cano, M.B., Perry, P., Ashman, R. and Waite, K. (2017), The influence of image interactivity upon user engagement when using mobile touch screens, *Computers in Human Behavior*, **77**, 406-412.

Cavallo, A. (2017). Are online and offline prices similar? Evidence from large multi-channel retailers. *American Economic Review*, **107**(1), pp.283-303.

Chafkin, M. (2017), Amazon Needs to Watch What it Eats, Bloomberg Businessweek, https://www.bloomberg.com/news/articles/2017-07-31/amazon-needs-to-watch-what-it-eats, [Accessed 1st August 2017].

Clay, X. (2014), It is Wrong to Photograph your Food in Restaurants? *The Telegraph*, 19th February, http://www.telegraph.co.uk/foodanddrink/restaurants/10648419/Is-it-wrong-to-photograph-your-food-in-restaurants.html, [Accessed 1st August 2017].

Consultancy.uk (2016), Top 10 Digital Trends 2016 to Watch for Design Thinking, http://www.consultancy.uk/news/3162/top-10-digital-trends-2016-to-watch-for-design-thinking [Accessed 1st August 2017]

Court, D., Elzinga, D., Mulder, S. and Vetvik, O.J. (2009), The consumer decision journey, *McKinsey Quarterly*, https://www.mckinsey.com/business-functions/marketing-and-sales/our-insights/the-consumer-decision-journey [Accessed 4th August 2017].

Csikszentmihalyi, M. (1997), *Finding Flow: The Psychology of Engagement with Everyday Life*, Basic Books, New York.

Dailey, L. (2004), Navigational web atmospherics: explaining the influence of restrictive navigation cues, *Journal of Business Research*, **57**(7), 795-803.

Daunt, K.L. and Harris, L.C. (2012), Exploring the forms of dysfunctional customer behaviour: a study of differences in servicescape and customer disaffection with service, *Journal of Marketing Management*, **28**(1-2), 129-153.

Deleersnyder, B., Geyskens, I., Gielens, K. and Dekimpe, M.G. (2002), How cannibalistic is the internet channel? a study of the newspaper industry in the United Kingdom and the Netherlands, *International Journal of Research in Marketing*, **19**(4), 337–48.

Edelman, D.C. and Singer, M. (2015), Competing on customer journeys, *Harvard Business Review*, **93**(11), 88-100.

Engel, J.F., Kollat, D.T. and Blackwell, R.D. (1973), *Consumer Behavior,* Holt, Rinehart and Einston, New York.

Forlizzi, J. and Battarbee, K., (2004), Understanding Experience in Interactive Systems, In Proceedings of the 5th conference on Designing interactive systems: processes, practices, methods, and techniques (261-268), ACM.

Gao, L. and Bai, X. (2014), Online consumer behaviour and its relationship to website atmospheric induced flow: insights into online travel agencies in China, *Journal of Retailing and Consumer Services*, **21**(4), 653-665.

Gentile, C., Spiller, N. and Noci, G. (2007), How to sustain the customer experience: an overview of experience components that co-create value with the customer, *European Management Journal*, **25**(5), 395-410.

Greenwald, M. (2017) From Storytelling to VR "Storyliving": Future marketing communications, *Forbes Magazine*, https://www.forbes.com/sites/michellegreenwald/2017/07/31/from-storytelling-to-vr-storyliving-future-marketing-communications/#5b8414c435e2 [Accessed 31st July 2017]

Hasan, B. (2016), Perceived irritation in online shopping: the impact of website design characteristics, *Computers in Human Behavior*, **54** (Jan), 224-230.

Hoffman, D.L. and Novak, T.P. (2009), Flow online: lessons learned and future prospects, *Journal of Interactive Marketing*, **23**(1), 23-34.

Holbrook, M.B. and Hirschman, E.C. (1982), The experiential aspects of consumption: consumer fantasies, feelings, and fun, *Journal of Consumer Research*, **9**(2), 132-140.

Howard, J.A.S. and Sheth, J. N. (1969), *The Theory of Buyer Behavior*, John Wiley, New York.

Hsu, C.L., Chang, K.C. and Chen, M.C. (2012), The impact of website quality on customer satisfaction and purchase intention: perceived playfulness and perceived flow as mediators, *Information Systems and e-Business Management*, **10**(4), 549-570.

Kapko, M. (2017), A Guide to the 10 Next Hot Jobs in Digital Marketing, and for Several Years to Come, *Adweek*, http://www.adweek.com/digital/a-guide-to-the-10-next-hot-jobs-in-digital-marketing-and-for-several-years-to-come/ [Accessed 31st July 2017].

Kotler, P. (1973), Atmospherics as a marketing tool, *Journal of Retailing*, **49**(4), 48-64.

Lee, S., Ha, S. and Widdows, R. (2011), Consumer responses to high-technology products: product attributes, cognition, and emotions, *Journal of Business Research*, **64**(11), 1195-1200.

Lemon, K.N. and Verhoef, P.C. (2016), Understanding customer experience throughout the customer journey, *Journal of Marketing*, **80**, 69-96.

Luo, M.M., Chen, J.S., Ching, R.K. and Liu, C.C. (2011), An examination of the effects of virtual experiential marketing on online customer intentions and loyalty, *Service Industries Journal*, **31**(13), 2163-2191.

Mehrabian, A. and Russell, J.A. (1974), *An Approach to Environmental Psychology*, The MIT Press, Boston.

Meyer, C. and Schwager, A. (2007), Customer experience, *Harvard Business Review*, **85**(2), 1-11.

Norton, D.W. and Pine, B.J., (2013), Using the customer journey to road test and refine the business model, *Strategy and Leadership*, **41**(2), 12-17.

Perez-Vega, R., Waite, K. and O'Gorman, K. (2016), Social impact theory: an examination of how immediacy operates as an influence upon social media interaction in Facebook Fan Pages, *Marketing Review*, **16**(3), 299-321.

Pine, B.J. and Gilmore, J.H. (1998), Welcome to the experience economy, *Harvard Business Review*, 76 (Jul-Aug), 97-105.

Pine, B.J. and Gilmore, J.H. (2011), *The Experience Economy*. Harvard Business Press, Boston.

Poncin, I. and Mimoun, M.S.B. (2014), The impact of 'e-atmospherics' on physical stores, *Journal of Retailing and Consumer Services*, **21**(5), 851-859.

Rigby, D., (2011), The future of shopping, *Harvard Business Review*, **89**(12), 65-76.

Rowe, G. P. (1987), *Design Thinking*, The MIT Press, Cambridge.

Schybergson, O. (2015) 10 design trends CMOs should watch for in 2016, *Forbes Magazine* 17th December, https://www.forbes.com/sites/onmarketing/2015/12/17/10-design-trends-cmos-should-watch-for-in-2016/#b521316674b7 [Accessed 1st August 2017].

Stein, A. and Ramaseshan, B. (2016), Towards the identification of customer experience touch point elements, *Journal of Retailing and Consumer Services*, **30**, 8-19.

Tombs, A. and McColl-Kennedy, J.R. (2003), Social-servicescape conceptual model, *Marketing Theory*, **3**(4), 447-475.

Van Noort, G., Voorveld, H.A. and Van Reijmersdal, E.A. (2012), Interactivity in brand web sites: cognitive, affective, and behavioral responses explained by consumers' online flow experience, *Journal of Interactive Marketing*, **26**(4), 223-234.

Verhoef, P. C. (2012), Multi-channel customer management strategy, in *Handbook of Marketing Strategy*, Shankar V. and Carpenter G., eds. Cheltenham: Edward Elgar Publishing Limited, 135-150.

Verhoef, P.C., Kannan, P.K. and Inman, J.J. (2015), From multi-channel retailing to omni-channel retailing: introduction to the special issue on multi-channel retailing, *Journal of Retailing*, **91**(2), 174-181.

Verhoef, P.C., Lemon, K.N., Parasuraman, A., Roggeveen, A., Tsiros, M. and Schlesinger, L.A. (2009), Customer experience creation: determinants, dynamics and management strategies, *Journal of Retailing*, **85**(1), 31-41.

Vizard, S. (2017) Digital Ad Budgets See Biggest Rise in Almost 10 years, *Marketing Week*, https://www.marketingweek.com/2017/07/19/digital-ad-budget-bellwether [Accessed 31st July 2017].

Waite, K. and Rowley, J., (2015), E-servicescapes in online banking in Harrison, T. and Estelami, H. (eds), *The Routledge Companion to Financial Services Marketing*, 346-364, Routledge, Abingdon.

Wang, L.C. and Hsiao, D.F., (2012), Antecedents of flow in retail store shopping, *Journal of Retailing and Consumer Services*, **19**(4), 381-389.

Wilson, A., Zeithaml, V.A., Bitner, M.J. and Gremler, D.D., (2008), *Services Marketing: Integrating Customer Focus Across the Firm*. McGraw Hill, Columbus.

3

4 Digital Service Quality

Digital channels are an established means of accessing information and goods. The online marketplace has considerable economic significance. In response to the pervasive use of technology the idea of the *market-space* is used instead of traditional *marketplace* term (Rayport and Sviolka, 1994). A market-space is where "products and services exist as digital information and can be delivered through information based channels" (Rayport and Sviokla, 1995:14). It is estimated that the market-space was worth €430bn to the EU economy in 2012, and in the UK, the use of Google Search and AdWords generated at least £11 billion in economic activity in 2014 (House of Lords Select Committee, 2014). However market-space competition is getting stiffer (WSI, 2013), and ensuring that customers are satisfied with the online experience is critical in order to avoid loss of customers to competitors.

One strategy open to digital marketers is to ensure repeat custom through offering a quality e-service that delivers customer satisfaction. In offline service research the argument is that a satisfied customer is more inclined to return to a service outlet, to repurchase, to spread favourable word of mouth, and to be less sensitive to price competition (Berry and Parasuraman, 2004). These outcomes are also present within empirical research into the use of digital technology, which shows that overall satisfaction with digital technology performance has a positive effect on the intention to continue use (Rowley, 2001).

Customer satisfaction and service quality

The concepts of customer satisfaction and service quality are both defined as being customer judgments. Customer satisfaction is a "judgement that a product or service feature, or the product or service itself, provided (or is providing) a pleasurable level of consumption-related fulfilment" (Oliver 1996:13). Service quality is a "judgement about an entity's overall excellence or superiority" (Parasuraman et al., 1988: 5). The concept of electronic service quality (e-SQ) has been developed for digital channels, and is the "extent to which a website [or other digital channel] facilitates efficient and effective shopping, purchasing and delivery" (Parasuraman et al., 2005:5). However, as the Internet has developed, e-SQ has been redefined as a judgement of the service experience provided in the online marketplace (Sousa and Voss, 2006).

The exact relationship between service quality and satisfaction is uncertain (Sureshchandar et al., 2002). Some researchers argue that service quality leads to a judgement of satisfaction (Parasuraman et al., 1985) whilst others state that in fact customer satisfaction comes before a judgement of service quality (Cronin and Taylor, 1992). However, a key difference is that customer satisfaction is transaction- and time-specific, whilst service quality is a long-term attitude; this means service quality is considered to be source of differentiation and competitive advantage for services (Giese and Cote, 2000).

E-service

Digital channels provide remote rather than direct delivery; any interaction with the product or service is technology-mediated and is similar to a service experience (Shostack, 1977). E-service encompasses the "deeds, efforts or performances whose delivery is mediated by information technology" (Rowley, 2006:341) and is delivered through self-service technology (SST). SSTs include both on-site options, such as supermarket self-service check-outs and ATMs, and online channels accessed in the home (Dabholkar and Bagozzi, 2002). When using SSTs customers are uncertain about the consequences of making mistake which can reduce both trust and loyalty (Meuter et al., 2000).

In addition, online purchase increases the intangibility of goods as there is limited customer capacity to make a direct assessment through feel, touch and detailed visual inspection (Jiang and Benbasat, 2004). According to

Signaling Theory (Spence 1973), in such situations individuals will make use of extrinsic cues or signals to make a quality assessment. This means that digital marketing mix elements (i.e. product brand, place, pricing and communications) act as signals of quality to reduce uncertainty and risk and to increase transactional trust (Wells et al., 2011).

Exercise 4.1

Select two websites, one where you have transactional trust and one where you do not. Identify how the different elements of the digital marketing mix are acting as signals that increase or reduce your feelings of uncertainty.

4

Expectancy-Disconfirmation Theory

Service quality and satisfaction measures are based on Expectancy-Disconfirmation theory which proposes that customers make assessments of product performance based on a comparison of expectations with perceptions (Oliver, 1996). Customer expectations are beliefs formed before service delivery that serve as standards or reference points against which perceptions of actual service are judged (Zeithaml et al., 1993). This means that online customers are making constant comparisons between the e-service they expect and the e-service they are receiving. Each comparison results in either (1) a positive disconfirmation where the service experience exceeds expectation; (2) a negative disconfirmation where service is below standard that expected; or (3) a zero disconfirmation where expectation standards are met (Oliver, 1996). Upon completion of the transaction the customer would be either satisfied or dissatisfied and would make a service quality judgement (Parasuraman et al., 1985).

The service quality literature identifies four reasons for mismatching expectations and perceptions (Wilson et al., 2008) (Table 4.1). A mismatch between performance and promises is the most complex gap to close. Expectations can be raised as a result of not only promotional materials but also through brand positioning and previous experience that the customer has gained offline.

Table 4.1: Mismatching expectations and perceptions

Mismatch	Action
A company does know what customers expect from their website	Conduct primary research
Incorrect design and standards	Commission a redesign of the website
The website does not deliver well across all devices	Ensure that technical specifications are met
The performance of the service does not match the brand promise	Evaluate digital channel fit with the strategic brand plan

Measuring E-service quality

SERVQUAL measures the gaps between customer expectations and perceptions across five areas, or dimensions, which are considered to contribute
to an overall service quality judgement. This is also known as the RATER
model (Parasuraman et al., 1988) (Table 4.2). SERVQUAL is a survey with
22 questions about expectations and perceptions in each the RATER model
dimensions. Quantitative analysis techniques are used to calculate and
aggregate the gap between expectations and perceptions and correlate these
to a measure of the customer's overall service quality assessment.

Table 4.2: Dimensions of SERVQUAL. (Adapted from Buttle, 1991; Wilson et al., 2008)

Dimension	Definition
Reliability	The service is performed as promised resulting in a judgement of the organisation being dependable and accurate
Assurance	The employees demonstrate knowledge and courtesy resulting in a judgement of trust and confidence
Tangibles	The physical facilities, equipment, personnel and communications result in a judgement of them being appealing and up-to-date
Empathy	Customers receive caring and individualised attention resulting in a judgement of that needs are understood
Responsiveness	Response to customer requests are prompt and constructive resulting in a judgement of flexibility and the ability to customise the service

To ensure validity, the SERVQUAL instrument needs to be adapted for
particular service contexts, e.g. financial services, health services etc. (Carman,
1990). Parasuraman et al. (2005:215) state that "studying e-SQ requires a scale
development that extends beyond merely adapting offline scales" and so
they create E-S-QUAL to assess the quality of websites using two scales:

- The E-S-QUAL which relates core service quality to efficiency, fulfilment, system availability and privacy;

- The E-ReS-QUAL that is applied when customers experience non-routine encounters that require an online service recovery process that is responsive, offers compensation and personal contact.

There should be careful consideration regarding the provision of channel features, as research indicates that more features may not be perceived by customers as better, and that an ideal point of provision exists for each transaction stage (Hooi Ting, 2004). Zeithaml et al. (2002) identify that there is "curvilinearity" in e-SQ dimensions. Curvilinearity is like an upside down smile, i.e. there is an increase in satisfaction with additional provision until over-provision becomes a source of dissatisfaction. For example, when placing an order customers may value a text confirmation but not frequent updates as to the progress of the parcel. In addition, a customer may trade-off different features; for example, by accepting reduced functionality on a mobile-optimised site. It is costly for organisations to have to support all target platforms and devices equally so developing appropriate e-SQ measures provides insight to help balance the costs of implementation vs benefit of customer quality judgement.

Decompose e-SQ

There is renewed interest in how service quality can inform experience design (XD) (Shin et al., 2012). The scope of e-SQ has widened to include digital devices (i.e. mobile phone) and different platforms (i.e. Web 2.0 as well as Web 1.0). To gain clarity, a technique from computer science known as object-orientated decomposition is used to break down the growing complexity of e-service into smaller parts or components which each contribute to an e-SQ judgement (Figure 4.1). Support for object-orientated decomposition is found within the information systems literature where information quality (judgement of content) and system quality (judgement of the technology function) are measured as distinct elements rather than grouping them together into one set of measures that predict information system success (DeLone and McLean, 2003).

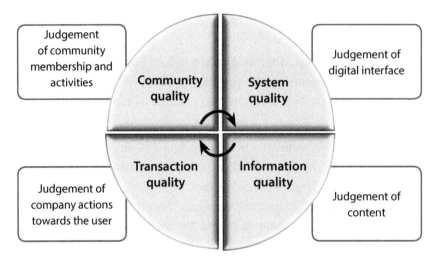

Figure 4.1: Components of e-Service Quality

■   System quality

System quality is a judgement of the digital interface. Assessing system quality enables a company to identify whether there are bugs in the system, the contribution of the interface to ease of use, and the ability to withstand hackers (Seddon 1997). There are three dimensions of system quality: system availability, system efficiency, system reliability and system security. (Figure 4.2)

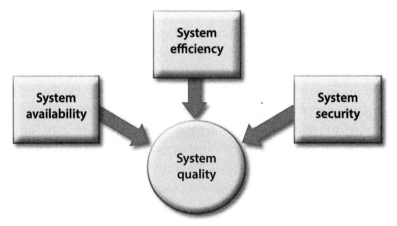

Figure 4.2: Dimensions of system quality

System availability focuses upon whether the digital channel is available and functioning correctly. Customer judgement is formed in response to whether the digital channel launches quickly, and does not crash or freeze. In addition, judgement may be formed in response to system use across multiple devices (such as mobile phones and tablets) and also formed based on the capacity of the system to allow the user access when the device is not online, i.e. offline functionality. System availability can be affected by restricted computing power, battery limitations and the telecoms network provision, and thus can be outside the direct control of digital marketing managers (Chalmers and Sloman, 1999).

System efficiency focuses upon the channel ease of use, speed of access and accessibility. It is important that information is well organised so that customers can locate products, find relevant information and check out effortlessly (Wilson et al., 2008). These features are also known as information architecture, which is the practice of how to organise information spaces to make them usable (Ding and Lin, 2009). Faceted navigation allows users to drill down to a relevant product by selecting different product attributes. A company may structure information so that the most frequently purchased products, new additions and those on special offer are prominent. When selecting how pages interconnect there are two approaches (Table 4.3). Whichever approach is chosen a rule of thumb is there should be only three clicks to reach any section of the site. This rule is of particular importance when serving pages in response to the initial search to reduce the bounce rate. Therefore digital marketers may need to consider designing separate landing pages for specific search terms to improve system efficiency.

Table 4.3: Faceted navigation approaches

Approach	Definition	Impact on selection	Impact on clicks
Narrow and deep	Shows a few links or choices on each page, typically a tightly defined range of information, e. g. women's high-heeled shoes	Easier for the user to make their selection	More clicks are required to reach a particular piece of information
Broad and shallow	Shows a larger number of links and choices on each page, typically a wide range of information, e. g. all women's shoes	Harder for the user to choose between competing information	Fewer clicks required at each stage of the search

System security is how sensitive user information is kept secure during transmission and storage. Sensitive information includes personal history and payment information. Judgement is formed in response to two dimensions: technical controls and operational controls (Stoneburner et al., 2002). Technical controls include "products and processes (such as firewalls, antivirus software, intrusion detection, and encryption techniques)" that are installed in the system (Baker and Wallace, 2007:37). Operational controls are used to control actions outside the system and are "enforcement mechanism and methods of correcting operational deficiencies that various threats could exploit", for example lack of physical access controls (e.g. passwords), absence of backup capabilities, and protection from environmental hazards (e.g. enabling unprotected devices to access the system) (Baker and Wallace, 2007:37).

Poor system security can result in a database being hacked enabling criminals to hijack customer accounts, for example AirBnB accounts were compromised by burglars who used the guest profiles to gain access to accommodation to commit theft. As a result of this scam AirBnB tightened their security to include two-step authentication process for ID changes and a text warning if a profile is altered (BBC News, 2017). Users may not have strong perceptions that a digital channel provides a secure connection as this is a background condition to the primary intent to use, however enforcement mechanisms such as requesting passwords are a stronger signal of system security quality (Waite and Rowley. 2015).

■ Information quality

Information quality is a judgement of the content provided on the digital channel. Information quality is important since it reduces bounce rate, prolongs browsing activity and will persuade the customer to move towards purchase. There are three dimensions that contribute to information quality: intrinsic quality, contextual quality and representational quality (Figure 4.3). (NB: you may find some studies that include information availability (Lee et al., 2002) but we argue that this is a dimension of system quality).

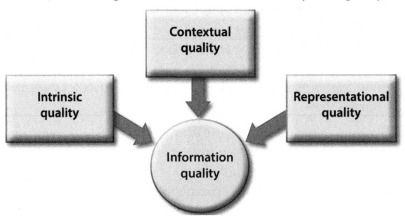

Figure 4.3: Dimensions of information quality

Intrinsic quality focuses upon the accuracy, believability and objectivity of the information. Judgement is formed in response to the extent of any content errors (e.g. incorrect facts), believability (the trustworthiness of the source), objectivity (whether content is evidence based and draws upon verifiable facts) and consistency (whether content is logical and is consistent with the brand voice) (Wang and Strong, 1996). Intrinsic quality judgements may be shaped the environment in which the information is being used and by whom (Rieh, 2002). For example, higher levels of objectivity may be required for information that students present in an academic essay compared to information that they post in their social media pages.

Contextual quality focuses upon the appropriateness and helpfulness of the information for a specific task or application (Nelson et al., 2005). Judgement is formed in response to the relevance, completeness, quantity and currency of the information (Wang and Strong, 1996). Relevance refers to strength of the connection between information and the information need of the user (Saracevic, 1975). Completeness refers to the extent that the needs of each user are met. It is important for digital marketers to understand the information needs of each target user segment, for whilst information might be complete in the eyes of one group of users, it may be incomplete for others (Nelson et al., 2005). Quantity refers to the number of information items that are present (Keller and Staelin 1987). Currency refers to the degree to which the information is up-to-date and assessment depends on task and user characteristics (Ballou et al., 1998). For example, the information currency of online exam timetables is more important to current students compared to prospective students or alumni.

Representational quality focuses upon the way in which the content is presented, meaning how content is formatted to make it understood or readable and not how a user might navigate between different information spaces (this is a dimension of system efficiency). Judgement of representational quality is formed in response to colour, graphics, video, audio, punctuation and font. For example, making it clear that text contains a hyperlink by using a different colour and underlining the words. If representational quality does not correspond to brand image then we may judge the site as fake and distrust it (Fogg et al., 2001). For example, fake news is defined as content that is manipulated to resemble credible journalism and attract maximum attention and with it advertising revenue (Hunt, 2016). Whilst originally intended as humorous satire (Marchi, 2012), fake news is now used with serious intent to persuade and mimic the representational quality of reputable news, making it believable (Stanford History Education Group, 2016).

We want to stop the spread of false news on Facebook. Learn more about the work we're doing. As we work to limit the spread, here are some tips on what to look out for:

1 Be skeptical of headlines. False news stories often have catchy headlines in all caps with exclamation points. If shocking claims in the headline sound unbelievable, they probably are.

2 Look closely at the URL. A phony or look-alike URL may be a warning sign of false news. Many false news sites mimic authentic news sources by making small changes to the URL. You can go to the site to compare the URL to established sources.

3 Investigate the source. Ensure that the story is written by a source that you trust with a reputation for accuracy. If the story comes from an unfamiliar organization, check their "About" section to learn more.

4 Watch for unusual formatting. Many false news sites have misspellings or awkward layouts. Read carefully if you see these signs.

5 Consider the photos. False news stories often contain manipulated images or videos. Sometimes the photo may be authentic, but taken out of context. You can search for the photo or image to verify where it came from.

6 Inspect the dates. False news stories may contain timelines that make no sense, or event dates that have been altered.

7 Check the evidence. Check the author's sources to confirm that they are accurate. Lack of evidence or reliance on unnamed experts may indicate a false news story.

8 Look at other reports. If no other news source is reporting the same story, it may indicate that the story is false. If the story is reported by multiple sources you trust, it's more likely to be true.

9 Is the story a joke? Sometimes false news stories can be hard to distinguish from humor or satire. Check whether the source is known for parody, and whether the story's details and tone suggest it may be just for fun.

10 Some stories are intentionally false. Think critically about the stories you read, and only share news that you know to be credible.

Figure 4.4: Facebook: Tips for Spotting Fake News (Adapted from Thomas, 2017)

Exercise 4.2

In 2017 Facebook posted a warning 10 tips informing users how to spot fake news (Figure 4.4). Can you identify how these tips correspond to each dimension of information quality?

■   Transaction quality

Transaction quality is a judgement of how the company provides services that are important to customers during and after the marketing exchange. A marketing exchange does not have to involve a purchase, for example, if the customer is seeking to exchange information with the company by providing user-generated content in order to gain recognition. Several dimensions within this component (responsiveness and compensation) correspond with the E-RecS-Qual of post-purchase e-service as proposed by Parasuraman et al. (2005) (Figure 4.5).

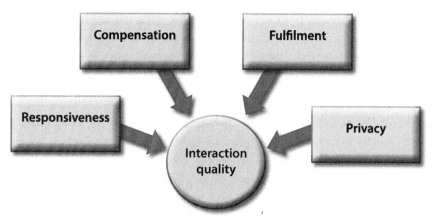

Figure 4.5: Interaction quality dimensions

Responsiveness focuses upon the communication exchange between the company and the customers. Judgement is formed in response to promptness, appropriateness and flexibility (Wolfinbarger and Gilly, 2003). Promptness focuses on the speed of response to queries. When using digital channels customers expect fast response times and acknowledgement of their communication within one hour (Sousa and Voss, 2006). Appropriateness focuses on the suitability of the message content and tone of voice in the context of communication. Griffiths (2017) argues that customers expect an "online customer service that actually speaks to them" and not an automated response. She argues that light-hearted humour can be appropriate, but warns that when dealing with a customer in a great deal of distress there should be consideration of "how much inconvenience has been caused before you start cracking jokes". Flexibility focuses on the degree to which an interaction is able to be adapted to fit with the customer's requests (Parasuraman et al., 2005). Kuo et al. (2009) find that a mobile phone company's ability to alter a contract whilst maintaining a friendly attitude results in a positive customer judgement.

Compensation focuses upon the distributive justice in any exchange of value between the customer and the company. Distributive justice refers to perceptions of fairness in resource allocation and the outcome of the exchange (Chebat and Slusarczyk, 2005). There are three dimensions of compensation: the price paid, the refund received, the reparation for service problems and reward. The price paid is what the customer pays for a good or service (including shipping) and the refund received is the amount which will be received if items are returned (Zeithaml et al., 2002). Reparation refers to the amount that the customer receives if a complaint is upheld (Collier and Bienstock, 2006); in some situations this may be a refund of the total or part of the amount paid for the goods. Reward is the value that a customer gains from providing services to the company, for example through contributing user-generated content (UGC). Consumers produce UGC in return for rewards such as prizes, social status and also feelings of achievement (van Dijck, 2009)

Fulfilment focuses upon the physical delivery of products and services. Judgement is formed in response to the extent how and when the goods are received in terms of delivery timing, stock availability and product quality (Field et al., 2004). Delivery timing involves the speed with delivery is despatched, the duration of its transit and the time at which it is delivered. Stock availability involves having product in stock so that it is available for delivery. Product quality involves the actual product received matching its description in the digital channel. Fulfilment links both online and offline operations, for example online information regarding product availability needs to be matched to offline warehouse stock control procedures.

Privacy focuses upon how personal information is gathered and how it is shared with others. Judgement is formed in response to privacy notices, request legitimacy and anonymity. Privacy notices inform consumers about who has control and who will make use of digital data. Privacy notices help consumers decide whether or not to engage with a digital channel (Milne and Culnan, 2004). Customers are dissatisfied when their data is used for purposes beyond the initial transaction (Foxman and Kilcoyne, 1993). Request legitimacy is related to the exchange and perceived as necessary to carry out the function (Li et al., 2011). Customers tend to perceive that irrelevant sensitive information might be used to unfairly discriminate against or target them in future (Stone-Romero et al., 2003). Anonymity is the degree to which the user has the ability to withhold or remove identifying information; it is slightly different from information control which relates to information that has been collected. Individual needs for online anonymity varies according to personality traits, such as being introverted or extroverted, and perceived social pressure (Hughes et al., 2012).

■ Community quality

Community quality is a judgement of how the membership and interactions with a brand community meet customer expectations, and is an emerging online area of research (Brodie et al., 2013). There are two dimensions that contribute towards a judgement of community quality: interaction and membership (Figure 4.6).

Figure 4.6: Community quality dimensions

Interaction focuses upon how community members interact in order to create value for each other and for the brand (Schau et al., 2009). Judgement is formed in response to interaction range, frequency and dispersion. A healthy brand community supports a range of interactions including welcoming new members, discussing how the brand can be used and celebrating significant events (Schau et al., 2009). Interactions can be functional, e.g. asking questions about brand use, or non-functional, e.g. socialising (Brodie et al., 2013), the richness and meaningfulness of interaction results in a judgement of community satisfaction (Casalo et al., 2010). Interaction frequency refers to the time between interactions; a community with high interaction frequency meets the information and social needs of its members (Kuo and Feng., 2013). Interaction dispersion refers to the number of different contributors to a conversation; narrowly focussed conversations that only involve a few individuals have a lesser impact (Godes and Mayzlin, 2004).

Membership focuses upon the composition of the brand community. Judgement is formed in response to membership homogeneity and community size. Membership similarity focuses upon the shared affective, cognitive and demographic characteristics of members and the target consumer. Interaction with people similar to oneself satisfies an emotional need for group belonging (Schau et al., 2009), and generates a feeling of "we-ness"

(Scarpi, 2010:16)). Where a brand community is homogenous but dissimilar to the target customer then there is a negative judgement; in such situations it is better to keep identifying characteristics ambiguous (Naylor et al., 2012). Community size focuses upon the number of people who belong to the online community. Members of small communities (those with less than 100 members) show a much stronger sense of loyalty to the community but within large communities (more than 1000 members) there exists a stronger sense of loyalty towards the brand (Scarpi, 2010).

Summary

Increasing competition in the marketspace means that it is important to ensure that customers make judgements of e-service quality and satisfaction when using a digital channel. Digital managers need to make careful choices regarding which features to include in the channel design in order to control implementation costs. This chapter provides a decomposed e-SQ model containing components of system quality, information quality, transaction quality and community quality to support managerial action.

Exemplar paper

Waite, K. and Harrison, T., (2002), Consumer expectations of online information provided by bank websites, *Journal of Financial Services Marketing*, **6**(4), 309-322.

An empirical paper that reports on the process of generating and testing items related to information quality in the specific context of online banking. Data is gathered using a focus group and a survey of young adult Internet users. The analysis shows that the most and least important attributes, and reveals that those contributing to decision-making convenience are preferred over the technological entertainment value of the site. The results provide an indication of the website features and design most likely to attract and retain customers.

■ **Additional reading**

Xu, J.D., Benbasat, I. and Cenfetelli, R.T. (2013), Integrating service quality with system and information quality: an empirical test in the e-service context, *MIS Quarterly*, **37**(3), 777-794.

Lin, H.H. (2012), The effect of multi-channel service quality on mobile customer loyalty in an online-and-mobile retail context, *Service Industries Journal*, **32**(11), 1865-1882.

References

4

Baker, W.H. and Wallace, L. (2007), Is information security under control?: investigating quality in information security management, *IEEE Security & Privacy*, **5**(1).

Ballou, D.P., Wang, R., Pazer, H. and Tayi, G.K. (1998), Modeling information manufacturing systems to determine information product quality, *Management Science*, **44**(4), 462-484

BBC News (2017), Airbnb Account Hijackers Burgle Homes, http://www.bbc.co.uk/news/technology-39589241, 13th April, [Accessed on 14thApril 2017].

Berry, L.L. and Parasuraman, A. (2004), *Marketing Services: Competing Through Quality*, Simon and Schuster, London.

Brodie, R.J., Ilic, A., Juric, B. and Hollebeek, L. (2013), Consumer engagement in a virtual brand community: an exploratory analysis, *Journal of Business Research*, **66**(1), 105-114.

Buttle, F. (1996), SERVQUAL: review, critique, research agenda, *European Journal of Marketing*, **30**(1), 8-32.

Carman, J.M. (1990), Consumer perceptions of service quality: an assessment of the SERVQUAL dimensions, *Journal of Retailing*, **66**(1), 33-55.

Casaló, L.V., Flavián, C. and Guinalíu, M. (2010), Determinants of the intention to participate in firm-hosted online travel communities and effects on consumer behavioral intentions, *Tourism Management*, **31**(6), 898-911.

Chalmers, D. and Sloman, M. (1999), A survey of quality of service in mobile computing environments, *IEEE Communications Surveys*, **2**(2), 2-10.

Chebat, J.C. and Slusarczyk, W. (2005), How emotions mediate the effects of perceived justice on loyalty in service recovery situations: an empirical study, *Journal of Business Research*, **58**(5), 664-673.

Collier, J.E. and Bienstock, C.C. (2006), Measuring service quality in e-retailing, *Journal of Service Research*, **8**(3), 260-275.

Cronin Jr, J.J. and Taylor, S.A. (1992), Measuring service quality: a reexamination and extension, *Journal of Marketing*, **56**(3), 55-68.

Dabholkar, P.A. and Bagozzi, R.P., (2002), An attitudinal model of technology-based self-service: moderating effects of consumer traits and situational factors, *Journal of the Academy of Marketing Science,* **30**(3), 184-201.

Delone, W.H. and McLean, E.R., (2003), The DeLone and McLean model of information systems success: a ten-year update, *Journal of Management Information Systems*, **19**(4), 9-30.

Ding, W. and Lin, X. (2009), *Information Architecture: The Design and Integration of Information Spaces*, Morgan and Claypool.

Field, J. M., Heim G. R., and Sinha K. K. (2004), Managing quality in the e-service system: development and application of a process model, *Production and Operations Management*, **13**(4), 291–306.

Fogg, B.J., Marshall, J., Laraki, O., Osipovich, A., Varma, C., Fang, N., Paul, J., Rangnekar, A., Shon, J., Swani, P. and Treinen, M. (2001), What makes web sites credible? a report on a large quantitative study, in *Proceedings of the SIGCHI Conference on Human Factors in Computing Systems* (61-68). ACM.

Foxman, E.R. and Kilcoyne, P., (1993), Information technology, marketing practice, and consumer privacy: ethical issues, *Journal of Public Policy & Marketing*, **12**(1), 106-119.

Giese, J.L. and Cote, J.A. (2000), Defining consumer satisfaction, *Academy of Marketing Science Review*, **4**(2), 1-27.

Godes, D. and Mayzlin, D. (2004), Using online conversations to study word-of-mouth communication, *Marketing Science*, **23**(4), 545-560.

Griffiths, K., (2017), Dealing with Customer Complaints using Humour, *Online Retail*. http://www.onlyretail.com/blog/make-em-laugh-dealing-with-customer-complaints-using-humour, [Accessed 25th March 2017].

Hooi Ting, D., (2004), Service quality and satisfaction perceptions: curvilinear and interaction effect, *International Journal of Bank Marketing*, **22**(6), 407-420.

House of Lords Select Committee (2014), Make or break: The UK's digital future, https://www.publications.parliament.uk/pa/ld201415/ldselect/lddigital/111/111.pdf [Accessed 31st March 2016].

Hughes, D.J., Rowe, M., Batey, M. and Lee, A. (2012), A tale of two sites: Twitter vs. Facebook and the personality predictors of social media usage, *Computers in Human Behavior*, **28**(2), 561-569.

Hunt, E., (2016), What is fake news? how to spot and what you can do to stop it, *The Guardian*, https://www.theguardian.com/media/2016/dec/18/what-is-fake-news-pizzagate, [Accessed 14th April 2017].

Jiang, Z. and Benbasat, I. (2004), Virtual product experience: effects of visual and functional control of products on perceived diagnosticity and flow in electronic shopping, *Journal of Management Information Systems*, **21**(3), 111-147.

Keller, K.L. and Staelin, R. (1987), Effects of quality and quantity of information on decision effectiveness, *Journal of Consumer Research*, **14**(2), 200-213.

Kuo, Y.F. and Feng, L.H. (2013), Relationships among community interaction characteristics, perceived benefits, community commitment, and oppositional brand loyalty in online brand communities, *International Journal of Information Management*, **33**(6), 948-962.

Kuo, Y.F., Wu, C.M. and Deng, W.J. (2009), The relationships among service quality, perceived value, customer satisfaction, and post-purchase intention in mobile value-added services, *Computers in Human Behavior*, **25**(4), 887-896.

Lee, Y.W., Strong, D.M., Kahn, B.K. and Wang, R.Y. (2002), AIMQ: A methodology for information auality assessment, *Information and Management*, **40**(2), 133-146.

Li, H., Sarathy, R. and Xu, H. (2011), The role of affect and cognition on online consumers' decision to disclose personal information to unfamiliar online vendors, *Decision Support Systems*, **51**(3), 434-445.

Marchi, R. (2012), With Facebook, blogs, and fake news, teens reject journalistic objectivity, *Journal of Communication Inquiry*, **36**(3), 246-262.

Meuter, M.L., Ostrom, A.L., Roundtree, R.I. and Bitner, M.J. (2000), Self-service technologies: understanding customer satisfaction with technology-based service encounters. *Journal of Marketing*, **64**(3), 50-64.

Milne, G.R. and Culnan, M.J. (2004), Strategies for reducing online privacy risks: why consumers read (or don't read) online privacy notices, *Journal of Interactive Marketing*, **18**(3), 15-29.

Naylor, R.W., Lamberton, C.P. and West, P.M. (2012), Beyond the 'like' button: the impact of mere virtual presence on brand evaluations and purchase intentions in social media settings, *Journal of Marketing*, **76**(6), 105-120.

Nelson, R.R., Todd, P.A. and Wixom, B.H. (2005), Antecedents of information and system quality: an empirical examination within the context of data warehousing, *Journal of Management Information Systems*, **21**(4), 199-235.

Oliver, R. L. (1996), *Satisfaction: A Behavioural Perspective on the Consumer*, McGraw Hill, New York.

Parasuraman, A., Zeithaml, V.A. and Berry, L.L. (1985), A conceptual model of service quality and its implications for future research, *Journal of Marketing*, **49**(4), 41-50.

4

Parasuraman, A., Zeithaml, V.A. and Berry, L.L. (1988), SERVQUAL: A multiple-item scale for measuring consumer perceptions of service quality. *Journal of Retailing*, **64**(1), p.12-40.

Parasuraman, A., Zeithaml, V.A. and Malhotra, A. (2005), ES-QUAL a multiple-item scale for assessing electronic service quality, *Journal of Service Research*, **7**(3), 213-233.

Rayport, J.F. and Sviokla, J.J. (1994), Managing in the marketspace, *Harvard Business Review*, 72, 2-11.

Rayport, J.F., and Sviokla, J.J. (1995), Exploiting the virtual value chain, *Harvard Business Review*, 73, 14-24

Rieh, S.Y. (2002), Judgment of information quality and cognitive authority in the Web. *Journal of the American Society for Information Science and Technology*, **53**(2), 145-161.

Rowley, J. (2001), Remodelling marketing communications in an internet environment, *Internet Research*, **11**(3), 203-212.

Rowley, J. (2006), An analysis of the e-service literature: towards a research agenda, *Internet Research*, **16**(3), 339-359.

Saracevic, T. (1975), Relevance: A review of and a framework for the thinking on the notion in information science, *Journal of the American Society for Information Science*, **26**(6), 321-343.

Scarpi, D. (2010), Does size matter? an examination of small and large web-based brand communities, *Journal of Interactive Marketing*, **24**(1), 14-21.

Schau, H.J., Muñiz Jr, A.M. and Arnould, E.J. (2009), How brand community practices create value, *Journal of Marketing*, **73**(5), 30-51.

Seddon, P.B. (1997), A respecification and Eextension of the DeLone and McLean model of IS success, *Information Systems Research*, **8**(3), 240-253.

Shin, D.H., Jung, J. and Chang, B.H. (2012), The psychology behind QR codes: user experience perspective, *Computers in Human Behavior*, **28**(4), 1417-1426.

Shostack, G.L. (1977), Breaking free from product marketing, *Journal of Marketing*, **41**(2), 73-80.

Sousa, R. and Voss, C.A. (2006), Service quality in multichannel services employing virtual channels, *Journal of Service Research*, **8**(4), 356-371.

Spence, M. (1973), Job market signaling, *Quarterly Journal of Economics*, **87**(3), 355-374.

Stanford History Education Group (2016) Evaluating Information: The Cornerstone of Civic Online Reasoning, at https://sheg.stanford.edu/upload/V3LessonPlans/Executive%20Summary%2011.21.16.pdf [Accessed 14th April 2017].

Stoneburner, G., Goguen, A. and Feringa, A. (2002), *Risk Management Guide for Information Technology Systems*, National Inst. of Standards and Technology, US Dept of Commerce, http://csrc.nist.gov/publications/nistpubs/800-30/sp800-30.pdf [Accessed 15th March 2016]

Stone-Romero, E. F., Stone, D. L. and Hyatt, D. (2003), Personnel selection procedures and invasion of privacy, *Journal of Social Issues*, 59(2),343-368.

Sureshchandar, G.S., Rajendran, C. and Anantharaman, R.N. (2002), The relationship between service quality and customer satisfaction–a factor specific approach, *Journal of Services Marketing*, **16**(4), 363-379.

Thomas, D. (2017), Facebook to Tackle fake news with educational campaign, http://www.bbc.co.uk/news/technology-39517033, [Accessed 4th April 2017].

Van Dijck, J. (2009), Users like you? theorizing agency in user-generated content, *Media, Culture and Society*, **31**(1), 41-58.

Waite, K. and Rowley, J. (2015), E-servicescapes in online banking: towards an integrated conceptual model of the stimuli contributing to the online banking experience. In T. Harrison, & H. Estelami (Eds.), *The Routledge Companion to Financial Services Marketing*, pp. 346-363, Abingdon, Routledge.

Wang, R.Y. and Strong, D.M. (1996), Beyond accuracy: what data quality means to data consumers, *Journal of Management Information Systems*, **12**(4), 5-33.

Wells, J.D., Valacich, J.S. and Hess, T.J. (2011), What signal are you sending? how website quality influences perceptions of product quality and purchase intentions, *MIS Quarterly*, **35**(2), 373-396.

Wilson, A., Zeithaml, V.A., Bitner, M.J. and Gremler, D.D. (2008), *Services Marketing: Integrating Customer Focus Across the Firm*, McGraw Hill, Maidenhead.

Wolfinbarger, M., and Gilly, M. C. (2003), ETailQ: dimensionalizing, measuring and predicting etail quality, *Journal of Retailing*, **79**(3), 183–198

WSI (2013), *Digital Minds: 12 Things Every Business Needs to Know about Digital Marketing*, Friesen Press, Victoria.

Zeithaml, V.A., Berry, L.L. and Parasuraman, A. (1993), The nature and determinants of customer expectations of service. *Journal of the Academy of Marketing Science*, **21**(1), 1-12.

Zeithaml, V.A., Parasuraman, A. and Malhotra, A. (2002), Service quality delivery through websites: a critical review of extant knowledge, *Journal of the Academy of Marketing Science*, **30**(4), 362-375.

5 Online Consumer Engagement

For digital marketing practitioners, online consumer engagement (OCE) is one of the most desirable outcomes from digital marketing activity (eMarketer, 2015). Gaining a detailed understanding of engagement is important. There a number of different ways of conceptualising engagement which help to develop insight into OCE. In addition, a useful way of understanding process and drivers of OCE within social networks is to apply Social Impact Theory (Latane, 1981) to social media activity; this enables us to identify how social influence shapes consumer decision making.

Consumer engagement

Consumer engagement can be associated with positive outcomes such as consumer trust (Hollebeek, 2011), satisfaction and loyalty (Bowden, 2009) and commitment (Chan and Li, 2010) all of them strong indicators of long-term sales, word-of-mouth and brand advocacy. However, the concept of consumer engagement is relatively new in the marketing literature, and research efforts to define the concept and understand its antecedents and consequences are increasing. An accepted definition by Van Doorn et al. (2010) is that consumer engagement is the "behavioural manifestation toward the brand or firm, beyond purchase, resulting from motivational drivers". It is important to note that consumer engagement can occur offline as well as online.

Online consumer engagement refers to interactive experiences between consumers and the brand, and/or other consumers, and that occur in digital environments such as online brand communities (Dessart et al., 2016). Online brand communities (OBC) are defined as "a network of relationships between consumers and the brand, product, fellow consumers, and the marketer" (McAlexander et al., 2002:39). From a marketing perspective, OBCs are of special interest because they enable new and extended forms of consumer interaction, and the development of consumer-brand relationships (Brodie et al., 2013).

Consumer engagement is distinct from the concepts of consumer involvement and consumer commitment. Consumer *involvement* is defined as the perceived importance that a consumer gives to a focal object – a product or brand (Mittal, 1995). Note how involvement does not suggest any behavioural outcomes, instead if remains at the cognitive and affective level within the mind of the consumer. Similarly, consumer *commitment* relates to the willingness to sustain a relationship with the product or brand, which again does not necessarily means that the consumer will go beyond purchasing the product in the long-term (Goldsmith and Horowitz, 2006). Therefore, consumer *engagement* is more active and involves the consumers within cognitive, affective but also behavioural dimensions.

A consumer can be engaged with not only the brand. The literature argues that consumer engagement can occur not only between a consumer and a firm but also between consumers, depending on the platforms where the process is occurring (Brodie et al., 2011). For example, consider how highly engaged Apple consumers try to 'evangelise' others to join the brand, and defend it against its detractors. This means that consumer engagement may change according to context and will also be responsive to the ongoing dynamics of the interactions and the motivations whilst being engaged.

Brands may not have complete control of how and when consumer engagement occurs. Many customer-to-customer engagements occur in blogs and forums that are not controlled by the brand/firm, but that relate to them. As Solis (2010) points out, people are already speaking about and advocating the brands they like and discouraging others from using the brands they do not, and this is happening regardless of the official presence of that brand. Brand communities are another example of such activity. Brand communities are defined as "specialised, non-geographically bound communities, based on a structured set of social relationships among admirers of a brand"(Bagozzi and Dholakia, 2006:45). Brand communities are environments where social interaction is not initiated by the brand but is driven by the participation of its members due to the commitment that they feel to the brand.

Exercise 5.1: iOS or Android?

Two of the major operating systems for smartphones are Apple's iOS and Google's Android. Search for "Google vs iOS" and idenfity links to forums on the topic. Click on any of them and examine whether the definition of brand communities suggested by Bagozzi and Dholakia (2006) can apply.

Which of the two groups (i.e. Google or iOS customers) seems to be more engaged? List the activities that you can find, beyond purchase, as examples of consumer engagement.

Different manifestations of consumer engagement

It is accepted that consumer engagement results in behavioural outcomes, however prior to such behaviour there are cognitive and affective states (Figure 5.1). This means that consumer engagement is multi-dimensional and includes cognitive and emotional components (Vivek et al., 2012).

Table 5.1: Dimensions of manifestation of consumer engagement

Dimension	Definition	Example
Cognitive	The level of absorption of consumers' thoughts in relation to the brand	A customer thinking he made the right choice by purchasing insurance for his smartphone from company X as it was good value for money.
Emotional	The range of emotions that consumers experience as a result of interacting with the brand.	A customer feeling relieved that he bought insurance when his mobile was stolen during a night out.
Behavioural	The actions consumers take in relation to the brand.	The customer writes a review of his experience with the insurance brand on Google and recommends it to others when he has the chance.

The cognitive dimension of engagement is the "level of absorption and vigour that individuals demonstrate" in their interactions with a brand (e.g. the focal object) (Patterson et al., 2006:.4). A consumer's brand-related thoughts do not necessarily have to be positive; they can also be negative suggesting a valence of engagement. The emotional dimension of engagement is the consumer sense of belonging to a group, and the pride, enthusiasm, enjoyment and passion that consumers can experience as a result of branded interactions which includes purchase (Dessart et al., 2016; Patterson et al., 2006).

The emotional dimension of engagement can also have a positive or negative valence, leading to feelings of attraction or repulsion to the focal object (Hollebeek and Chen, 2014). An example of negative emotional engagement can be the crisis that United Airlines experienced earlier in 2017 when their personnel dragged off the plane a paying customer due to overselling tickets. A twitter search using the hashtag #AmericanAirlines still shows evidence of the negative feelings that other customers felt towards the brand. Finally, the behavioural dimension of engagement is the visible outcomes of online consumer engagement. The psychological states associated with online consumer engagement, such as trust and commitment (Bansal et al., 2004), brand experience (Brakus et al., 2009), consumer identification (Ahearne et al., 2005), brand-consumer connections (Fournier, 1998) and loyalty (Jahn and Kunz, 2012) have a behavioural outcomes. A natural behavioural outcome sought by marketers from engaged consumers in social media is purchase (Zhang et al., 2017). Cognitive and emotional manifestations of engagement can be hard to measure, as they usually remain in the mind of the consumer. On the other hand, behavioural manifestations are more easily traceable, especially when they occur online.

Table 5.2: Components and metrics for online consumer engagement. Adapted from: Haven and Vittal, 2008.

Component	Metric
Involvement	Number of visitors
	Time spent on the site
Interaction	Click-through rates
	Online transactions
	Uploaded videos/pictures
Intimacy	Sentiment measurement
	Blog posts
	Blog comments
	Discussions in forums
Influence	Brand awareness
	Loyalty
	Affinity
	Repurchase
	Satisfaction ratings

Digital marketers use a behavioural metrics to assess the extent of online consumer engagement because these measurements are easy to capture. Engagement measures can be collected both online and offline. Haven and

Vittal (2008) identify four areas of metrics that are used to assess online customer engagement in the areas of involvement, interaction, intimacy, and influence (Table 5.2). It is worth noting that the metrics are behavioural in nature, such as visits or time spent on a site. Engagement is also demonstrated by clicks and participation with the online community (uploading videos or photos), as well as word-of-mouth communication in the form of blog posts and comments.

Levels of engagement

There are a range of online consumer engagement behaviours and each will require different degrees of effort from consumers. This means that the outcomes and value of each type of engagement behaviour will not be identical in terms of brand benefits. One way to think of this concept is to use the metaphor of diving, where the deeper you go, the cognitive, affective and behavioural processes involved in keeping you engaged in the activity increase (Figure 5.1). In this example, giving ratings is at the shallow level of the dive, as minimum effort is required to rate a product or a service from 1 to 5. As we dive deeper, producing an online review requires more cognitive effort since it involves remembering the experience, as well as extensive efforts in typing a review. At the deepest level of the engagement dive, consumers will engage in the processes of service delivery or even in the co-creation of products. Deep engagement is present at MyStarbucksIdea.com where consumers are asked to providing ideas about service process improvement (e.g. reducing waiting time during rush hours). Consumers can also submit new product ideas to be implemented by the brand.

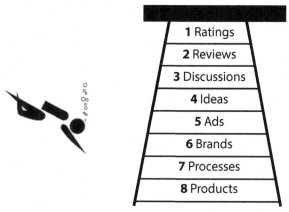

Figure 5.1: The engagement dive

Motivations for online consumer engagement

Brands seek to increase the level of engagement to the deepest level and thus it is important to understand what motivates consumers to engage. Some consumers will engage in order to receive financial rewards such as discounts, points, rebates, etc. However, research has found that financial benefits are only part of the motivations that drive engagement in online settings (Oh and Syn, 2015). Consumers can also be motivated by feelings of altruism (helping others). Altruism is one motivation for posting reviews, in order to prevent others making a purchasing mistake, or encourage brand use if the product was satisfactory. Another motivation is reputation, by which becoming engaged sets consumers apart from other members of an online community and makes them feel special. Finally, consumers can be motivated by the enjoyment they gain when they draw on their creativity and individuality to create content.

Brands can use insights into what motivates consumer engagement to generate a range of engagement management tactics. For example having spaces that invite and facilitate engagement (e.g. My Starbucks Idea website) is a productive way to motivate consumers to express creative feelings. In addition, having spaces where consumers can post reviews to help others (e.g. forums, enabling reviews in a website) and recognising consumers when they engage (e.g. Badges for top contributors, or ratings by other users based on the perceived value of their contribution) are ways in which brands can facilitate engagement behaviour.

Online consumer engagement and social influence

Brands encourage engagement by creating fan pages on social media channels. Fan pages are spaces where brand fans can share their enthusiasm about the brand with other members of the brand community. Within fan pages the effect of social influence changes consumer behaviour, attitudes and beliefs through their interaction with others (Cialdini and Goldstein, 2004). The literature on social influence is extensive, and even though interest on this phenomenon started within the field of social psychology, marketing academics have been interested on how others influence consumer behaviour.

One of the most notable studies on social influence is the one developed by Solomon Asch in the early 50s. He presented a group of students with a card that had a black line printed on it (Card 1 in Figure 5.2). He then showed Card 2 and the task was to find the same line as shown previously in Card 1. Each participant was asked to say out loud what they thought was the correct answer. However, in some of the groups there were actors pretending to be students and they were asked to choose the wrong answer (i.e. options 1 or 3). In the groups with no actors, the error rate was less than 1%. However, in the groups where actors gave wrong answers first, this error rate increased to 36.8% (Asch, 1961)

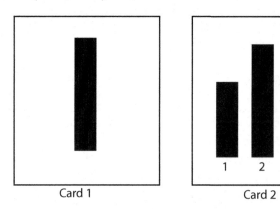

Card 1   Card 2

Figure 5.2: Social Influence Experiment. Adapted from Asch (1955)

The experiments by Asch suggest that the influence of others changes behaviour. These conformity studies, rooted in the field of social psychology, led to other psychologist to challenge Ash's views that that majority size did not have much effect beyond a minimal number of three (Bond, 2005). However, what Asch was able to establish in his initial experiments was that people can change their behaviour based on what others do, which led to further investigation on social influence processes and new theories that are discussed in this chapter.

If we transfer these findings to the context of online marketing, we can hypothesise that fan page followers might be influenced to like or dislike a brand depending on the opinions of others. Research into word-of-mouth (WOM) communication indicates that product perceptions remain positive, even if the consumer is exposed to negative information from other media (Bone, 1995). These effects are also present within social media (Perez-Vega et al., 2016).

Social influence processes

According to Kelman (1961) there are three processes that govern an individual's response to social influence: internalisation, identification, and compliance (Table 5.3)

Table 5.3: Processes governing social influence response. Adapted from Kelman (1961)

Process	Definition	Illustration
Internalisation	When an individual accepts influence because the induced behaviour is congruent with his/her value system	Influence occurs because behaviour is intrinsically rewarding, it helps the individual to find solutions to his or her problems, or because their own value system demands it.
Identification	When an individual adopts behaviour derived from another person or group because this behaviour is associated with a satisfying self-defining relationship to this person or group	Influence occurs because the individual wants to be a member of the group thus becomes a way to maintain the desired relationship with others
Compliance	When an individual accepts influence from another person or a group because he hopes for a favourable reaction from the other	Compliance occurs because the target of influence is looking to either get a reward or avoid negative outcomes, as a result of complying.

For internalisation to occur, the characteristics of the source are important because they elicit influence, in particular regarding the credibility or strength of this source of influence (Bagozzi and Lee, 2002). Internalisation of certain behaviour in the digital context can be achieved in different ways. For example, if every comment receives feedback from most of the members of the group, an individual may feel rewarded. In some other cases the reward can come not from the members, but from the platform itself. Google and other platforms relying on online reviews try to encourage participation by awarding their members badges depending of their level of expertise, which is directly tied to the level of participation on the platform.

Source characteristics are also important for identification. For example, vloggers rely on the identification that the viewers feel towards the vlogger. It is not uncommon that vloggers ask their followers to share videos or take part in other participatory behaviours. Marketers are keen to leverage the identification of a vlogger's follower base to encourage certain behaviours towards the brands that they manage. This may result in a vlogger visiting certain types of businesses or using certain brands of clothing or camera. For a reciprocal relationship to exist, there needs to be a mutually shared expectation of one another's behaviour, so that the both participants can behave in line with the requirements of that particular relationship. Followers are willing to engage with activities with their vlogger, but in exchange they expect the vlogger to reply to their messages on their videos, or interact with them in other social networking platforms such as Twitter.

In addition, consumers who feel they identify with a brand will be more likely to interact with that brand in online environments and will have a more positive perception of the other community members (Tsai and Men, 2013). Identification with a focal community should lead to normative behaviour from the target of influence, leading the individual to adapt or mimic the behaviour that is rewarded by the community.

Unlike in the process of internalisation, where the reward is in the content of the induced behaviour, in *compliance*, the content is less important, but rather the social effect attached to that content is instrumental in the production of a positive outcome for the target. This also means that cognitive and behavioural changes are only expressed when the source of influence can observe them. In the digital context, compliance to certain behaviours may occur when they are publicly available. For example, consider how you may write a public message on a board or on Facebook, where you know that family and friends can see it, as opposed to private or anonymous messages, where you may comply less with social norms. Lee (1996) found that in digital environments, anonymity relieves people from public consequences and may encourage speech that under other circumstances is considered harmful or offensive.

Behavioural goals and social influence susceptibility

In parallel with the processes of social influence, it is important to understand how the goals of the person make them susceptible to social influence. Cialdini and Goldstein, (2004) identify three main goals: accuracy, affiliation and self-concept.

■ Goal of accuracy

One of the reasons why people are subject to influence from others is because they try to fill the gaps of information that they may have regarding a focal behaviour or object. Cialdini and Goldstein (2004) argue that letting others fill in that missing information allows people to achieve their goals in a more efficient and rewarding manner. Hence, according the goal of accuracy, the individual will conform to information supplied by others when reconstructing memories of a certain stimulus as this is the most efficient way to fill in gaps (Walther et al., 2002). Sometimes the desire for accuracy may result in a change in judgement (Wood, 2000). For example a consumer may be on holiday and trying to decide where to go for dinner. Under the goal of accuracy, and by trying to fill the gap in information underpinned by a lack of knowledge of local places to eat out, the consumer may go to other sources of information such as online reviews or ratings.

Interestingly, even after someone collects experiences about a place, word-of-mouth communication like reviews can challenge the individual's experience with a product and increase the likelihood of re-evaluating their experience (Allsop et al., 2007). The goal of accuracy may also underpin the desire to join a fan page. Such online brand communities enable consumers to exchange brand experiences and increases the information available (Adjei et al., 2010). Research shows that consumers join online brand communities to gain insights on high involvement products before buying them, as well as to get to know how to use the products (Algesheimer et al., 2005; Cheung et al., 2008).

■ Goal of affiliation

The goal of affiliation also increases receptiveness to social influence. Individuals are motivated to create and maintain meaningful social relationships with others (Cialdini and Goldstein, 2004) and to engage in certain behaviours that will gain the approval of others or which signal belonging to a certain referent group. One of the clearest examples of our desire to affiliate is that the more we like and approve a person or a group, the more likely we are to take actions to maintain that relationship with them or to start imitating their behaviour. In addition, the norm of reciprocation, which obliges someone to repay to others what they have received from them, also a makes an individual susceptible to social influence.

Affiliation to online brand communities provides consumers with social, functional and experiential value (Brodie et al., 2013; Sicilia and Palazón, 2008). As participants in online brand communities, consumers create and nurture meaningful connections with other consumers and the brand (Muniz and Schau, 2005). Brand community identification is considered to be an antecedent of engagement behaviours (Algesheimer et al., 2005). The fact that social value is one of the motivators of consumers to engage in brand communities further supports a social influence approach to explaining some of the engagement behaviours that occur in these environments.

■ Goal of self-concept

The goal of self-concept relates to the need to be consistent about behaviours, commitments, beliefs and self-ascribed traits (Cialdini and Goldstein, 2004). An example of this is the need to be consistent with previous behaviours and commitments. For example, Cioffi and Garner (1996) found that making an active and open choice in written form tends to be consistent with holding extreme views on that position later in time when the respondent is asked again. Thus public commitment tends to be more persistent than a private one. Within the goal of self-concept, research into minorities and majorities has found that the degree of identification with the views of a certain group – regardless of whether that group belongs to the majority or minority – affects the processing strategies employed by the target of the influence, and also its final outcome (Haslam et al., 2000).

There is evidence that possession of branded products can be used to satisfy the need to build and grow a person's self-concept (Escalas and Bettman, 2005). Also, as discussed with respect to the previous goal of affiliation, the association with online brand communities serves the purpose of reflecting social ties from which self-concept can also be reinforced (Muniz and O'Guinn, 2001). In this regard, empirical research supports the argument that consumers use brand choices to construct their self-identities and present themselves to others (Escalas and Bettman, 2003; Ferraro et al., 2011). Thus, engagement behaviours with brands, such as 'Following' a brand presence in social media, could also be part of the construction of the self-concept, as these elements are usually displayed within the user's online profile. Furthermore, sharing content from a certain brand would also provide elements with which to construct and present the self to others.

Social Impact Theory

An understanding of social influence helps digital marketing managers to identify the processes and motivations that shape engagement behaviour but Social Impact Theory (SIT) provides a framework to facilitate the design and management of online content to stimulate engagement. Social Impact Theory was developed by Latané (1981) to explain the changes in behaviour, attitudes and beliefs of individuals. The theory is grounded on the principle of interaction between people. The main principle of this interaction is that there is a source (or several sources) that exerts an influential force on a target based on three components: strength, immediacy, and number of sources. Keep in mind that the source of influence can be a person, a brand, or an institution looking for a change of behaviour, attitudes or feelings from another person (i.e. the target of influence).

■ Strength of influencing source

Strength refers to the characteristics held by a source which plays a role in influencing a target, e.g. salience, importance, or intensity (Latané, 1996, 1981). In marketing communications terms the source will be the sender of the message. Characteristics of strength can be trans-situational or situation specific. Trans-situational characteristics are those that are relatively stable across different contexts and time. Examples of trans-situational forms of strength can be age, gender, physical characteristics, and perceived intelligence, among others. When this type of strength is identified in a source, the characteristic is assumed to be 'stable', regardless of the situation where the source is situated. The concept of strength as trans-situational has been empirically tested in a wide range of forms that are more diverse than Latané's initial proposition, for instance, in the form of personality traits, social status and voice tone or the type of clothing that a source is wearing. There are also situation-specific types of strength, and these take into consideration the context where the target of influence is interacting in relation to the characteristic that that specific situation is giving to the source.

To better understand how strength translates to online environments, let's consider an example of a series of online reviews in a travel website (Figure 5.3). Trans-situational characteristic of strength would be the gender and age of the person giving the review, and how that influences the social impact that they have on your decision making. Perhaps you would be more willing to listen to someone that is your age and gender for certain products?

Furthermore, situation-specific traits, in this case, would be a review coming from someone who is considered a "top reviewer" on that platform. This element of strength only applies to that context and situation. If we look at the sample online reviews, both customers have situation-specific strength elements as they have both stayed in that hotel. In addition, some websites also display other trans-situation traits of their reviewers. In Figure 5.3, we know that both Tom and Lisa are based in the UK, which will have a special effect if the person reading the review is UK based.

Figure 5.3: Sample review

■ Immediacy of influencing source

Immediacy can be defined as the distance relationship that exists between a source, the object being communicated about, the receiver of the communication (Nowak et al., 1990). SIT conceptualises immediacy as a set of related factors, summarised in closeness in space or time, as well as the absence of intervening barriers or filters and physical proximity between source and target, and clarity and richness of communication channels. Three types of immediacy are identified: physical or geographical, temporal, and social. Digital environments offer a particularly interesting context to examine the effects of immediacy on social impact (Perez-Vega et al., 2016). The Internet allows for interactions to occur regardless of the geographical distance. Evidence suggests that the level of influence diminishes when we know people are on the other side of the world (Miller and Brunner, 2008). Certain websites display the geographical place where the reviewer is posting to provide further information to the reader and influence behaviour.

If we take temporal distance, the Internet also allows for both synchronous and asynchronous interactions. Synchronous interaction occurs in real time, while asynchronous one happens at different points in time. An example of an online communication that is both synchronous and asynchronous can be a tweet. We can reply to a tweet that was just published a few seconds ago in real time (synchronous interaction) or we can join a conversation on Twitter that occurred three months ago (asynchronous interaction). Finally, regarding social distance, social networking sites like Facebook use social advertising to push messages that are being artificially sponsored as appearing to be linked to or recognised by your friends. When you read a post from someone socially close to you (e.g. a friend or family member), this will also affect the impact that the review has on your attitudes towards a given product.

■ Number of influencing sources

The third element relates to the number of sources exerting influence. The theory suggests that as the number of sources of influence increases, this will have a multiplying effect on the final impact. Asch (1961) found that individuals tended to conform more to the views of others was when the majority numbered three. In his experiments, whenever the number of sources increased further, no increase in conformity could be found. However, this view is challenged by several other authors, including Latané and Wolf (1981) and Tanford and Penrod (1984), both suggesting that the influence of a majority does not stop but continues to increase once the number in the group reaches three. A context in which the number of sources has an important role is social media. For example, consider the effect that the number of likes, or number of views of a YouTube video has on the perception of that object in terms of popularity and attention given to it when scrolling down your mobile. Likewise, the number of members of an online community can be used as a cue for a new member to decide whether or not to join in.

Exercise 5.2

Go to Trip Advisor or another online review site and read the reviews. Identify how the strength, immediacy and number of reviews shape your willingness to purchase the product that is being reviewed. Consider the difference in influence if the online review is negative, published yesterday versus one published four years ago, and how the geographical location of the reviewer provide cues that affects your assessment.

Online customer engagement and decision making

We can use SIT to build tactics into our online campaigns to influence consumer decision making (Table 5.4)

Table 5.4: Influencing consumer decision making

Stage	Campaign tactic
Need recognition	Use social ads that with low social distance and high source number
Search	Promote reviews that are high in temporal immediacy
Evaluation	Feedback on the number of sources who are booking and the temporal immediacy of the present offer (i.e. how much is left at the current price).
Purchase	Ask for customer to post online that they have just purchased the product so that they can influence friends.
Post-purchase	Request review, indicate how many others post reviews. Invite to join online brand community.

During the need recognition stage, being exposed to social ads on Facebook is more effective than website banner ads (Li et al., 2012). Social ads usually show the number of likes (source number) following the page and sometimes they show icons with the faces of friends of the target (strength and social immediacy). During the information search and evaluation process, evidence suggests that strength (number) and immediacy (temporal) influence the effect of ratings and reviews (a form of electronic word-of-mouth) on attitudes and behaviours (Chu and Kim, 2011). A negative review has weaker impact if it was posted nine years ago versus nine minutes ago.

A very good example of the effect of immediacy during the purchase decision stage would be the case of e-commerce websites. Many of them display information at the check-out stage regarding how many purchases have been made, or a time limit in which the price will be valid in order to exert influence on the users and lead them to act. Upon purchase customers may be asked to post online. Strong influencing sources are friends and members of social networks who are similar, i.e. more socially immediate in socio-demographic characteristics such as gender, race and age, as well as in perceptual attributes such as beliefs and attitudes (Gilly et al., 1998).

SIT also would recommend that marketer seek to increase engagement of users in brand communities after purchase. Algesheimer et al. (2005) found that consumer and community characteristics accentuate the online brand community's influence on its members. They argue that consumer characteristics, brand knowledge, and the community size are significant determinants of influence, i.e. numbers of influencers and also the strength (attractiveness and expertise). Consumer characteristics and brand knowledge are manifestations of strength within SIT. Moreover, the number of members is also accounted as a determinant of influence within this theory. This supports the premise that social influence forces are determinants of consumer engagement behaviours.

Summary

In the context of digital marketing, eliciting online consumer engagement will remain one of the key priorities. The benefits associated from an engaged consumer not only improve the brand value and financial prospects of a company, but engagement also generates opportunities to co-create value, products, and ideas. In this chapter, it argued that an understanding of social influence principles, and in particular the application of social impact theory in different digital contexts can be a productive tool to harness engagement across digital environments.

Exemplar paper

Perez-Vega, R., Waite, K. and O'Gorman, K., (2016), Social Impact Theory: an examination of how immediacy operates as an influence upon social media interaction in Facebook fan pages, *The Marketing Review*, **16**(4), 299-321.

A conceptual paper that reviews the literature on social influence and presents Social Impact Theory as an appropriate theory to explain consumer engagement behaviour on Facebook fan pages. The paper looks at the types of interactions that occur with Facebook fan pages and the associated meaning of these interactions. The paper argues for a need to develop the concept of immediacy in online contexts and proposes that physical, social and temporal immediacy can have different effect on engagement behaviours in social media settings. The paper presents a framework to be tested empirically.

■ Additional reading

Brodie, R. J., Hollebeek, L. D., Jurić, B. and Ilić, A. (2011), Customer engagement: conceptual domain, fundamental propositions, and implications for research, *Journal of Service Research*, **14**(3), 252-271.

Maslowska, E., Malthouse, E. C. and Collinger, T. (2016), The customer engagement ecosystem, *Journal of Marketing Management*, **32**(5-6), 469-501.

References

Adjei, M. T., Noble, S. M. and Noble, C. H. (2010), The influence of C2C communications in online brand communities on customer purchase behaviour, *Journal of the Academy of Marketing Science*, **38**(5), 634-653.

Ahearne, M., Bhattacharya, C. B. and Gruen, T. (2005), Antecedents and consequences of customer-company identification: expanding the role of relationship marketing, *Journal of Applied Psychology*, **90**(3), 574-585.

Algesheimer, R., Dholakia, U. M. and Herrmann, A., (2005) The social influence of brand community: Evidence from European car clubs, *Journal of Marketing*, **69**(3), 19-34.

Allsop, D. T., Bassett, B. R. and Hoskins, J. A. (2007), Word-of-mouth research: principles and applications, *Journal of Advertising Research*, **47**(4), 398-411.

Asch, S.E. (1961), Effects of group pressure upon the modification and distortion of judgments, in Henle, M. (Ed.), *Documents of Gestalt Psychology*, University of California Press, Berkeley, 222–236.

Bagozzi, R. P. and Dholakia, U. M. (2006), Antecedents and purchase consequences of customer participation in small group brand communities, *International Journal of Research in Marketing*, **23**(1), 45-61.

Bagozzi, R. P. and Lee, K. H. (2002), Multiple routes for social influence: the role of compliance, internalization, and social identity, *Social Psychology Quarterly*, **65**(3), 226-247.

Bansal, H. S., Irving, P. G. and Taylor, S. F. (2004), A three-component model of customer to service providers, *Journal of the Academy of Marketing Science*, **32**(3), 234-250.

Bond, R. (2005), Group size and conformity, *Group Processes and Intergroup Relations*, **8**(4), 331-354.

Bone, P. F. (1995), Word-of-mouth effects on short-term and long-term product judgments, *Journal of Business Research*, **32**(3), 213-223.

Bowden, J. L. H. (2009), The process of customer engagement: a conceptual framework, *Journal of Marketing Theory and Practice*, **17**(1), 63-74.

Brakus, J. J., Schmitt, B. H. and Zarantonello, L. (2009), Brand experience: Whatis it? How is it measured? Does it affect loyalty? *Journal of Marketing*, 73(3), 52-68.

Brodie, R. J., Hollebeek, L. D., Jurić, B. and Ilić, A. (2011), Customer engagement: conceptual domain, fundamental propositions, and implications for research, *Journal of Service Research*, **14**(3), 252-271.

Brodie, R. J., Ilic, A., Juric, B. and Hollebeek, L. (2013), Consumer engagement in a virtual brand community: an exploratory analysis, *Journal of Business Research*, **66**(1), 105-114.

Chan, K. W. and Li, S. Y. (2010), Understanding consumer-to-consumer interactions in virtual communities: the salience of reciprocity, *Journal of Business Research*, **63**(9), 1033-1040.

Cheung, C. M., Lee, M. K. and Rabjohn, N. (2008), The impact of electronic word-of-mouth: the adoption of online opinions in online customer communities, *Internet Research*, **18**(3), 229-247.

Chu, S.C. and Kim, Y. (2011) Determinants of consumer engagement in electronic word-of-mouth (eWOM) in social networking sites. *International Journal of Advertising*, **30**(1), 47-75.

Cialdini, R. B. and Goldstein, N. J. (2004), Social influence: compliance and conformity, *Annual Review of Psychology*, **55**(1), 591-621.

Cioffi, D. and Garner, R. (1996), On doing the decision: effects of active versus passive choice on commitment and self-perception, *Personality and Social Psychology Bulletin*, **22**(2), 133-147.

Dessart, L., Veloutsou, C. and Morgan-Thomas, A. (2016), Capturing consumer engagement: duality, dimensionality and measurement, *Journal of Marketing Management*, **32**(5-6), 399-426.

eMarketer (2015), Increasing Audience Engagement Key Objective in Social Media, https://www.emarketer.com/Article/Increasing-Audience-Engagement-Key-Objective-Social-Media-Marketing/1013148 [Accessed 08-12-17].

Escalas, J. E. and Bettman, J. R. (2005), Self-construal, reference groups, and brand meaning, *Journal of Consumer Research*, **32**(3), 378-389.

Escalas, J. E. and Bettman, J. R. (2003), You are what they eat: the influence of reference groups on consumers' connections to brands, *Journal of Consumer Psychology*, **13**(3), 339-348.

Ferraro, R., Escalas, J. E. and Bettman, J. R. (2011), Our possessions, our selves: domains of self-worth and the possession–self link, *Journal of Consumer Psychology*, **21**(2), 169-177.

Fournier, S. (1998), Consumers and their brands: developing relationship theory in consumer research, *Journal of Consumer Research*, **24**(4), 343-373.

Gilly, M. C., Graham, J. L., Wolfinbarger, M. F. and Yale, L. J. (1998), A dyadic study of interpersonal information search, *Journal of the Academy of Marketing Science*, **26**(2), 83-100.

Goldsmith, R. E. and Horowitz, D. (2006), Measuring motivations for online opinion seeking. *Journal of Interactive Advertising*, **6**(2), 2-14.

Haslam, S. A., Powell, C. and Turner, J. (2000), Social identity, self-categorization, and work motivation:rrethinking the contribution of the group to positive and sustainable organisational outcomes, *Applied Psychology*, **49**(3), 319-339.

Haven, B. and Vittal, S. (2008), Measuring engagement: fours steps to making engagement measurement a reality, https://www.forrester.com/report/Measuring+Engagement/-/E-RES44421 [Accessed 14-2-17].

Hollebeek, L. D. and Chen, T. (2014), Exploring positively-versus negatively-valenced brand engagement: a conceptual model, *Journal of Product and Brand Management*, **23**(1), 62-74.

Hollebeek, L. D. (2011), Demystifying customer brand engagement: exploring the loyalty nexus, *Journal of Marketing Management*, **27**(7-8), 785-807.

Jahn, B. and Kunz, W. (2012), How to transform consumers into fans of your brand, *Journal of Service Management*, **23**(3), 344-361.

Kelman, H. C. (1961), Processes of opinion change, *Public Opinion Quarterly*, **25**(1), 57-78.

Latané, B. (1981), The psychology of social impact, *American Psychologist*, **36**(4), 343-356.

Latané, B. and Wolf, S. (1981), The social impact of majorities and minorities, *Psychological Review*, **88**(5), 438-453.

Latané, B. (1996), Dynamic social impact: the creation of culture by communication, *Journal of Communication*, **46**(4), 13-25.

Lee, G. B. (1996). Addressing anonymous messages in cyberspace, *Journal of Computer-Mediated Communication*, **2**(1).

Li, Y. M., Lee, Y. L. and Lien, N. J. (2012), Online social advertising via influential endorsers, *International Journal of Electronic Commerce*, **16**(3), 119-154.

McAlexander, J. H., Schouten, J. W. and Koenig, H. F. (2002), Building brand community, *Journal of Marketing*, **66**(1), 38-54.

Miller, M. D. and Brunner, C. C. (2008), Social impact in technologically-mediated communication: an examination of online influence, *Computers in Human Behavior*, **24**(6), 2972-2991.

Mittal, B. (1995), A comparative analysis of four scales of consumer involvement, *Psychology and Marketing*, **12**(7), 663-682.

Muniz, A. M. and O'Guinn, T. C. (2001), Brand community, *Journal of Consumer Research*, **27**(4), 412-432.

Muniz Jr, A. M. and Schau, H. J. (2005), Religiosity in the abandoned Apple Newton brand community, *Journal of Consumer Research*, **31**(4), 737-747.

Nowak, A., Szamrej, J. and Latané, B. (1990), From private attitude to public opinion: a dynamic theory of social impact, *Psychological Review*, **97**(3), 362-376.

Oh, S. and Syn, S. Y. (2015), Motivations for sharing information and social support in social media: a comparative analysis of Facebook, Twitter, Delicious, YouTube, and Flickr, *Journal of the Association for Information Science and Technology*, **66**(10), 2045-2060.

Patterson, P., Yu, T. and De Ruyter, K. (2006), Understanding customer engagement in services. In *Advancing Theory, Maintaining Relevance, Proceedings of ANZMAC 2006 Conference*, Brisbane,4-6.

Perez-Vega, R., Waite, K. and O'Gorman, K. (2016), Social Impact Theory: an examination of how immediacy operates as an influence upon social media interaction in Facebook fan pages, *The Marketing Review*, **16**(3), 299-321.

Sicilia, M. and Palazón, M. (2008), Brand communities on the Internet: A case study of Coca-Cola's Spanish virtual community, *Corporate Communications: An International Journal*, **13**(3), 255-270.

Solis, B. (2010), *Engage: The Complete Guide for Brands and Businesses to Build, Cultivate, and Measure Success in the New Web*, Wiley, Hoboken, NJ.

Tanford, S. and Penrod, S. (1984), Social Influence model: a formal integration of research on majority and minority influence processes, *Psychological Bulletin*, **95**(2), 189-225.

Tsai, W. H. S. and Men, L. R. (2013), Motivations and antecedents of consumer engagement with brand pages on social networking sites, *Journal of Interactive Advertising*, **13**(2), 76-87.

Van Doorn, J., Lemon, K. N., Mittal, V., Nass, S., Pick, D., Pirner, P., and Verhoef, P. C. (2010), Customer engagement behavior: Theoretical foundations and research directions, Journal of service research, 13(3), 253-266.

Vivek, S. D., Beatty, S. E. and Morgan, R. M. (2012), Customer engagement: exploring customer relationships beyond purchase, *Journal of Marketing Theory and Practice*, **20**(2), 122-146.

Walther, E., Bless, H., Strack, F., Rackstraw, P., Wagner, D. and Werth, L. (2002), Conformity effects in memory as a function of group size, dissenters and uncertainty, *Applied Cognitive Psychology*, **16**(7), 793-810.

Wood, W. (2000), Attitude change: persuasion and social influence, *Annual Review of Psychology*, **51**(1), 539-570.

Zhang, Y., Trusov, M., Stephen, A. T. and Jamal, Z. (2017), Online shopping and social media: friends or foes? *Journal of Marketing*, **81**(6),24-41.

6 Crowdsourcing and Crowdfunding

The growth of Web 2.0 has created a sustained emphasis on interaction between customers and organisations. In 2006 *Wired Magazine* editor and author Jeff Howe created the term "crowdsourcing" to define the practice of "taking a job traditionally performed by a designated agent (usually an employee) and outsourcing it to an undefined, generally large group of people in the form of an open call" (Saxton et al., 2013: 3). Marketers use crowdsourcing for marketing activities such as product design and promotion. A related but distinct concept is "crowdfunding", which is defined as "an open call, mostly through the Internet, for the provision of financial resources" (Belleflamme et al., 2014:4). Crowdfunding has been popular amongst arts and music communities as well as entrepreneurs and is linked to an established subscription-based business model, for example in 1885 Carnegie financed the Statue of Liberty plinth by asking for donations through a newspaper advertisement. Whilst crowdsourcing and crowdfunding offer many opportunities, there are several challenges that face the marketer in terms of quality, control and the ethical treatment of participants.

The concept of crowdsourcing

Crowdsourcing is an umbrella term within which there are several variants that can be distinguished according to four key criteria: (1) the nature of the crowd; (2) the nature of the task; (3) the nature of the reward; and (4) the ownership of the output (Zhao and Zhu, 2012). We will look at each of these criteria in turn.

■ The nature of the crowd

Early definitions of crowdsourcing identified that a crowd is formed of a large set of anonymous individuals (Schenk and Guittard, 2011; Saxton et al., 2013), however organisations can also draw on crowds composed of professional specialists. Open innovation is a variant of crowdsourcing, where a company seeks outside knowledge in order to source ideas to advance processes and technology (Chesbrough, 2003). For example, Unilever uses open innovation to gather ideas from external sources. Unilever circulate an innovation brief to a specialist crowd, found at either at a conference, by soliciting certain companies or by using brokerage agencies. A typical project might be soliciting input into the formulation of a new enzyme from amongst bio-tech firms, therefore an open call is being made to a known crowd. Outsourcing occurs when a company contracts out a business process externally and may be initiated by an open call (Contractor et al., 2010). Typically, outsourcing was considered as different from crowdsourcing because it involved a smaller number of people and is undertaken by professionals (Gefen and Camell, 2008).

The growth in crowdsourcing platforms for creative work, such as www.designcrowd.co.uk or www.designhill.com, means that it is a variant of crowdsourcing activity. Individuals are not anonymous, as within these platforms designers create profiles and seek to generate positive reviews of their work to boost their online reputation and improve their chances of being successful (Schorpf et al., 2017). Where crowdsourcing activity involves encouraging interaction amongst crowd members to create final output, a new relationship is created that changes the dyadic relationship of participant and organisation to being a triadic relationship of participant, organisation and community. For example, for Lego Ideas crowd members create and submit an idea but also comment and vote on the ideas of others. In these instances it is strategically important to build a supportive and engaged online community.

■ The nature of the task

Tasks are either micro or macro. Micro tasks are simple and repetitive but due to a degree of complexity, variability or needing judgement are not able to be easily automated (Vondrick et al., 2013). For example, the Smithsonian museum needed to decipher the handwriting of its collection of historical documents, so they could be digitised for devices such as the Kindle. Micro tasks are easy to complete when only a few in number, however large numbers of micro tasks require an organisation to dedicate a lot of resources, and in this situation crowdsourcing increases organisational task execution capacity by enabling task completion to be performed simultaneously by a large number of participants (Schenk and Guittard, 2011). The Smithsonian Museum launched a Digital Volunteer centre (https://transcription.si.edu/) which to date has recruited over 8,800 participants who have transcribed more than 300,000 documents.

There are commercial platforms that provide a marketplace within which organisations can recruit individuals to perform micro tasks in return for payment. One platform is MTurk or 'mechanical Turk' that enables individuals and businesses (known as Requesters) to recruit people (called 'providers' or 'Turkers') to perform micro tasks known as HITS (human intelligence tasks). Tasks are given a time in which to complete and a monetary reward per task completed. Requesters can specify that Turkers have attained certain qualifications, such as first completing an online test and sample HIT, in order to ensure that completed tasks meet a specified quality.

6

Exercise 6.1

Visit www.mturk.com and view some of the HITS. Search for the task with the highest reward and requiring the highest level of qualification (note you can filter HITS by qualification and sort by various criteria). Go to the Qualifications tab and look at the nature of the required qualifications that need to be attained. Are there any HITS would you consider accepting, which would you definitely reject? Why these HITS and not others?

Macro tasks are bigger in scope than micro-tasks and may require a high degree of time investment, creativity and customisation; while a micro task may take seconds to complete, a macro task will take much longer. It is sometimes possible for a macro task to be divided into separate micro tasks, for example the conversion of a whole speech into digital text (macro task) could be divided into conversion of single sentences (micro tasks) (Cheng et al., 2015). Macro tasks may also be characterised in requiring a high degree of innovation, customisation and individual input requiring specialist skills (Li et al., 2016). Frequently an organisation will use competitions or contests to complete macro tasks (Zheng et al., 2011). For example, open innovation is a form of macro task; the US federal government website (https://www.challenge.gov/list/) invites crowd participation in solving major challenges set by the Department of Homeland Security (passenger screening), the National Oceanic and Atmospheric Administration (ways of automating counts of sea lions) and the Air Force Research Lab (design of a portable weather station). In this way through requesting the crowd to produce a number of competing solutions, the organisation increases its task execution capacity.

■ The nature of the reward

As crowdsourcing involves a form of 'working', several academics have used Human Resource theory to help understand how the nature of the reward offered can either motivate or de-motivate the participants in the crowd. Self Determination Theory (Deci and Ryan, 1985) classifies motivation into two broad types: intrinsic and extrinsic. Intrinsic motivation is driven by internal individual psychological needs, whereas extrinsic motivation is created by the existence of external rewards (White, 1959; Ryan and Deci, 2000). In the context of crowdsourcing, intrinsic motivation includes the need to experience feelings of competency, distraction and belonging to a group with a shared aim, whereas extrinsic rewards include industry recognition of skill levels and payment (Bauer and Gegenhuber, 2015) (Table 6.1).

Table 6.1: Example of crowdsourcing rewards

Type of reward	Explanation	Example
Money	*Extrinsic reward* which is a strong motivator of individuals of with limited financial resources, particularly in poorer countries	Payment per HIT on MTurk, competition prize money
Skill development	*Extrinsic reward* when individuals are given the opportunity to engage in a specialised professional setting that can aid career advancement and expand networks	Open innovation where participants contribute to complex projects at www.innocentive.com
Recognition of competency	*Extrinsic rewards* which signals that achievement to others	Badges or awards for contribution, e.g. Trip Advisor levels
Social interaction and sharing of ideas	*Intrinsic reward* which provides also a sense of achievement and recognition amongst one's peers.	Ability to vote and share ideas with others for comments, e.g. Lego Ideas
Feeling of helping others	*Intrinsic reward* associated with providing outcomes that benefit society and makes the individual feel that they have meaning	Contributing to a digital archive at the Smithsonian museum
Distraction	*Intrinsic reward* for individuals requiring effortless tasks to pass time, e.g.when commuting	MTurk tasks

The nature of the reward determines the size, commitment and skill level of the crowd (Goh et al., 2017): too low a reward will result in a lack of interest and too high a reward might result in high numbers of speculative submissions that will be of low quality and take time to assess. Research shows that positive emotions such as pleasure, excitement and happiness are linked to reward structures which are appropriate and result in participants investing more time, which also can lead to higher task quality (Goh et al., 2017).

■ The ownership of the output

Different forms of crowdsourcing leads to different ownership outcomes. At the conclusion of the task, the ownership rights might reside with the company initiating the call or with the crowd who participate. For example, open-sourcing is a method of collaboratively generating knowledge for the benefit of a community or public where the output is free and open to all, and there is limited formal managerial control (Milberry and Anderson, 2009). An example of open-sourcing is Wikipedia, which is a free online encyclopaedia where individuals propose topic entries and generate content. This contrasts with forms of crowdsourcing where the benefit is not shared and belongs to the company or individual making the call, and there is clear managerial control (Belleflamme et al., 2014). At the conclusion of open innovation tasks, the ownership rights are usually held by the organisation; for example at the conclusion of Lego ideas (https://ideas.lego.com/dashboard) the winning design is put into production and the creator gets 1% of the royalties.

Concepts of co-creation and collaboration

Crowdsourcing participation involves behaviour that is conceptualised as co-creation and collaboration. Co-creation is when additional value is realised as a result of the interaction between the company and the customer, and between the customer and other customers (Prahalad and Ramaswamy, 2004). A key component of co-creation is allowing the customer to be able to customise the experience to suit their own needs or experience. We can see this present in a crowdsourcing activity that asks for customers to submit their own ideas for a pizza; for example Domino's Pizza Legends asks customers to create a pizza which is then available to other customers to order and vote for entry into the Pizza Legends Hall of Fame. (https://www.dominos.co.uk/blog/pizza-legends-hall-of-fame/)

Collaboration is a sub-set of co-creation activity where the customer is asked to comment on the company processes rather than customise an output to meet their needs. The focus is still on the company and customer working together, however here instead of customisation to individual need, the focus is upon the gaining insight from consumer knowledge in order to improve the overall product, for example collaboration is present in open source crowdsourcing activity. There is considerable variation in the extent and nature of collaboration that occurs within crowdsourcing platforms, with some such as Amazon's MTurk not involving any collaboration at all as they follow a process of 1) Find 2) Finish and 3) Earn with no further interaction (Saxton et al., 2013). We will now look at the components of the process of crowdsourcing.

The crowdsourcing process

Despite growing trends towards the use of crowdsourcing there is limited detailed understanding about its effectiveness, best practices, challenges and implications (Marjanovic et al., 2012). A crowdsourcing process has five stages (Figure 6.1) (Zhao and Zhu, 2014). There are multiple stakeholder groups involved in this process, and these are: the solution seekers, the solution providers, any intermediary brokerage platform which is used, and finally the public (Marjanovic et al., 2012).

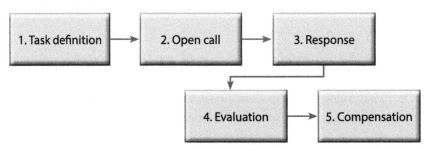

Figure 6.1: The crowdsourcing process. Adapted from Zhao and Zhu, 2014

Stage 1: Task definition

Task definition begins by recognising the strategic need for crowdsourcing activity by the solution seeker. This need relates to a particular gap in execution capacity and the ability of the solution seeker to complete a particular function. Task definition might be prompted by a gap in employee numbers, a gap in ideas or a gap in market awareness (since crowdsourcing activity can be used to generate positive PR) (Brabham, 2012). Task definition involves determining whether the job being crowdsourced should be positioned as a macro or micro task. Task definition informs the later stages of compensation and response management since micro tasks require lower levels of skill and effort from solution providers compared to macro tasks. Micro tasks are in essence subtasks for an overall macro task, e.g. digitalising text is a subtask for the macro tasks of digitising the whole library. When breaking down a macro task into micro tasks, it is important to determine the workflow of tasks and how they link together to solve the overall task; workflow might be iterative (batches of tasks are completed, checked, then progressed) or parallel (all tasks are worked on together) (Allahbakhsh et al., 2013).

Stage 2: Open call

An invitation to participate in the task is made through an open call, which may be placed within the solution seekers' owned communication channels and/or a paid channel such as an established crowdsourcing provider, e.g. Kickstarter, Wikipedia or MTurk. Established communication frameworks should be used to inform this decision, i.e. formulation of call content and choice of channel in terms of its audience numbers, audience composition and cost. Call content is a short description of the task, the type of tasks, e.g. transcription, the time limitations, the qualification requirements and reward (Allahbakhsh et al., 2013). The clarity and the precision of the call are important for task outcome quality (Chen et al., 2011). Channel choice should be related to the task requirements and quality of output. There are several areas which are task sensitive, including the size of the crowd, the level of skills required and the level of homogeneity (sameness) between solution providers (Estelles Arolas and Gonzalez-Ladron De Guevara., 2012). They note that for Boeing, the optimal size of the crowd is 100, but that for Lego an optimal crowd is in the region of thousands. This means that sometimes the call does not go to the general public but to a group with connection to the company, such as its own customers or suppliers (in the case of Boeing). Audience education attainment should be considered since tasks might require solution providers capable of innovation; there is evidence that in some crowds the majority are educated to postgraduate level (Buecheler et al., 2012).

Stage 3: Response

Two key elements are volume and quality of response. Response volume is determined by the effectiveness of call communication and also by participation incentive. Research shows that tasks compete for the attention of solution seekers, who themselves assess several factors such as likelihood of gaining the reward (DiPalantino and Vojnovic, 2009). Tasks performed under contract by employees or providers give a solution seeker greater control than crowdsourced solutions; this means that quality control is an important consideration.

In business practice, organisations usually benefit from sustaining a working relationship with a small number of employers, however response quality declined in Dell's Ideastorm system when it was using same panel of solution providers to solve macro tasks (Bayus, 2013). This suggests that response quality falls when the call goes to the same audience; Dell found for example that solution providers repeatedly submitted the same idea, and solution providers whose ideas were implemented tended to return with additional ones that were very similar to their first suggestions. Micro tasks can also suffer issues of low quality as a result of worker boredom and fatigue. To increase engagement, brokerage platforms provide the opportunity for solution seekers to review the completed work. Solution solvers with good reviews are able to ask for higher levels of reward.

Quality and volume of solutions are important, but there needs to be consideration given to the level of engagement with the call message. For example, there was public negative engagement when McDonalds created a call for heart-warming stories using the hashtag #McDStories, to generate positive content. The response from the public was to share complaints or make fun of the brand. According to Forbes magazine, the hashtag became a *'bashtag'* as the tweets included highlighting poor food hygiene, highlighting bad employment practices and accusing the chain of making poor quality products (Hill, 2012).

Stage 4: Evaluation

Task quality is evaluated upon completion. Quality control issues relate to the quality and the timeliness of the crowd-work. This may vary according to degree of skill and ability within the target market of the company. Micro task evaluation might be done by the brokerage platform and the solution seeker. Macro contest-based tasks might be evaluated by the public, and while this can result in the final solution being a good fit to market demand, there is a danger that the selected option is not the best fit with the image of the solution provider. For example, the National Environment Research Council sought a name for its new exploration vessel using the hashtag #nameourship. Once a short list of suggestions had been crowdsourced, the final stage of evaluation and selection of the winning solution was done by public vote. However, the winning name was *RRS Boaty McBoatface* which NERC rejected as being unsuitable for the main vessel, choosing instead the name *RRS Sir David Attenborough*, though after a public outcry they did use the winning name for one of the underwater vehicles (https://en.wikipedia. org/wiki/RRS_Sir_David_Attenborough). Whilst there may be a desire to control crowdsourcing projects it is important to ensure that management control does not stifle the creativity, innovation and flexibility that characterise crowdsourcing.

Stage 5: Compensation

Compensation can be distributed directly for each completed task or can be awarded competitively, i.e. one reward given to the best completed task. The amount of compensation can vary from being a substantial financial reward to non-existent. The appropriateness of the incentives and the detail in the compensation policy will influence the performance of solution providers and affect task quality (Allahbaksh et al., 2013). Solution seekers need to consider how they can combine one or more of the reward structures in Table 6.1., particularly since a combination of intrinsic and extrinsic rewards can increase task motivation (Mason and Watts, 2010). Whilst monetary rewards are commonly offered, research shows that it is important to also consider payment amount and method. Whilst the reward amount affects the speed of task completion, it does not affect task quality, but the payment method does (Chen et al., 2011; Mason and Watts, 2010).

6

The challenges and benefits of crowdsourcing

There are a range of risks that companies need to address when considering crowdsourcing. Marjonovic et al. (2012) identify that various risks exist for all the stakeholders which include "disclosure of competitive intelligence; upfront investment of time and effort with no guarantee of reward; and the dependence of the commercial viability of the brokers' business model on a critical mass of solutions" (p12). They note that these risks can be managed through "formal mechanisms (terms and conditions, legal frameworks, IP policies) and informal mechanisms (relationships of trust)". It is important to note that this contrasts with the idea that crowdsourcing is low cost and easy to implement. One of the challenges that a solution seeker must consider is that there will be an increase in management effort in both task identification and also management of a process. Second there are trust issues, particularly related to innovation where the solution seeker provides access to sensitive functions and innovation to allow for successful completion of the task. As we have seen there are several instances where damage limitation skills are needed when a crowdsourcing task goes wrong. This may involve PR skills after the event as well as before. Even if the crowdsourcing task flows according to plan, at the least there will need to be staff resource allocated to manage the queries and questions that might arise from the crowd. Also there will be costs associated with promoting the crowdsourcing project to the crowd.

A second challenge are the ethical considerations associated with crowdsourcing activity. Key questions to consider are the extent to which a crowd based approach reduces genuine employment opportunities. There are several instances where the use of the crowd tends to devalue the work done by professionals who have invested in training and accreditation, for example Stockphoto is an image platform brokerage which is identified as undermining the work done by professional photographers (Howe, 2006). There is also ongoing debate surrounding crowdsourced provision of holiday accommodation (Airbnb) and taxi transport (Uber). An example where service jobs are replaced by customers can be found in Vodafone Service Friends which was launched in 2014 and is designed to shift work away from store reps. Requests are sent to tech support members who are crowdsourced and customers pay an hourly rate for support. The tech support is given in your own home or in another convenient location, i.e. you put in your postcode, exchange texts and the service rep visits you. Vodafone Service Friends are vetted by Vodafone and reviewed by customers.

A third challenge is sustaining public interest and support for the crowdsourcing activity. Lucyna and Hanna (2016) suggest that the public is becoming increasingly aware that low cost solutions are being crowdsourced to deliver high value business success. Solution providers, particularly where these are the solution seekers' customer base, can become frustrated and bored with calls to participate in tasks such as providing reviews or inventing new product names or formulations. Solution providers can have bad experiences of rewards not being delivered fairly, e.g. a lack of clear and transparent criteria as to why the prize winner was given the prize, or perceptions that the competitions are open to professionals or highly trained amateurs and that it is not a "level playing field".

However there are a range of benefits which make overcoming these challenges worthwhile. For a solution seeker, crowdsourcing provides a more flexible and lower risk route to problem-solving when working on a solution in-house involves high uncertainty (e.g. no solution is possible) or cost (e.g. requires new skills, take up too much time) (Marjanovic et al., 2012). Crowdsourcing provides a rich source of ideas and skills, scale of production and flexibility of work since an international crowd of solution providers can contribute across time zones. For solution providers, participation in crowdsourcing activity brings benefits such as a boost of esteem, feelings of being close to the brand, fun, mental challenge and financial rewards and ultimately can lead to feelings of empowerment (Djelassi and Decooperman, 2013) .

Crowdfunding

Crowdfunding is distinct from crowdsourcing in that instead of task completion the focus is upon accumulation of finance. There are two dominant crowdfunding mechanisms: (1) reward-based, for example, pre-ordering where the customer purchases the proposed product if sufficient funding is received for it to be made; (2) profit-sharing, where the individuals are promised a share of future profits or a share of equity if funding is achieved (Belleflamme et al., 2014). Other forms of crowdfunding are a debt-based (receiving a loan) or a donation (Kuppsuwamy and Bayus, 2015). The process is similar to that outlined in Figure 6.1. However instead of task definition the solution seeker has to define the nature of reward offered to the crowd.

In all forms there are 'extra benefits' from being part of a community of funders which enhances the consumption experience and gaining individual recognition from the company (Gerber et al., 2012). These extra benefits are important since they increase the fun of participating in a crowdfunding project. Sometimes this sense of enjoyment is all that the individual participant receives since not all crowdfunding initiatives succeed, for example only 36% of Kickstarter projects succeed (Statista, 2017). Crowdfunding calls are placed upon crowdfunding broker sites (Table 6.2), with some sites specialising in a particular sort of funding call. Broker sites provide solution providers with valuable information on how others in the crowdfunding community are acting. Kuppuswamy and Bayus (2015) examine funded projects listed on Kickstarter and show that social information (i.e. other crowdfunders' funding decisions) plays a key role in the success of a project.

Table 6.2: Top four crowdfunding sites. Compiled from www.alexa.com

No	Name	Alexa Rank	Fee	Remit
1	Kickstarter	534	5%	Goods and services only; not personal fundraising
2	Patreon	722	5%	Creative projects only; subscription funding
3	Gofundme	1285	5%	Personal fundraising
4	indiegogo	1521	5%	Funds for ideas, charity or start-up business

Crowdfunding has become a valuable alternative source of funding for entrepreneurs (Belleflamme et al., 2014). There can be legal limitations to crowdfunding initiatives when it is used by entrepreneurs seeking external financing, particularly if it involves offering shares or equity (Belleflamme et al., 2014). For example, companies can be limited as to the number of private investors in some countries (Schwienbacher and Larralde, 2012). To overcome this restriction entrepreneurs can offer alternative rewards. For example, the 2012 campaign to develop an Ostrich pillow did not offer shares to its backers. Instead, the company offered products, special features on the website, and special distribution treatment to backers of their product (Kickstarter, 2012).

A key component of crowdfunding is pre-ordering – paying for an item before it is produced and available to be shipped. The benefit of pre-ordering is that it provides the entrepreneur with valuable marketing information, particularly in seeing which package of benefits are most attractive to which customer segment; the entrepreneur gains insight into willingness to pay (Belleflamme et al., 2014). Pre-ordering usually involves offering the basic product plus enhancements, which may or may not attract a price premium above the regular purchase price. The choice of mechanism depends on the amount of funds being sought. Where the amount is relatively small the entrepreneur typically prefers pre-ordering as it means that they can charge a premium price to extract benefit from the crowdfunding community. However when the amount sought is large, the entrepreneur would have to lower pre-ordering prices in order to attract the necessary volume of crowd-funders or risk not being able to raise sufficient funds.

For a customer, a drawback of pre-ordering is the inability to judge product quality; this is particularly true in profit sharing schemes where they may not ever be in direct receipt of the product (Belleflamme et al., 2014). Therefore it is important to understand what determines funder satisfaction. Research by Xu et al. (2016) finds that crowdfunding comprises two stages: the funding stage and the implementation stage. In their study they explore funder satisfaction after the implementation stage. They find that delivery timeliness, product quality, project novelty, sponsorship participation and entrepreneur attractiveness are all influences upon sponsor satisfaction. The information that goes from the entrepreneur to the crowd is very important. Ahlers et al. (2015) analyse equity crowdfunding (i.e., crowdfunding involving equity issuance), presenting evidence that successful crowdfunding initiatives rely on credible signals, quality of the start-up, and sound information disclosure to the crowd. Xu et al. (2016) present research which they have conducted in the Chinese market place which examines how these elements influence satisfaction with the product. Interestingly they find differences according to gender and age. This means that as the crowdfunding market place grows it is important that companies understand who they are most likely to attract as funders and to manage the rewards accordingly.

Exercise 6.2

Look at a range of campaigns seeking crowd funding on the brokerage platforms in Table 6.2, and see if you can identify where the influences proposed by Xu et al. (2016) are in operation.

6

Summary

Crowdsourcing and crowdfunding are becoming established as Web 2.0 phenomena, however there is limited understanding of the limitations and processes of these approaches to harnessing the power of the online crowd. Whilst there are several instances of organisations and online communities benefiting from the ability to outsource a range tasks to online solution providers, there are also challenges present as seen in examples where the lack of control has lead to poor output quality, and examples which lead to questions about the ethics of replacing paid employment with crowdsourced labour. This chapter has identified these benefits and challenges and provided an account of the processes and mechanisms that marketers can use to manage these activities.

Exemplar paper

Bal, A. S., Weidner, K., Hanna, R. and Mills, A. J., (2017), Crowdsourcing and brand control, *Business Horizons*, **60**(2), 219-228.

> This is a conceptual paper that draws together research on crowdsourcing and brand community activity. The paper discusses the managerial implications to propose a typology to enable strategic brand management.

■ Additional reading

Wilson, M., Robson, K. and Botha, E. (2017), Crowdsourcing in a time of empowered stakeholders: lessons from crowdsourcing campaigns, *Business Horizons*, **60**(2), 247-253.

Prpić, J., Shukla,P.P., Kietzmann, J.H. and Mccarthy, I.P. (2015), How to work a crowd: developing crowd capital through crowdsourcing, *Business Horizons*, **58**(1), 77-85.

References

Ahlers, G. K., Cumming, D., Günther, C. and Schweizer, D. (2015), Signaling in equity crowdfunding, *Entrepreneurship Theory and Practice*, **39**(4), 955-980.

Allahbakhsh, M., Benatallah, B., Ignjatovic, A., Motahari-Nezhad, H. R., Bertino, E., & Dustdar, S. (2013). Quality control in crowdsourcing systems: Issues and directions. IEEE Internet Computing, 17(2), 76-81.

Bauer, R. M., and Gegenhuber, T. (2015), Crowdsourcing: Global search and the twisted roles of consumers and producers, Organization, 22(5), 661-681.

Bayus, B. L. (2013), Crowdsourcing new product ideas over time: An analysis of the Dell IdeaStorm community. *Management Science*, **59**(1), 226-244.

Belleflamme, P., Lambert, T. and Schwienbacher, A. (2014), Crowdfunding: tapping the right crowd, *Journal of Business Venturing*, **29**(5), 585-609.

Brabham, D.C. (2012), The myth of amateur crowds: a critical discourse analysis of crowdsourcing coverage, *Information, Communication and Society*, **15**(3), 394-410.

Buecheler, T., Sieg, J. H., Füchslin, R. M. and Pfeifer, R. (2010), Crowdsourcing, open innovation and collective intelligence in the scientific method-a research agenda and operational framework, In: *Artificial Life XII – Twelfth International Conference on the Synthesis and Simulation of Living Systems*, Odense, 679-686.

Chen, J. J., Menezes, N. J., Bradley, A. D. and North, T. A. (2011), Opportunities for crowdsourcing research on Amazon Mechanical Turk, *Interfaces*, **5**(3), 1-4.

Cheng, J., Teevan, J., Iqbal, S. T. and Bernstein, M. S. (2015), Break it down: a comparison of macro-and microtasks, In *Proceedings of the 33rd Annual ACM Conference on Human Factors in Computing Systems*, 4061-4064.

Contractor, F.J., Kumar, V., Kundu, S.K. and Pedersen, T. (2010), Reconceptualizing the firm in a world of outsourcing and offshoring: the organizational and geographical relocation of high-value company functions, *Journal of Management Studies*, **47**(8), 1417-1433.

Deci, E. L. and Ryan, R. M. (1985), The general causality orientations scale: Self-determination in personality, *Journal of Research in Personality*, **19**(2), 109-134.

DiPalantino, D. and Vojnovic, M. (2009), Crowdsourcing and all-pay auctions, In *Proceedings of the 10th ACM conference on Electronic Commerce*, 119-128.

Gefen, D. and Carmel, E. (2008), Is the world really flat? A look at offshoring at an online programming marketplace, *MIS Quarterly*, **32**(2) 367-384.

Gerber, E. M., Hui, J. S. and Kuo, P. Y. (2012), Crowdfunding: why people are motivated to post and fund projects on crowdfunding platforms, in *Proceedings of the International Workshop on Design, Influence, and Social Technologies: Techniques, Impacts and Ethics*, 11-22.

Goh, D. H. L., Pe-Than, E. P. P., and Lee, C. S. (2017), Perceptions of virtual reward systems in crowdsourcing games, *Computers in Human Behavior*, **70**(1), 365-374.

Hill, K. (2012), #McDStories: When a Hashtag Becomes a Bashtag, *Forbes Magazine*, https://www.forbes.com/sites/kashmirhill/2012/01/24/mcdstories-when-a-hashtag-becomes-a-bashtag/#470c636ded25 [Accessed 1st July 2017]

Howe, J. (2006), The rise of crowdsourcing, *Wired magazine*, **14**(6), 1-4.

Kickstarter (2012). Ostrich Pillow. Available from: https://www.kickstarter.com/projects/studio-banana/ostrich-pillow [Accessed: 21-11-2017].

Kuppuswamy, V. and Bayus, B. L. (2015), Crowdfunding Creative Ideas: The Dynamics of Project Backers in Kickstarter (November 2), versioned in Hornuf, L. and Cumming, D. , (eds.), (2017), The Economics of Crowdfunding: Startups, Portals, and Investor Behavior, https://ssrn.com/abstract=2234765 or http://dx.doi.org/10.2139/ssrn.2234765 [Accessed 15th August 2017]

Li, G., Wang, J., Zheng, Y. and Franklin, M.J. (2016), Crowdsourced data management: a survey, *IEEE Transactions on Knowledge and Data Engineering*, **28**(9), 2296-2319.

Lucyna, W. and Hanna, H., (2016), Prosumption use in creation of cause related marketing programs through crowdsourcing, *Procedia Economics and Finance*, **39**, 212-218.

Mason, W. and Watts, D. J. (2010), Financial incentives and the performance of crowds, *ACM SigKDD Explorations Newsletter*, **11**(2), 100-108.

Marjanovic, S., Fry, C. and Chataway, J., (2012), Crowdsourcing based business models. In: *Search of Evidence for Innovation 2.0, Science and Public Policy*, **39**(3), 318-332.

Milberry, K. and Anderson, S. (2009), Open sourcing our way to an online commons: contesting corporate impermeability in the new media ecology, *Journal of Communication Inquiry*, **33**(4), 393-412.

Ryan, R. M. and Deci, E. L. (2000), Self-determination theory and the facilitation of intrinsic motivation, social development, and well-being, *American Psychologist*, **55**(1), 68.

Saxton, G.D., Oh, O. and Kishore, R., (2013), Rules of crowdsourcing: models, issues, and systems of control, *Information Systems Management*, **30**(1), 2-20.

Schörpf, P., Flecker, J., Schönauer, A. and Eichmann, H., (2017), Triangular love–hate: management and control in creative crowdworking, *New Technology, Work and Employment*, **32**(1), 43-58.

Schenk, E. and Guittard, C. (2011), Towards a characterization of crowdsourcing practices, *Journal of Innovation Economics & Management*, **7**(1), 93-107.

Schwienbacher, A. and Larralde, B. (2012), Crowdfunding of small entrepreneurial ventures. In: Cumming, D.J. (Ed.), *The Oxford Handbook of Entrepreneurial Finance*, Oxford University Press, Oxford

Statista (2017) Percentage of Successfully Funded Kickstarter Projects as of January 2017, https://www.statista.com/statistics/235405/kickstarter-project-funding-success-rate/ [Accessed March 25th 2017].

Vondrick, C., Patterson, D. and Ramanan, D. (2013), Efficiently scaling up crowdsourced video annotation, *International Journal of Computer Vision*, **101**(1), 184-204.

White, R. W. (1959), Motivation reconsidered: The concept of competence. *Psychological Review*, **66**(5), 297.

Xu, B., Zheng, H., Xu, Y. and Wang, T. (2016), Configurational paths to sponsor satisfaction in crowdfunding, *Journal of Business Research*, **69**(2), 915-927.

Zhao, Y. and Zhu, Q. (2014), Evaluation on crowdsourcing research: current status and future direction, *Information Systems Frontiers*, **16**(3), 417-434.

7 Digital Content Planning

Marketing communications are messages sent to a target audience in order to achieve marketing goals. Marketing communications should inform, persuade and remind the target audience about the product and services that the brand offers (Bell and Taheri, 2017). Prior to the widespread adoption of digital technology the direction of these messages was depicted as a one-to-many model whereby marketing communications were formulated and sent by the brand to be received and decoded by the customer. However developments in digital communications channels enable consumers to engage not only in communication with a brand but also with each other.

Communication models

The digitisation of marketing communication challenges the existing one-to-many marketing communications model. To reflect the changing communications landscape, marketing communication models have evolved from a one-to-many to a many-to-many communication models (Table 7.1). The *one-to-many* model represents a broadcast communication process where a message is formulated, sent, received and decoded. This does not account for the interactivity that characterises digital media. Interactivity can be represented by a two-way communications model, where the source sends a message which is received and a response is sent, this is called a *dialogue*. A many-to-many model is where consumers can interact with other consumers and with the brand (Hoffman and Novak, 1996). This is called a *trialogue* (Chaffey and Ellis-Chadwick, 2012).

Table 7.1: Communications models. Adapted from Chaffey and Ellis-Chadwick, 2012

Communication model	Description	Example
One to many model 	One source contacts many receivers with one message, the medium does not allow the customers to respond to the brand	Television advert
One to one model 	One source contacts each recipient with a different personalised message and the customers can each respond to the source through the same medium	E-mail advert
Many to many model 	One source sends a different message to each participant , customers can each send a message to each other, response to each sender- receiver can be made through the same medium	Social media post

Reactions to online communications in the form of a dialogue and trialogue are instances of *online consumer engagement* (OCE). OCE is a key measurement of the success of digital marketing communications (Morgan-Thomas and Veloutsou, 2013). OCE can be either active or passive. *Active engagement* behaviour would be participating in message creation, content sharing and commenting on the content provided by others (Casalo et al., 2007); and *passive consumer engagement* behaviour would be liking a fan page and viewing content.

Selection criteria for an organisation's communication channels are the level of control that each channel allowed to the marketer (Fill, 2009). As the level of interactivity decreases the degree of control increases, for example, earned media has the highest level of interactivity and the least amount of control. There is brand risk associated with the lack of message control in digital environments since social media enables consumers to complain or praise the products of an organisation and take a more active role in creating and sending communications within the brand space (Ward and Ostrom, 2006). Lack of control of social media activity by other users is a common fear among marketers (Pfeffer et al., 2014). We will now consider each of the three digital classifications in more detail.

Owned media

Owned media is branded content which is present online because the company has established ownership of specific digital pages. Owned digital media includes e-mail, website, company blogs and social media sites (Figure 7.1).

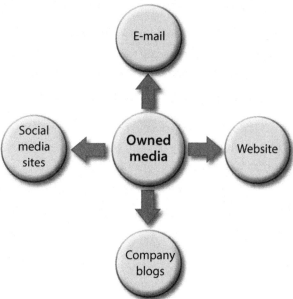

Figure 7.1: Range of owned media

E-mail marketing usually takes the form of newsletters that are sent to a database on a periodic time (Table 7.2). Sending and receiving e-mails is the top online activity among adults in the UK, and it is expected to reach 90% usage among Internet users by 2019 (Office for National Statistics, 2016; Campaign Monitor, 2017). E-mail marketing is an effective way to reach prospects and to manage existing customers' relationships. Whenever running an e-mail marketing campaign, it is important also to consider the average expected opening and click-through rates, as evidence from e-mail marketing providers find that these vary depending on the industry. For example, according to MailChimp (2017), a popular e-mail marketing supplier, the click-through rates (CTRs) of restaurant industries is among the lowest (1.25%) whereas Hobbies and Media and Publishing industries are among the highest industries regarding CTRs (5.13% and 4.70% respectively). Such benchmarks help a digital marketer to plan and evaluate an e-mail marketing campaigns.

Table 7.2: Types of e-mail marketing campaigns

Newsletters	Commonly used to inform a company's audience about news happening around the company and that can be of interest to their customers. Newsletters are usually sent periodically (weekly, monthly). Examples: New product lines or services, achievements of the company.
Offers and promotions	Since e-mails are sent to an existing database, customised offers can be sent to segments that have disengaged with the company or other attractive segments to encourage a behavioural outcome.
Announcements	Usually used to communicate news, this might not necessarily be positive. Some companies keep their customers informed via e-mail as part of the service recovery strategies when there is service failure.
Events	E-mail marketing can be used to promote events organised by a company. Since it is possible to track who opened an e-mail, it can also be used to facilitate conversions by offering discounts to segments that may be prone to purchase only with this type of promotions.
Surveys	Getting feedback from customers via e-mail is also a common practice. This can be after the service was provided, or as part market research activities during new product development.

Weblogs or *blogs* are personalised, easy-to-manage websites with content presented in reverse chronological order (Schiano et al., 2004). Reading blogs is very popular; over 409 million people read 23.7 billion blog pages each year (Wordpress, 2017), which means that blogs are an important media channel. A survey conducted by Hubspot (2017) found that blogs are a central part of a content marketing strategy, with 53% of marketers using blogs to disseminate content. Blogs provide brands with the means to build communities that contribute towards success.

Singh et al. (2008) identify four key benefits for brands that blog.

■ The first benefit is being relevant to their customers. Brands can use blogs to communicate on things that matter to customers and provide content that resonates with them. For example, Innocent's blog (http://www.innocentdrinks.co.uk/blog) is used to communicate messages about where their ingredients are sourced, as well as post about company culture.

■ A second benefit is the ability to gather insight into how consumers access information and interact with contents. Linking back to the example of Innocent's blog, since the brand owns the blog, they can also gather information about which posts generated more interest, which in turn can inform future marketing activities to fit those interests. Receiving firsthand feedback in the form of comments to a blog post is one of the most valuable benefits of having a blog!

- A third benefit is that blogs reach younger consumers (Singh et al., 2008). For example, 21 to 35-year olds represent 53.3% of those who interact with and write blogs (Sysomos, 2017). Brands targeting a younger target audience should consider blogging as a communication channel.

- A fourth and final benefit is that by blogging, a brand can build a deeper connection with the audience, especially when a brand spokesperson is the blogger.

Para-social interaction is defined as the interpersonal involvement between the media user and the media that he or she consumers (Lee and Watkins, 2016). Para-social interaction occurs when company partners are considered experts, since this will enhance the relationship that exists between the consumer, the blogger, and the brand. This can manifest in the form of seeking guidance from the media personality, perceiving personalities as friends, or imagining being part of their social world.

Blogging occurs in a written form. However, social media channels such as YouTube have also extended this practice to video blogging or *vlogging*. There are several celebrity vloggers with several million subscribers. A brand may form a partnership with a celebrity vlogger but there may be mixed results (e.g. Zoella's 2017 advent calendar would be an example of a partnership that didn't work out well due to poor decisions in pricing). A good match between a vlogger and a brand can produce positive outcomes for the brand, such as higher purchase intentions and higher perceived brand value (Lee and Watkins, 2016).

There are three factors that are important to consider when choosing a vlogger: social attractiveness, physical attractiveness and attitude homophily. *Social attractiveness* refers to the 'likeability' of the person (Dufner et al., 2013). *Physical attractiveness* refers to the degree in which physical features are considered aesthetically pleasing or beautiful. Finally, *attitude homophily* refers to the perceived similarity that exists between the attitudes of the vlogger and the consumer. However, the challenge for marketers is determining accurately how the target audience views the vlogger, which is why vloggers with higher audiences (i.e. celebrity vloggers) are usually the preferred choice for a brand.

Social networking sites have facilitated the proliferation of *online brand communities* (OBCs). These are defined as "a network of relationship between consumers and the brand, product, fellow consumers, and the marketer" (McAlexander et al., 2002:39). OBCs differ from traditional communities as they reflect the members' common interest for a brand, combined with commercial distinctiveness. Commercial distinctiveness turns traditional communities into "specialised consumer communities" (Zaglia, 2013: 217).

■ Approaches to community management

There are two approaches to community management: reactive and proactive approaches. *Reactive approaches* focus on containing negative behavioural outcomes that can damage the brand value and reputation. A common characterisation of this behaviour is negative electronic word-of-mouth. Corporate wrongdoings, public gaffes, and unsatisfactory service that originate offline migrate into the social media sphere within minutes in the form of angry posts, wall-based conversations, and activist-orchestrated attacks (Champoux et al., 2012). *Proactive approaches* look to plan actions to generate positive engagement and co-create value with consumers.

Reactive approaches to community management use many of the skills from the domain of Public Relations. Crisis in online communities can be initiated by a combination of online and offline events. A negative experience with a product purchased by a consumer can elicit a complaint on twitter or on the brand's fan page. Sometimes consumers appropriate brand activities on social media to express their discontent with the product or service that the brand is offering. For example, in 2012 McDonalds decided to run a twitter campaign behind the hashtag #McDStories. However, users started to share negative feedback about the McDonald's product or funny stories about the company. The volume and speed of this negative engagement means that it is classed as an *online firestorm* (Pfeffer et al., 2014). A reactive approach in this case was to change the hashtag, and stop calling consumers to participate using #McDStories.

Online firestorms are initiated by service failures originated by the brand. For example, in 2012 Italian cruise ship Costa Concordia capsized and sank after striking an underwater rock off Isola del Giglio, Tuscany. This later generated a backlash on social media under the hashtag #costaconcordia. In the days following the accident, it was clear that the brand had no plan for resolving the firestorm. The brand's Facebook page continued to offer the usual updates on trips, deals and specific ships, while the Facebook wall became packed with several hundred comments expressing questions, fears, anger and compassion (Engler, 2012).

DiStaso et al. (2015) identify three strategies that brands can use when reacting to a crisis on social media: apology, sympathy and information (Table 7.3).

Table 7.3: Proactive strategies to crises on social media. Adapted from Distaso et al. (2015)

Strategy	Example
Apology	We accept responsibility for the incident that occurred this week resulting in nine deaths. We hope those who were affected can forgive us.
Sympathy	We are deeply saddened by the incident that occurred this week resulting in nine deaths. Our thoughts and prayers go out to those affected
Information	On April 7, 4 patients, a nurse and 2 doctors died from a highly contagious virus. The hospital is investigating the cause of the outbreak

An *apology strategy* involves the acknowledgement and acceptance of the responsibility. A brand following this strategy would normally ask for forgiveness from its consumers, as well as a promise that the event won't repeat again in the future. Evidence suggests that an apology strategy is better than denial (Kim at al., 2009). The apology strategy is the most commonly used. In fact the majority of Fortune 500 companies applied this strategy on Facebook to communicate with their consumers when a crisis occurred (Ki and Nekmat, 2014). The *sympathy strategy* involves a brand having a high degree of attentiveness for crisis-affected stakeholders. Finally, an *information strategy* occurs when the brand only reports what happened. DiStaso et al. (2015) investigated the effects of these three strategies in a crisis on reputation, credibility and trust. Their findings show that an apology and information strategy can have a better impact on trust and reputation than a sympathy strategy. However, posting facts (information strategy) had a positive effect on credibility, and posts containing facts are more likely to be shared, which can be useful when the dissemination of information can reduce the negative impact of the situation.

Proactive strategies require an understanding of consumer's motivations to engage online. Consumers engage in OBCs for different reasons, and the role of the community manager is to design strategies that cater for different motivations. Reasons to engage with a brand vary according to context (Portilla Irastorza and Perez-Vega, 2016). Common motivational factors for engagement in OBCs found in the literature are:

- **Functional**, where consumers obtain utilitarian benefits for engaging in the brand community (Wirtz et al., 2013);

- **Affective**, when engaging in the brand community elicits enjoyment feelings (Dessart et al.,2016);

- **Behavioural**, when engaging in activities is the main driver for being part of that community, e.g. by sharing, connecting or helping others (Dessart et al, 2016; Baldus et al., 2015);

- **Social**, when being part of the community becomes part of the social identity of the consumer; and

- **Cognitive**, when engaging in the brand community serves to be inspired for new ideas and generate a feeling of absorption (Portilla Irastorza and Perez-Vega, 2016).

It is important to note that within the same OBCs, users can have different motivations. For example, an online forum of a digital device like the iPhone X, might have users who are there to learn how to take advantage of its features (i.e. functional motivation). Others are there because they like to help others (i.e. behavioural motivation) and by doing so they get a sense of validation of being part of the iPhone community (i.e. social motivation).

Exercise 7.1

Visit the social media pages of a brand across different channels (i.e. Facebook, Instagram, Twitter). Examine the posts and determine the primary motive. Identify if there are any differences across channel and between consumers.

Proactive approaches to community management will focus on creating value through the interaction with consumers in OBCs. Schau et al. (2009) identify three key practices applied to the context of social networking that can create and enhance ties among brand community members: welcoming, empathising, and governing. *Welcoming* is the first practice to which members are exposed. Community managers can easily adopt this practice, and recent members can enact this practice with newer members. *Empathising* creates value by providing affective resources within a sympathetic social network. This support system acts as a significant switching cost for consumers who come to depend on it. Finally, the practice of *governing* articulates the behavioural expectations within the brand community.

Paid media

Paid media is defined as branded content which is present online because the company has made payment. Paid digital media includes paid search placement, programmatic advertising and paid affiliates (Figure 7.2).

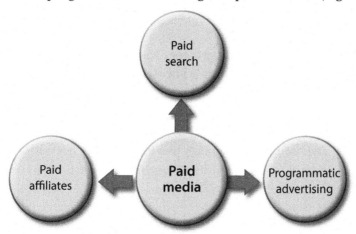

Figure 7.2: Paid media types

Paid search (also known as paid advertising, pay-per-click or PPC) is a digital channel that leverages on the use of search engines to navigate the Internet. According to Internet Live Stats (n.d.), there were 1.2 trillion searches on Google in 2012. Search engines like Google sell advertising space in the Search Engine Results Page (SERP) to businesses. This is usually made via a bidding process for keywords that users type when they search for things online, with the higher bidder appearing at the top of the result list (Rutz and Bucklin, 2011). Marketers pay for search engines to serve text advertisements in response to keyword searches that are generic (e.g., "hotels"). A text advertisement from a company will appear in the top results if the keyword and bidding beat that of other businesses interested in showing their ads, and advertisers will only be charged when someone clicks on the ad (hence the term 'pay-per-click'). The market for this type of digital channel was estimated to be worth 83.06 billion US dollars in 2016 (Statista, 2017).

Programmatic advertising is one of the most recent innovations in digital advertising. Before programmatic advertising, media buying agencies contacted websites to buy space on behalf of their clients for a period of time, or a number of impressions. This process had several disadvantages for both buyers and sellers of online space. From the buyer's perspective, it required media planning, negotiating skills, and relied on skill in choosing websites where the audience of interest would be. However, this approach was an inflexible way of buying advertising space as it did not allow for a reactive change in approach if alternative placement sites were found later that were a better fit to the target audience. There were also inefficiencies for the website owner who was selling the advertising space, as they would sell space to the first bid and this would exclude and subsequent brands who might have been willing to pay more.

With programmatic advertising, the process of media buying is automated through digital platforms such as *real-time bidding exchanges* (RTB) and *demand-side platforms* (DSP) (Elmeleegy et al., 2013). RTB exchanges auction ad space in real time on behalf of the media owners and demand-side platforms respond with bids on behalf of brands for that particular ad space on the website. The entire process takes less than 250 milliseconds. To optimise the buying decision, data, including user data, advertiser data, and contextual data plays a central role.

Affiliates are online sources (e.g. blogs or a link in an online newspaper) that link their content to other websites (Google, 2017). During browsing activity a consumer might follow links and click between websites. This activity is classified by website analytics software as *referral traffic*. Links can either be added spontaneously by other website owners due to the relevance of the content or might have been placed through an affiliate programme, in which a third-party owner agrees to host links with the intention of getting a benefit from conversions and traffic. In this way bloggers would gain revenue from the content they are creating.

■ Bidding strategies

A bidding strategy determines how a brand's online advertising budget will be spent, and aligns expenditure to campaign goals. Bidding strategies focus on three outcomes: clicks, impressions, and conversion (Figure 7.3).

A focus on clicks is suitable when the goal is to build website traffic. There are two click-based bidding strategies: *manual cost-per-click* (CPC) and the *automated maximise clicks* bidding. In manual cost-per-click, the marketer chooses how to spend per keyword based on estimated competitor demand which is published by platforms like Google Adwords. The 'maximise clicks' bidding strategy adjusts bidding automatically to bid higher or lower, based on the probability of a consumer click. The click predictions are based on analysing historical data of user profile groups reactions to particular ad campaigns. This is an example of the applications of machine learning to online advertising.

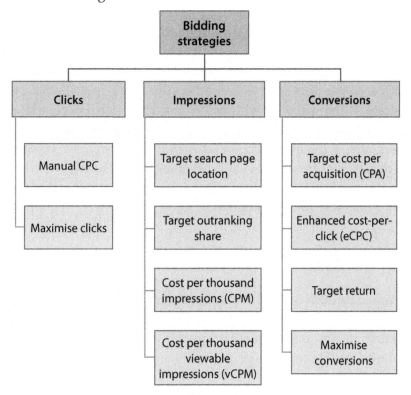

Figure 7.3: Bidding strategies

A focus on impressions is suitable when generating awareness of the brand. There are four bid strategies: target search page location, target out-ranking share, cost-per-thousand impressions (CPM), and cost-per-thousand viewable impressions (vCPM). *Target search page location* is an automated bid strategy that sets bids to increase the chances that an ad appears at the top or on the first page of search results. *Target outranking share* is an automated bid strategy that lets the marketer choose a search domain in which to outrank a competitor, in this instance the brand ad is displayed above the competitor's ad, or shows when the brand's ad does not outrank a competitor for that search term. It is possible to determine how often an ad aims to outrank in that search domain. The *cost-per-thousand impressions* (CPM) is used for display (e.g. banners) campaigns. Under this bid strategy the marketer pays when an ad is displayed every thousand times. Similarly, in a *cost-per-thousand viewable impressions* (vCPM) bid strategy, the marketer pays when an ad can be seen by potential consumers. This means bidding on the value of the ad appear in a viewable position on a given placement.

A focus on *conversions* makes use of machine learning, and lets the ad broker automate the bidding strategies based on the different conversion goals. Automated bidding strategies linked to conversion on the website require a piece of code to be added to the sidebar in order to be able to measure those conversions. There are four bidding strategies under this category: target cost-per-acquisition (CPA), target return-on-ad-spend (ROAS), maximise conversions, and enhanced cost-per-click (eCPC). With a *target CPA* strategy, the marketer will look to maximise conversion while targeting a specific cost per acquisition. *Target ROAS* increases conversion value while targeting a specific return on ad spend. A *maximise conversion* strategy will optimise for conversions, while spending the entire budget, instead of targeting a specific CPA. Finally, *enhanced CPC* automatically adjusts manual bids to try to maximise conversions.

Earned media

Earned media is defined as branded content which is present online for which no company payment has been made. Earned digital media includes organic search results, user-generated content, viral marketing and unpaid affiliate marketing (Figure 7.4).

Figure 7.4: Types of earned media

Organic search refers to traffic coming from search engines. Unlike paid search, traffic comes from clicks of the organic list of results that appear in the SERPs (Figure 7.5). The order of sites appearing in an organic search is based on a complex and search-engine specific algorithm, but in general terms, it takes into consideration the quality of the website for a particular search, as well as the relative importance of a particular website versus other alternatives (Yang and Ghose, 2010). There is evidence that organic search results have a stronger influence upon conversion amongst Internet users than paid search results, especially because they are considered to be more unbiased than paid results (Hotchkiss et al., 2004)

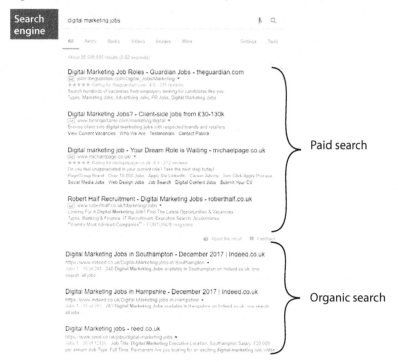

Figure 7.5: Paid and organic search results. Source: Google

User generated content (UGC) is content produced by the general public rather than paid professionals and which is distributed online. Proactively eliciting user generated content involves the design of strategies within the online community that facilitate the generation of this content. The different possible strategic options are a combination of an understanding of the motivations to engage, and social networking practices that can be applied to the online brand community.

Earned affiliate marketing refers to the links that other website owners put on their sites to channel traffic from their website. Affiliates are paid a fee if a transaction (e.g. subscription, purchase) is made from the traffic that they generated. Companies can actively organise affiliate events with bloggers to promote a particular product or service. Bloggers agree to attend these events in exchange of free products or financial rewards. Bloggers running this type of affiliate programmes also expect to have the editorial freedom to discuss their experience with the product. Having an independent review (i.e. electronic word-of-mouth) is beneficial for brands as they usually hold higher levels of trustworthiness and influence due to perceptions that the blogger writing the review is unbiased (Cheong and Morrison, 2008).

Viral marketing refers to any technique that encourages website owners and users to pass on marketing messages to other sites and users with the aim of creating a potentially exponential growth in the message visibility. Leskovec et al. (2007) argue that viral marketing is an effective tool, as it increases the likelihood of purchasing intent when a consumer receives messages from different sources. They also note the importance that online communities have to successful viral marketing campaigns, as these communities share messages about the focal interest of the community, but also exchange unrelated messages when the community members deem it valuable.

Marketers trying to initiate viral campaigns may pay prominent members (e.g. bloggers, or celebrities) in an online community to feed the message to the online community. The Advertising Standards Authority (ASA) regulates and provides a few guidelines for viral marketing practice in the UK (Advertising Standards Authority, 2017). ASA says that the Advertising code covers any marketing communications created by affiliates, members of the public acting as sales representatives and anyone contractually obliged to promote or advertise a company or product, and any paid marketing communication should be identified as such somewhere in the post content (#ad, sponsored by, etc.).

Designing digital content

Content marketing is a marketing technique of creating and distributing valuable, relevant and consistent content to attract and acquire a clearly defined audience (Content Marketing Institute, 2015). When designing content marketers need to consider factors such as the credibility of the content, the credibility of the content source, and the timeliness in which the content is released.

Content credibility refers to the believability of the content and/or its source (O'Keefe, 2002). *Source credibility* refers to the degree of competence that a person has to provide information on a specific subject (Brown et al., 2007). A person or a brand can be considered an expert because of deep knowledge on a subject (e.g. they have worked in the field for many years, or they have studied the subject). Trustworthiness is a further aspect of the source credibility and is established by continuously providing believable information. A brand that has hidden information (e.g. Volkswagen on carbon emissions) will lose its future trustworthiness.

Finally, a piece of content that is timely and relevant to consumers will have a higher impact as it will be more useful. *Timeliness* also results in higher levels of consumer engagement (Perez-Vega et al., 2016). Therefore, having a plan of all key dates that align with the brand is important. Commonly used dates are festivities like Christmas or Halloween, which offer an opportunity to align brand content proactively with customer celebrations. Sometimes content has to be planned reactively, for example, crisis situations require content to address emerging issues in a timely manner and to be focussed on the situation. There are several different types of content that brands can produce, and a few examples are illustrated in Table 7.4.

Table 7.4: Content type. Adapted from Tuten and Solomon, 2015.

Content type	Description	Example
"How to" article	Explains how to undertake a particular activity	How to make a winning podcast
Definition article	Defines a concept	What is a podcast?
Glossary article	Contains several definitions that are related to each other and creates a resource on the topic	A glossary of online video-making terms
Theory article	Offers some unique insight into the topic	Video needs audio
List article	Provides a top-ten list of topic items	Top 10 podcast editing software packages
Infographic	Visual representation of key facts and statistics	The rise of podcasts

Message appeal

An appeal is the sticky glue that hooks the reader or viewer to the advertising message. *Rational appeals* such as value, economy, popularity, convenience, health, performance, or durability emphasize the functional value of the brand. *Emotional appeals* such as humour, sex, guilt, nostalgia, pride, joy, or security stir feelings around the brand message (Dix and Merchegiani, 2013). There is substantial literature regarding advertising appeals. However, there is a lack of a consistent and comprehensive typology of appeals, which leads to a large but fragmented body of research that uses a range of classification schemes varying in aspects of size and form, and in levels and types (e.g. Resnik and Stern, 1977; Shimp, 1976; Shimp and Sharma, 1987). There is a rich range of approaches on which to draw, however it is important to ensure that the choice is consistent with the brand personality and is not arbitrary.

Enacting the brand

Aaker (1997, p.347) defines *brand personality* as "the set of human characteristics associated with a brand". A brand personality is something to which the consumer can relate; an effective brand increases its brand equity by having a consistent set of traits that a specific consumer segment enjoys. According to the literature, there are five main types of brand personalities: excitement, sincerity, ruggedness, competence and sophistication. *Excitement* is synonymous with a carefree, spirited and youthful attitude. *Sincerity* is highlighted by a feeling of kindness, thoughtfulness, and an orientation toward family values. *Ruggedness* is thought of as rough, tough, outdoorsy and athletic. *Competence*, in the mind of a consumer, is considered to be successful, accomplished and influential, highlighted by leadership. Finally, *sophistication* makes a brand seem elegant, prestigious and sometimes even pretentious. Consumers are more likely to purchase a brand if its personality is similar to their own (Aaker, 1997).

Exercise 7.1. Dove's brand personality

Dove is a personal care brand owned by Unilever originating in the United Kingdom. For this activity we will visit YouTube and the brand's Facebook page. Which personality is the brand trying to convey to consumers? Which elements in their videos and Facebook page made you decide for a particular type of personality?

Brand personality must be differentiated from *brand image*. Brand image denotes the tangible (physical and functional) benefits and attributes of a brand. Brand personality is the emotional associations of the brand (Aaker, 1997). Brand personality includes the personality features/characteristics and also demographic features like age, gender or class and psychographics, and the combination determines the nature of the brand-consumer relationship and also the means by which a consumer communicates their own identity. Brand personality develops brand equity (Kim et al., 2001). Brands are developed to achieve a particular brand position: to appeal to a particular audience for a particular purpose (Alden et al., 1999). *Brand positioning* sets out the characteristics, traits, or behaviours that express what is unique or distinctive about a brand (Sujan and Bettman 1989).

Brand personality is used to make the brand strategy come alive when it is implemented. It is a key input into the look and feel of any communication or marketing activity by the brand and differentiates brands from each other, specifically if they are otherwise alike in key areas, as might the case in the financial services sector (Aaker, 1997). Brand positioning and brand values are typically contained within a definitive statement of the brand – a *brand handbook*. The brand handbook is the definitive resource for making sure the brand 'stays put' in terms of how its employees and agencies develop all branded communications, including packaging and advertising.

A key aspect of digital marketing is ensuring that the brand personality is expressed in a written format using the appropriate *tone of voice*. Brand tone of voice ensures that the values, personality, or essence of the brand are uppermost in every situation in which people come into contact with the brand's language. Tone of voice refers to the language styles or registers that a company uses to express a distinctive personality or set of values that will differentiate its brands from those of competitors. Somewhat confusingly, tone of voice is becoming established as the term of choice to refer mainly to written language, although it may also be applied to speech. Other terms, such as verbal identity, brand language and language identity are also regularly used.

Integrating marketing communications

Integrated marketing communication is the combining of marketing campaigns to optimise the influence of the campaign and to ensure coherence and consistency of the communication (Fill, 2009). The concept involves linking communications in such a way that the content reinforces the overall message into a coherent whole. Awareness of the brand will be increased amongst the target audience through repetition and reinforcement of the central message. Integrated marketing communications provide a holistic approach to campaign planning and involve considering how the timing and content of messages ensures that different channels work together in the most effective and efficient way for the target audience. This might mean choosing a particular phrase or idea that facilitates not only an effective broadcast media campaign but which can also be adapted for a social media campaign that generates positive word-of-mouth.

One approach to integrating online and offline marketing communication activities would be to include the company's URL on every printed material, which could range from corporate cars to printed ads in magazine and billboards. More recently, QR (*Quick Response*) codes have emerged as an easy way to generate online traffic from offline activities. A QR code is a two-dimensional graphic designed to be read by smartphones through a QR reader application. An example of a QR code is presented in Figure 7.6 and if you download a QR code reader and scan this, it will take you to the Amazon's page of this book.

Figure 7.6: A Quick Response (QR) code.

The advantage of a QR code is that it can simplify the task of accessing complex or long URLs (as in the case of our book). QR codes facilitate a range of responses such as downloading an app, liking a page on social media, or sending a text message or e-mail. Research on the adoption of QR codes by users has found that the interactivity is one of the main drivers of intention to use the codes (Shin et al., 2012). Users perceive QR codes not only as a channel to search for information but also expect elements of entertainment due to the interactive nature of scanning the code, as well as socialisation and education (Shin et al., 2012). From a marketing perspective, designing offline campaigns using QR codes that embed more interactive and entertaining activities in campaigns offers the opportunity to position the brand as being both useful and fun.

Integration might result in *transmedia communication* which creates a narrative or story that is designed to be followed by piecing together different forms of media (i.e. film, game, blog, audio) across multiple media channels (both digital and offline) (Jenkins, 2006). Digital technology has facilitated the flow and adaptation of content across multiple media channels and has resulted in a *convergence culture*, which depends upon consumer active participation in sharing and commenting upon the story as it unfolds (Jenkins,

2006). Transmedia marketing campaigns are designed to stimulate brand interest amongst consumers and in particular to reward fans.

A transmedia marketing campaign was used in 2007 by Warner Brothers to promote the Batman film *The Dark Knight*. A game was created that directed all activity to a website called: 'I believe in Harvey Dent' which encouraged street campaigning for the fictional character (http://www.whysoseriousredux.com/dent/ibihd/home.htm). Online fans were encouraged to meet and search for clues offline which included calling phone numbers written in the sky by planes and going to GPS co-ordinates to locate mobile phones baked in cakes. The campaign resulted in 11 million participants worldwide and gained much coverage in specialist and mainstream press. In this way, transmedia communication offers a highly immersive experience of the brand.

Summary

The diversification of communication models in digital media gives marketers a wide range of media channels from which to choose when creating and disseminating content. In general terms, these channels can be classified as owned, paid, and earned media. Once the media channels are selected, designing digital content to reach marketing objectives requires a good understanding of the effects of different types of content, messages, and sources of content; as these will have an impact on the consumer and its perception of the brand. Finally, an important aspect to consider is the integration of all these communication channels and messages, in order to magnify their potential impact and to guard the brand's positioning across this diverse ecosystem.

Exemplar paper

Barcelos, R.H., Dantas, D.C. and Sénécal, S. (2018), Watch your tone: how a brand's tone of voice on social media influences consumer responses, *Journal of Interactive Marketing*, **41**, 60-80.

This study shows how brand tone of voice influences purchase intentions on social media. The research contrasts the effect of human and corporate tone of voice. The findings show that the effectiveness of each tone depends upon the consumer frame of mind and whether page comments are positive or negative. The authors present a set of guidelines to help digital marketers determine an appropriate tone of voice.

Further reading

Keller, K. L. (2016). Unlocking the power of integrated marketing communications: how integrated is your IMC program? *Journal of Advertising*, **45**(3), 286-301.

Shin, D. H., Jung, J. and Chang, B. H. (2012), The psychology behind QR codes: user experience perspective, *Computers in Human Behavior*, **28**(4), 1417-1426.

References

Aaker, J. L. (1997), Dimensions of brand personality, *Journal of Marketing Research*, 34(3), 347-356.

Advertising Standards Authority (2017). Remit: Social Media, Available from: https://www.asa.org.uk/advice-online/remit-social-media.html [Accessed: 5-12-2017]

Alden, D. L., Steenkamp, J. B. E. and Batra, R. (1999), Brand positioning through advertising in Asia, North America and Europe: The role of global consumer culture, *Journal of Marketing*, **63**(1), 75-87.

Baldus, B. J., Voorhees, C. and Calantone, R. (2015), Online brand community engagement: scale development and validation, *Journal of Business Research*, **68**(5), 978-985.

Bell, G. and Taheri, B. (2017) (eds), *Marketing Communications: An Advertising, Promotion and Branding Perspective*, Goodfellow Publishers, Oxford.

Brown, J., Broderick, A. J. and Lee, N. (2007), Word of mouth communication within online communities: conceptualizing the online social network, *Journal of Interactive Marketing*, **21**(3), 2-20.

Campaign Monitor (2017), The Modern Guidebook to Email Marketing, https://www.campaignmonitor.com/resources/guides/modern-guidebook-email-marketing/ [Accessed 9 December 2017].

Casaló, L., Flavián, C. and Guinalíu, M. (2007), The impact of participation in virtual brand communities on consumer trust and loyalty: the case of free software, *Online Information Review*, **31**(6), 775-792.

Chaffey, D. and Ellis-Chadwick, F. (2012), *Digital Marketing: Strategy, Implementation and Practice*, Pearson Education, Harlow.

Champoux, V., Durgee, J. and McGlynn, L. (2012), Corporate Facebook pages: When "fans" attack, *Journal of Business Strategy*, **33**(2), 22-30.

Cheong, H. J. and Morrison, M. A. (2008), Consumers' reliance on product information and recommendations found in UGC, *Journal of Interactive Advertising*, **8**(2), 38-49.

Content Marketing Institute (2017), What is Content Marketing?, http://contentmarketinginstitute.com/what-is-content-marketing/ [Accessed 9 December 2017].

Dessart, L., Veloutsou, C. and Morgan-Thomas, A. (2016), Capturing consumer engagement: duality, dimensionality and measurement, *Journal of Marketing Management*, **32**(5-6), 399-426.

DiStaso, M. W., Vafeiadis, M. and Amaral, C. (2015), Managing a health crisis on Facebook: How the response strategies of apology, sympathy, and information influence public relations, *Public Relations Review*, **41**(2), 222-231.

Dix, S. and Marchegiani, C. (2013), Advertising appeals, *Journal of Promotion Management*, **19**(4), 393-394.

Dufner, M., Denissen, J., Sedikides, C., Van Zalk, M., Meeus, W. H. and Aken, M. (2013), Are actual and perceived intellectual self-enhancers evaluated differently by social perceivers?, *European Journal of Personality*, **27**(6), 621-633.

Elmeleegy, H., Li, Y., Qi, Y., Wilmot, P., Wu, M., Kolay, S., Dasdan, A. (2013), Overview of Turn data management platform for digital advertising, *Proceedings of the VLDB Endowment*, **6**(11), 1138-1149.

Engler, G. (2012), Retreat from social media backfires on Carnival after Italy ship disaster, *Ad Age*, http://adage.com/article/digitalnext/post-disaster-retreat-social-media-backfires-carnival/232723/ [Accessed: 30-11-2017].

Fill, C. (2009), *Marketing Communications: Interactivity, Communities and Content*, Pearson Education, Harlow.

Google (2017), Determine a Bid Strategy Based on Your Goals, https://support.google.com/adwords/answer/2472725?hl=en-GB [Accessed 9 December 2017].

Hoffman, D. L. and Novak, T. P. (1996), Marketing in hypermedia computer-mediated environments: conceptual foundations, *Journal of Marketing*, **60**(3), 50-68.

Hotchkiss, G., Garrison, M. and Jensen, S. (2004), Search engine usage in North America, Enquiro Search Solutions, https://www.richswebdesign.com/SearchEngineUsageinNorthAmerica.pdf [Accessed 9 December 2017].

Hubspot (2017), Content Marketing Statistics, https://www.hubspot.com/marketing-statistics [Accessed 9 December 2017].

Internet Live Stats (n.d.), Google Search Statistics, Online at http://www.internetlivestats.com/google-search-statistics/ [Accessed 03-01-2018].

Jenkins, H. (2006) *Convergence Culture: Where Old and New Media Collide*, NYU Press.

Ki, E. J. and Nekmat, E. (2014), Situational crisis communication and interactivity: usage and effectiveness of Facebook for crisis management by Fortune 500 Companies, *Computers in Human Behavior*, **35**, 140-147.

7

Kim, S., Haley, E. and Koo, G. Y. (2009), Comparison of the paths from consumer involvement types to ad responses between corporate advertising and product advertising, *Journal of Advertising*, **38**(3), 67-80.

Kim, C. K., Han, D. and Park, S. B. (2001), The effect of brand personality and brand identification on brand loyalty: applying the theory of social identification, *Japanese Psychological Research*, **43**(4), 195-206.

Lee, J. E. and Watkins, B. (2016), YouTube vloggers' influence on consumer luxury brand perceptions and intentions, *Journal of Business Research*, **69**(12), 5753-5760.

Leskovec, J., Adamic, L. A. and Huberman, B. A. (2007), The dynamics of viral marketing, *ACM Transactions on the Web* (TWEB), **1**(1), 1-46.

Mailchimp (2017), Email marketing benchmarks, https://mailchimp.com/resources/research/email-marketing-benchmarks/ [Accessed 9 December 2017].

McAlexander, J. H., Schouten, J. W. and Koenig, H. F. (2002), Building brand community, *Journal of Marketing*, **66**(1), 38-54.

Morgan-Thomas, A. and Veloutsou, C. (2013), Beyond technology acceptance: brand relationships and online brand experience, *Journal of Business Research*, **66**(1), 21-27.

O'Keefe, D. J. (2002), *Persuasion: Theory and Research* (Vol. 2), Sage: London.

Office for National Statistics (2017). Internet access – Households and Individuals: 2017, https://www.ons.gov.uk/peoplepopulationandcommunity/householdcharacteristics/homeinternetandsocialmediausage/bulletins/internetaccesshouseholdsandindividuals/2017#email-remains-the-most-common-internet-activity [Accessed 9 December 2017].

Perez-Vega, R., Waite, K. and O'Gorman, K. (2016), Social Impact Theory: an examination of how immediacy operates as an influence upon social media interaction in Facebook fan pages, *Marketing Review*, **16**(3), 299-321.

Pfeffer, J., Zorbach, T. and Carley, K. M. (2014), Understanding online firestorms: negative word-of-mouth dynamics in social media networks, *Journal of Marketing Communications*, **20**(1-2), 117-128.

Portilla Irastorza, M.D.M. and Perez Vega, R. (2017), Exploring motivations to engage in online brand communities: a comparative analysis, in 46th EMAC Annual Conference: Leaving Footprints, University of Groningen, Groningen, 23rd – 26th May 2017.

Resnik, A. and Stern, B. L. (1977), An analysis of information content in television advertising, *Journal of Marketing*, **41**(1), 50-53.

Rutz, O. J. and Bucklin, R. E. (2011), From generic to branded: a model of spillover in paid search advertising, *Journal of Marketing Research*, **48**(1), 87-102.

Schau, H. J., Muñiz Jr, A. M. and Arnould, E. J. (2009), How brand community practices create value, *Journal of Marketing*, **73**(5), 30-51.

Schiano, D. J., Nardi, B. A., Gumbrecht, M. and Swartz, L. (2004), Blogging by the Rest of Us. In *CHI'04 extended abstracts of the 2004 conference on Human Factors in Computing Systems*, 1143-1146.

Shimp, T. A. (1976), Methods of commercial presentation employed by national television advertisers, *Journal of Advertising*, 5(4), 30-36.

Shimp, T. A. and Sharma, S. (1987), Consumer ethnocentrism: Construction and validation of the CETSCALE, *Journal of Marketing Research*, **24**(3), 280-289.

Shin, D. H., Jung, J. and Chang, B. H. (2012), The psychology behind QR codes: user experience perspective, *Computers in Human Behavior*, **28**(4), 1417-1426.

Singh, T., Veron-Jackson, L. and Cullinane, J. (2008), Blogging: A new play in your marketing game plan. Business Horizons, **51**(4), 281-292.

Statista (2017), Paid search advertising expenditure worldwide From 2015 to 2017 (in billion U.S. dollars), https://www.statista.com/statistics/267056/paid-search-advertising-expenditure-worldwide/ [Accessed 9 December 2017].

Sujan, M., & Bettman, J. (1989), The effects of brand positioning strategies on consumers' brand and category perceptions: some insights from schema research, *Journal of Marketing Research*, **26**(4), 454-467.

Sysomos (2010), Inside blogger demographics: data by gender, age, https://sysomos.com/reports/blogger-demographics/ [Accessed 9 December 2017].

Tuten, T. and Solomon, M. (2015), *Social Media Marketing*, Sage Publications: London

Ward, J. C. and Ostrom, A. L. (2006), Complaining to the masses: the role of protest framing in customer-created complaint websites, *Journal of Consumer Research*, **33**(2), 220-230.

Wirtz, J., Den Ambtman, A., Bloemer, J., Horváth, C., Ramaseshan, B., Van De Klundert, J., Canli, G.Z. and Kandampully, J. (2013), Managing brands and customer engagement in online brand communities, *Journal of Service Management*, **24**(3), 223-244.

Wordpress (2017), About Wordpress, https://wordpress.org/about/ [Accessed 9 December 2017].

Yang, S. and Ghose, A. (2010), Analyzing the relationship between organic and sponsored search advertising: positive, negative, or zero interdependence?, *Marketing Science*, **29**(4), 602-623.

Zaglia, M. E. (2013), Brand communities embedded in social networks, *Journal of Business Research*, **66**(2), 216-223.

7

8   **Metrics and Analytics**

Organisations use metrics and analytics to continuously improve their digital content in order to better serve customer needs, maintain functionality and remain competitive. It is tempting to use the terms metrics and analytics interchangeably as if they have the same meaning but they are two distinct concepts. Metrics is the process of collecting data. For example, capturing the number of visitors. Analytics is the process of selecting, combining and relating metrics to produce answers to business questions. Analytics are used to inform promotion, content and processes. For example, how do we know if our digital content is succeeding? The answer to this question might involve combining several metrics such as the number of visitors, number of repeat visitors and value of sales. In this way, analytics use metrics to help create understanding of the user experience (Pakkala et al., 2012). Analytics range from simple statistics (e.g. average visitor numbers) to complex modelling of visitor behaviour (e.g. the correlation between search patterns, products in shopping cart, shopping cart abandonment, repeat visits) (Pakkala et al., 2012:504)

Metrics and analytics

Metrics involves identifying and collecting numerical data. Analytics involves selecting appropriate metrics and conducting numerical analysis to show significant patterns in the data. Figures 8.1 and 8.2 illustrate the differences between the concepts. In Figure 8.1 metrics involve deciding the data of interest and the process of collection. In addition, metrics may involve working out the best way to present data in visual form such as the composition of dashboards and infographics. Metrics increase a general understanding on patterns of use but may not provide business insight. In Figure 8.2 we see that analytics involves articulating the business question, selecting and combining appropriate metrics and then analysing to provide a solution. The process of analytics requires digital marketers to be able to "explore, digest, synthesise and explain" metrics (Micu et al., 2011: 219).

Figure 8.1: Constituents of metrics

Figure 8.2: Constituents of analytics

■ Data collection process

Data collection involves three stages: Capture, Understanding and Presenting or CUP (Fan and Gordon, 2014).

- ■ **Data capture** involves taking decisions on: the site of data capture, i.e. which channel; the focus of data capture, i.e. organisation only or competitors; and the duration of data capture, i.e. trend or single measure capture.

- ■ **Data understanding** involves selecting the appropriate analytics and determining whether the data used is valid and reliable.

- ■ **Data presenting** involves preparing reports that are easy to understand by the intended audience who may or may not be data analysis experts.

Any form of data collection process will cost the company in terms of time and money, and it is important that metrics are collected that relate to marketing activities and goals. For example, Jackson (2016:59) writes that "most business questions have a number as the answer". The role of analytics is to inform marketing actions. We can use the marketing mix framework to help us to identify a range of questions that can be informed by digital analytics (Table 8.1).

Table 8.1: Questions related to the marketing mix framework

Mix variable	Question
Pricing	How many customers purchase from us online? Which products do customers place in the basket? Is the basket abandoned? Do customers visit our website after viewing the website of a competitor?
Promotion	Which online messages gain the best response? Who is responding to these messages? Which links encourage click through?
Place	Which devices are used to access website? From which locations do our users arrive? How many customers view our website before buying in a retail outlet? How many customers buy online whilst visiting a retail store?
Product	Which information relating to product is read the most? From which search terms do people arrive?
Process	Is the process of checkout smooth and working correctly? Is the process of viewing the website on a mobile device satisfactory? How long does it take for our staff to answer a complaint or query on social media? How many customers use our website for customer support?

Website metric collection decisions

Website metrics can be gathered in two places, client side (also known as front-end), in the browser that is being used to access the website, or server-side (also known as back-end), by the server which is hosting the website. Beasley (2013) identifies two methods of collecting website metrics: log file analysis, which is server-side, and page tagging, which is client-side. Log file analysis is a longstanding technique. A log file is a text file of all the activity generated by the Web server and provides information on server performance and problems (Peterson, 2004). Log file analysis helps IT professionals manage bandwidth and measure server capacity. Log files contain metrics that can be of use to digital marketers, including the number of site visitors, the number of bytes sent and received, the time and date of the visit, the resource being requested, and the referring page. Whilst some log files metrics have business value, others are more technical with limited business value, such as the IP address of the web server serving the resource to each end user (Peterson, 2004).

An alternative to log file analysis is page tagging. Page tagging gathers metrics by adding in a small piece of programming code to individual web pages. Google Analytics is a popular and well known page tagging tool and analytics programme. When a web page is opened in a browser, a request is sent to the server storing the page tag which allows tracking of website user activity. A page tag is used to set cookies, which are items of code placed in the user's browser to remember information such as the contents of the shopping cart as the user navigates a website. A common page tag is in the form of an invisible image such as transparent GIF, with JavaScript code. A new form of page tag is a web beacon which sends data prior to the web page actually loading and thus prevents any drag on navigation speed. Page tags are gathered client-side by the browser that the website visitor is using. Page tags capture a range of information including: visitor context (such as the IP address of the visitor, the type of browser, the type of device, the site which referred the visitor, the time of visit); visitor profile (profile ID unique to that user), targeting criteria based on either previous search or data shared, (e.g. gender, age, location, family status) and visitor behaviour (the products or information viewed, the links clicked and the time spent on each page). Such, information can be used to compare the performance of individual websites and improve website design.

It is important to consider the advantages and disadvantages of log file analysis and page tagging as data collection methods. Table 8.2 and Table 8.3 consider the evaluative criteria of ease of use and usefulness from the Technology Acceptance Model (TAM) (Davis, 1993). Ease of use evaluates the effort involved in implementing collection processes, and usefulness considers the analytical pros and cons in terms of data content and accuracy. The pros and cons of data ownership are also discussed.

Table 8.2: Advantages and disadvantages of log file analysis. Adapted from Peterson (2004)

Criteria	Advantages	Disadvantages
Implementation (Ease of use)	Easier than tagging every page	There can be significant upfront costs in software and staff skills Load balancing devices means it is harder and more time intensive to get an overview Log files can take a long time to analyse
Data content & accuracy (usefulness)	Provides insight into whether page downloads completed, and which robots and spiders are visiting	Does not capture information pages that have been 'proxy cached' or 'browser cached'. IP addresses are a misleading indicator of user uniqueness Robots and spiders can inflate visitor numbers
Ownership of data	Data controlled within company	Smaller companies depending on external website hosting may not get access to log files. Data set size creates difficulty in sharing & storing

In terms of ease of use, log file metrics do not require any additional implementation since they are collected without having to tag every page on the website; however, there can be significant upfront costs for software and hiring of skilled staff, particularly for smaller companies without a dedicated IT department. In addition log files, because of their size can take significant space to store; if log files are archived then this has an impact on ease of historical reporting. In addition, data is sent and received from more than one computer and thus web traffic load is shared or balanced across a number of machines, which splits up log files. This means that there will be several log files that will need combining into a single file for analysis, and this requires skill, incurs costs and results in a longer report generation time.

In terms of usefulness, log files show how much of a file is sent, which means we can see how often visitors stop the download of a document, and as a result can focus upon improving download time or content. *Robots* and *spiders* are automated programmes that systematically browse the web, typically for the purposes of indexing pages for search engines. Log file analysis allows us to generate reports on the source and frequency of robot and spider visits, which will inform search engine optimisation strategy (discussed later in this chapter). However, confusing automated programmes with human visitors can result in inflating the number of human website visitors.

Another serious disadvantage is the information lost from proxy and browser caching. A proxy cache is when an Internet Service Provider (ISP) places frequently requested content on machines close to the end user rather than at the original location, which may be far away, in order to improve download speed. This results in data transfer not being recorded by the original web server. Browser caching is also technique for speeding up information delivery; this is where a browser such as Internet Explore puts data on the user's computer, so that when the back button is hit the page is delivered very quickly. This also results in this information not being captured by log file analysis since the original server is not involved. Further information loss occurs from using IP addresses, since proxy caching obscures the true geographic location of users. Peterson (2004) reports that up to 40% of log file information might be lost in this way.

In terms of data ownership, log files have the advantage of being stored and collected within the organisation. This may be an important consideration if data is particularly sensitive (for example passwords, unencrypted credit card authentication, access to controversial websites). Sole ownership means that the organisation also has access to historical data and controls how it is backed up, retained or deleted. However, smaller companies who depend on external website hosting might not be able to gain access to log file analysis. To guard against this situation there should be discussion about log file ownership and access as part of the service agreement. Ownership of data means that the organisation will be responsible for storing the data, which can result in cost, in addition an internal department, such as the IT department, may consider it owns the data and might be unwilling to share this with the marketing department. Finally the data set size means that such sharing is operationally very difficult to achieve.

Table 8.3: Advantages and disadvantages of page-tagging. Adapted from Peterson (2004)

Criteria	Advantages	Disadvantages
Implementation (Ease of use)	Needs less technical knowledge Lower costs	Effort of manually adding in page tags Extra code may slow website download speed
Data content & accuracy (Usefulness)	Can provide real time reporting Flexibility in terms of the nature of metrics gathered Does not count spiders & robots	Inflexibility in reporting formats User can disable cookies and Javascript Multiple browsers and deletion of cookies
Ownership of data		Data not owned, which raises issue if shifting between providers Privacy issues

Page tagging techniques are relatively easier for someone to implement with limited technical knowledge. Whilst there is considerable effort involved in adding page tags manually to each page, there are a range of website content management systems that provide the option of adding page tags automatically and a low cost, e.g. Wordpress. However, one disadvantage is that by adding in extra code the speed of the website loading may be reduced.

Page tagging provides useful reports very quickly. Website content management systems will quickly provide standard reports in an easy to read format. For example, Google Analytics is a website content management system that is versatile, gives useful information and requires only small effort and cost (Pakkala et al., 2012). Google Analytics can provide reports very quickly as users interact with the page, which enables almost real-time reporting. However, whilst standardised reports are provided as part of a content management package, there may be a premium fee to pay to generate customised reports. There is greater flexibility regarding the range of metrics gathered since front-end data is being collected when users interact with the webpage, rather than back end as the webpage with the server. For example data can include information on interaction according to product price, screen size and interaction with website tools and graphics (Booth and Jansen, 2009). Accuracy is improved as spiders and robots are not counted, because the website pages have to be downloaded to activate the page tag. However, accuracy problems still exist from visitors disabling cookies and Javascript in order to preserve their privacy, and also switching between different browsers, e.g. moving from Google to Netscape.

In terms of ownership, since the data is collected and stored client side the organisation does not own the data. This means that if a company wants to move from one content management system to another the historical data will be lost. The use of cookies is contested on privacy issues. A page tag is an "implicit data gathering, as it collects data on website visitor behaviour 'quietly behind the scenes'." (Peterson 2004:11). The alternative to implicit data collection would be explicit data collection in the form of surveys and usability studies, which as Peterson (2004:11) writes can be "prohibitively expensive" and risk "damaging the relationship you have with your online visitors" by surveying them "again and again". However there are questions about the ethics of implicitly gathering data in this way. There are concerns about the ability of organisations to track user behaviour, leading to privacy invasion and also concerns about the way in which data is used to discriminate against groups of individuals or subject them to unwanted marketing (Sipior et al., 2011). In 2009 the EU Privacy and Electronic Communications Directive stated that organisations had to gain the consent of web users before serving them web cookies.

Social media metric collection decisions

Social media analytics focus on monitoring both the level of social media activity and the substance of that activity. It is important to obtain reliable counts as these allow us to quantify activity in order to inform marketing action. There are three key challenges: the first is how to record the variety of data that is being produced, which includes both visual, audio and textual data. The second challenge is how to understand the precise meaning behind data, which can be highly nuanced, e.g. the word 'bad' can mean 'good' in certain contexts. The third challenge is how to manage data collection and analysis across multiple channels.

A social media page is not owned or controlled directly by an organisation, as is the case with a website page. This means that social media metric collection is undertaken by the social media provider. For example, Facebook Insights is available to any organization whose page has at least 30 fans. Twitter provides metrics to users of Hootsuite and Tweet Deck. Google provides Google Alerts, which automatically send an e-mail if one or several key words are mentioned online, e.g. the brand name, or the product. In addition there are a number of specialist tools that focus on key indicators for each channel. For example, Klout will provide a measure of social influence, and Booshaka will measure Facebook page interaction.

There are also several companies that provide tools that aggregate social media analytics to enable comparison across different channels. For example, Social Mention will track keywords across several social media sites. In addition there are companies that provide monitoring dashboards that use a suite of tools to allow marketers to plan, implement, tag, track and report on social media campaigns across several different channels. Such tools provide both customer analytics, such as likes and shares, as well as organisational analytics, such as time to reply. An example is Sprout Social. In addition to tools that focus upon the organisation's own performance, there are also tools that monitor all activity in a sector and allow the organisation to benchmark its performance against that of competitors, e.g. Radian 6 and Lithium. Digital marketers will need to determine which tool or combination of tools offers the best value to the organisation. Several tools provide free downloads, but a fee or subscription is required for the full service, with the highest fees being required by tools that provide benchmarking functionality. Tool selection should be based on whether the cost is justified. Table 8.4 suggest criteria for decision making.

Table 8.4: Criteria for social media metric tools

Criteria	Key questions
Implementation (ease of use)	Is training support required and available? Are there visual reports i.e. does the software prepare graphs? Can we act easily on the results? e.g. can we respond to real-time reporting?
Data content & accuracy (usefulness)	Does the software provide real-time reporting? Can we customise the reporting structure? Can the software give coverage of all the social media channels we use? i.e. some "free" packages are limited
Ownership of data	If we shift packages will we own the historic data? Would we be liable for privacy issues?

How metrics and analytics contribute to marketing

The range of digital metrics available to companies has resulted in the term 'big data', which is framed as an opportunity for business (Gandomi and Haider, 2015). The term 'big data' is used to describe information that has volume, variety and velocity (also known as the three Vs) (Laney, 2001). Big data is worthless in a vacuum and the true value is only unlocked when used to drive decision making (Gandomi and Haider, 2015). However, Leeflang et al. (2014) conducted a survey of business leaders. They identified that amongst their survey participants there was a perception that online measures are not easily related to financial impact. This means that it is not clear how these metrics relate to profit or loss. In addition, participants highlighted that it is difficult to understand what metrics measure. From this we can see that it is important for a data analyst to be able to explain metrics to managers and also to be able to relate online indicators to offline indicators, such as sales and satisfaction, particularly where these are related to financial results. There is a need for data analysts to develop the richness of the data that is being captured and to be able to understand how this can be translated into meaningful insight.

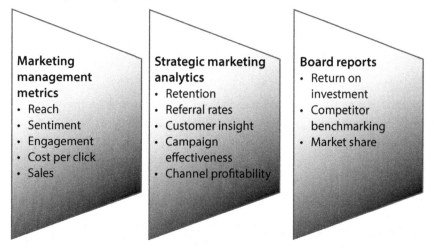

Figure 8.3: Layers of digital metric and analytic use. Adapted from Lenskold (2003)

Figure 8.3 shows three different layers of metric and analytic use which relate to three key areas of the marketing function. The first layer relates to the micro-management of digital marketing activity, the focus here is to quantify outcomes to track progress. The second layer analyses the first layer metrics gathered in order to assess how well marketing activity is performing in reducing costs whilst maximising value to the organisation. The third layer focuses on assessing the relative contribution of marketing activity to overall business strategy.

Digital customer lifecycle

Peterson (2004) identifies how analytics assess digital marketing success in reaching, acquiring, converting and retaining visitors. *Attraction* relates to gaining customer attention; *acquisition* relates to being successful in getting the visitor to your site; *conversion* is getting the visitor to complete a specified goal; and *retention* is getting visitors to return to the content or repeat the action. These four stages form the digital customer lifecycle (Lee et al., 1999) which is modelled as steps in a simplified customer journey in Figure 8.4.

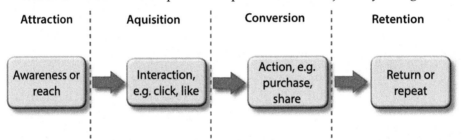

Figure 8.4: Simplified customer journey

Exercise 8.2

Consider how the metrics gathered at each stage of the customer journey might be used differently by brand managers for an established brand (such as Apple) and a newer brand (Huawei).

Developing customer insight: segmentation

Visitor segmentation involves dividing customers/mass market into groups that share characteristics that are meaningful and measurable, so that the marketing effort can be tailored to effectively and efficiently meet their needs. When we use website metrics we can select those groups with greater ease and precision. Meaningful metrics are those we can act upon. For example, if we sort individuals into groups according to the device which they use to access our website, we can see if it is sensible to invest in a mobile optimised website; or if we have a mobile optimised site, we benchmark this against competitors to see if that site or app is performing as it should.

A common approach is to use behavioural segmentation to determine which are new visitors, new customers, repeat visitor and repeat customers. Behavioural segments can also be created according to visitor source and content accessed. If visitors are incentivised to register on-site it is possible to build up more detailed profiles of behaviour for different demographic and lifestyle segments. Through allocating all visitors into different segments we can build up a picture of the 'average visitor', who we can describe in terms of frequency of visit, the average number of pages viewed, the average amount spent, etc.. It is also possible to develop personas or ideal customer profiles to help develop search engine marketing strategy.

Campaign effectiveness

Metrics can be gathered for multiple campaigns with distinct conversion goals over a period of time (Figure 8.5). For example, the first campaign might be designed to attract visitors to register with the website. Consider a situation where Hotel Chocolat posted paid content with influential bloggers and online publications in the form of an Easter Egg Hunt. The answers formed a coded message that needed to be entered, together with an e-mail address, into the Hotel Chocolat website in order to win a prize (conversion goal 1). The second campaign might focus upon e-mailing the competition participants with special offer codes for selected product with purchase (conversion goal 2).

Figure 8.5: Range of campaign metrics

An organisation may be running multiple campaigns at any time. Indeed it can be possible to track the online response to offline campaigns using special URLs and landing pages. Where there are multiple campaigns, website analytics tools are used to create progress overviews using various grouping criteria such as 'conversion goals', 'product category', 'message content', 'communication channel', 'duration', 'end date', 'geographic and demographic information', etc. There are various analytical dashboards available to help marketers, which pull metrics from multiple sources and report them in a single screen and which provide visual reporting aids such as charts, graphs and timelines.

Analytical accuracy is a challenge when choosing metrics since there is a risk of mis-attributing the credit for conversion. For example in the Hotel Chocolat campaign, the visitor may have clicked on a competition link on a blogger website but failed to register, however at a later point they might see the link in an online publication, click and return to complete the competition. In this instance the same person would be counted as two visitors and the conversion will be credited to the online publication, which would be last click attribution. A focus at this point on channel metrics might mean we draw the conclusion that the online publication was the most successful channel ,when in fact it was a combination of channels. When faced with this problem we might consider varying landing pages, which would result in subtle change in message or alternatively credit conversion across all channels. The choice over the method would be based on whether there was an important implication for financial resource allocation. For example, we might be paying significantly more for online publication content than blogger content and thus would like to evaluate the response to each separately.

Return on investment

Return on investment (ROI) is a calculation used to determine the extent to which the resources invested in a particular activity are increased or diminished as a result of that activity. ROI is calculated using a simple formula of dividing the value created by the costs of providing that activity. In a business context typically the value created is the profit (sales revenue – costs). When applied to website activity, working out a ROI can be more complex and involves gathering metrics on sales and costs associated with the website, e.g. server costs, staff costs, website promotion costs, software licence costs. In relation to website ROI, the key analytical challenge is to determine the degree to which it is related to other channels. This is a question of attribution. Attribution is the set of rules that determine how credit for sales and conversions is assigned to touchpoints in conversion paths. Hence there is an analytical decision to be taken regarding how the credit for sales should be assigned. Table 8.5 (page 150) summarises the different attribution models.

8

Summary

Digital metrics and analytics enable us to measure the success of digital marketing activity. The growth in the number of digital platforms and tools means that it is important for information on digital marketing trends to be available throughout the organisation. This chapter has explained the difference between metrics and analytics and has shown how this information can be applied to generate understanding of the digital customer life cycle. It has also discussed how to develop customer insight, assess campaign effectiveness and calculate return on investment.

Table 8.5: Different attribution models

Attribution model	Definition	Impact on ROI for website
Last interaction	Last touch point before conversion	None website receives 100% sale credit
Last click attribution	Credit for sale is given to last channel that customer clicked through before purchase	None if customer was direct visitor to website but if click-through was from social media or paid search then that would receive 100% of the sale credit.
First interaction model	The first touchpoint receives 100% of the sale	If this was not the website then it would receive zero credit for the sale
Linear attribution model	Gives each touchpoint leading to conversion an equal credit for the sale.	If the customer found the website using paid search and social media then the website would receive 30% of the sale credit
Time decay attribution model	Touchpoints closest in time to sale receive the most credit	The website will receive the majority of the credit but not if there were other channels used directly before purchase.
Position based attribution model	40% credit is assigned to first and last interaction and 20% distributed evenly across all other touchpoints	Website receives 40% of the sale credit

Exemplar paper

LaValle, S., Lesser, E., Shockley, R., Hopkins, M.S. and Kruschwitz, N., (2011), Big data, analytics and the path from insights to value, *MIT Sloan Management Review*, **52**(2), 21.

> Reports on research amongst business leaders to find out how organisations are using analytics. They classify organisations into three groups based on their adoption rates as being Aspirational, who are under prepared, Experienced who are developing and Transformed who have substantial experience of using analytics across a range of functions.

■ Additional reading

Hair Jr, J.F. (2007), Knowledge creation in marketing: the role of predictive analytics, *European Business Review*, **19**(4), 303-315.

Norton, D.W. and Pine, B.J. (2013), Using the customer journey to road test and refine the business model, *Strategy and Leadership*, **41**(2), 12-17.

References

Beasley, M. (2013). *Practical Web Analytics for User Experience: How Analytics Can Help You Understand Your Users*, Elsevier, Waltham.

Booth, D. and B.J. Jansen, B.J. (2009), A review of methodologies for analyzing websites in B.J. Jansen, A. Spink, I. Taksa (Eds.), *Handbook of Research on Web Log Analysis*, IGI Global, Hershey, NY, 141-163

Davis, F.D. (1993), User acceptance of information technology: system characteristics, user perceptions and behavioral impacts, *International Journal of Man-Machine Studies*, **38**(3), 475-487.

Fan, W. and Gordon, M.D, (2014), The power of social media analytics, *Communications of the ACM*, **57**(6), 74-81.

Gandomi, A. and Haider, M. (2015), Beyond the hype: big data concepts, methods, and analytics, *International Journal of Information Management*, **35**(2), 137-144.

Jackson, S. (2016), *Cult of Analytics: Data Analytics for Marketing*. 2nd Ed., Routledge, New York

Laney, D. (2001), 3-D data management: controlling data volume, velocity and variety, application delivery strategies by META Group Inc. (February 6), p. 949, http://blogs.gartner.com/doug-laney/files/2012/01/ad949-3D-Data-Management-Controlling-Data-Volume-Velocity-and-Variety.pdf, [Accessed on 18th May 2004).

Lee, J., Hoch, R., Podlasek, M., Schonberg, E. and Gomory, S. (1999), Analysis and visualization of metrics for online merchandising, web usage analysis and user profiling. In *Proceedings of the International WEBKDD'99 Workshop*, San Diego, USA, 126-141.

Leeflang, P.S., Verhoef, P.C., Dahlström, P. and Freundt, T. (2014), Challenges and solutions for marketing in a digital era, *European Management Journal*, **32**(1), 1-12.

Lenskold, J., (2003), *Marketing ROI: The Path to Campaign, Customer, and Corporate Profitability*, McGraw-Hill Professional, New York.

Micu, A. C., Dedeker, K., Lewis, I., Moran, R., Netzer, O., Plummer, J. and Rubinson, J. (2011).Guest editorial: the shape of marketing research in 2021, *Journal of Advertising Research*, **51**(1), 213–221.

Pakkala, H., Presser, K. and Christensen, T. (2012) Using Google Analytics to measure visitor statistics: the case of food composition websites, *International Journal of Information Management*, **32**(6), 504-512.

Peterson, E.T. (2004) *Web Analytics Demystified: A Marketer's Guide to Understanding How Your Website Affects Your Business*, Ingram.

Sipior, J.C., Ward, B.T. and Mendoza, R.A. (2011), Online privacy concerns associated with cookies, flash cookies, and web beacons, *Journal of Internet Commerce*, **10**(1), 1-16.

8

9 Website Metrics and Analytics

The ability to systematically measure and evaluate website marketing outcomes is highly valued. For example in the two year period between 2015 to 2017 the average salary of a web analytics manager in the UK increased by 11.7% from £45,000 to £52,500 (www.itjobswatch.co.uk). Sometimes website development is not considered as part of the marketing function because the process of gathering information on website performance requires technical skills (Aloha Ward, 2017). However, digital marketers need to understand how to measure website performance and link these outcomes to marketing activity at each stage of the digital customer lifecycle.

Attraction

Attraction is about getting the website to the attention of the user. A key metric is the page rank or the position of the content in search results. Search engines are programmes that match search terms to documents on the Internet. A search engine works by using a robot or spider to crawl through digital content and automatically index it very much like a library classifies books. When a search request is made a search engine selects the results to display on the search engine results page (SERP). The most popular search engine is Google which accounts for over 77% of the searches worldwide (Net Market Share, 2017); other search engines exist such as Yahoo and Bing. Ensuring that that a brand's website is listed in search results will succeed in gaining traffic. There is evidence to suggest a trend towards individuals preferring to enter search terms to locate a particular website rather than typing in the URL (Cabel, 2008).

Digital marketers should ensure that the brand website has visibility by being in the initial SERPS. When results are listed, consumers will only click on the highly ranked links. Studies show that over a third (37%) of searchers click through on links on the first page; this falls to just over a tenth on the second page. Internet users are becoming more skilled at online search. In 2012 Pew Internet research found that 91% of search engine users say they always or most of the time find the information that they are seeking when they use search engines, and 56% of searchers say they are very confident in their search abilities. Therefore people will not generally consider more than one page of search results.

The process of ensuring that a website has high visibility in the SERP is called Search Engine Marketing (SEM). SEM aims to ensure that a website has visibility and attracts appropriate visitors. A search engine ranks and scores documents in the index in terms of relevancy and recency of content, and the pages with the most relevant and recent are listed first on the SERP, in what are called the *organic* search results. SEO works since customers place greater trust in organic search results and are more likely to purchase from that brand (Malaga, 2009). The search engine will also display content that brands have paid to be displayed when specific search terms are entered. SEM involves pull and push media techniques (Table 9.1). Metrics and analytics measure the contribution of each of these routes in terms of costs for the quantity and quality of achieved visitors (Table 9.2).

Table 9.1: Comparison of pull and push media

Pull media	Push media
Search Engine Optimisation (SEO) designing a digital content so it is listed in the top results from a search engine as being the most recent and relevant to the searcher.	**Pay-per-Click (PPC)** or keyword advertising involves bidding to appear at in the top results. Payment is made when the ad is clicked.
	Paid placement or paid inclusion involves paying for an advertisement to appear in the search results. Payment is made when the ad is viewed.

Table 9.2: Key analytics: Attraction

Analytics	Calculation
Cost per visitor	Marketing expenses/visitors
Response rage	Responses/ total impressions
Cost per acquisition	Cost of campaign/ campaign respondents
Cost per click	Cost of campaign/ cost per response

Search engines as pull media

Keywords describe the content of each web page so that the search engine can match the page with the search query, and content should be relevant to the keyword supplied. Each search engine has its own requirements for determining relevance and recency (Sen, 2005). This is called the search engine *algorithm*. Chaffey and Smith (2013) give the example of Google's search ranking algorithm which has around 200 factors or signals. These include both positive signals which boost ranking (for example, clearly relevant content) and negative signals which reduce position (for example, pages that have not been updated for some time).

Appearing in the organic results was more important when Google placed organic results in the main body of the page starting from the top left, and PPC results in a box on the right hand side of the SERP. Eye-tracking research by Nielsen (2006) shows that website visitors focus on the top left corner of a webpage and pay limited attention to the right hand side. However, in 2016, in order to enhance the display of results on mobile and tablet devices, Google changed the layout of the SERPS, so that there were fewer advertisements on each page, but that the PPC results were displayed at the top and bottom of each page of organic results. As there were fewer PPC opportunities on each page, the advertising costs increased, and this increased the importance of selecting an appropriate strategy.

Keywords are chosen by website managers to describe the website to the search engine. Keywords should reflect as accurately as possible the words that individuals use when looking for the goods and services of the organisation, e.g. 'handbag'. In addition, there are qualifiers which are words that can be used to form keyword phrases or keyphrases. (Figure 9.1). Keyphrases let brands fine tune the website placement in the SERPS, so that it reaches customers who are best placed to make use of services, for example including geographic qualifiers enables a brand to reach those in the geographic area. A feature of search engines is auto-complete, where the search engine suggests to the user a keyphrase after the first words have been input in order to improve the relevance of the results. If a website manager can ensure these keyphrases appear in the content of the website or are included in a PPC campaign, then the website will be highly ranked since search engines attribute more relevance to a match with a combination of keywords rather than a single word (Chaffey and Smith, 2013).

9

Figure 9.1: Examples of qualifiers and phrases

Keywords are used in the title which is how the webpage is listed in the the SERP. The title should sell the content of the result as being relevant to the user. Keywords are used in the meta description which is how the webpage is described in the SERP (Figure 9.2). Digital marketers should avoid keyword stuffing, which is endlessly using a limited number of keywords in all elements of the page, as search engines are programmed to rate such pages lower in the SERPS.

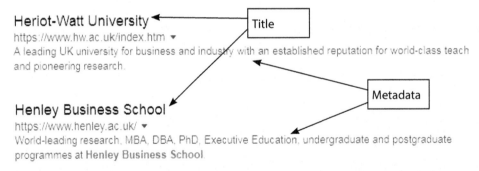

Figure 9.2: Titles and meta descriptions for the universities where the authors work.

Search engine optimisation

Optimising an organisational website so that it appears at the top of a SERP is an ongoingchallenge as the factors used by the search engines to determine ranking are constantly changing. The reasons for these changes are to ensure that genuinely authentic and relevant content is presented, and not content that has been specifically designed to appear first but which is not relevant.

There are four main factors that influence search engine ranking and which should be accounted for in any SEO strategy (Figure 9.3)

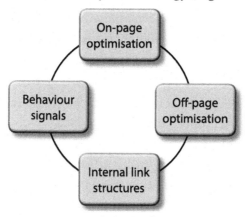

Figure 9.3: Search engine ranking factors

On-page optimisation is achieved by focussing on content-based techniques (what is placed on the page) and system-based techniques (page efficiency, availability and security) (Table 9.3). Developers use website crawler tools such as www.screamingfrog.co.uk to audit onsite SEO.

Table 9.3: Content-based and system-based techniques

Technique	Examples
Content-based	Matching commonly used search terms with keywords and actual page content
	Considering which keywords work for voice search, e.g. pronunciation
	Boosting keyword frequency by putting keywords in tabs at top of page, in sidebar, in body text, in hypertext anchors and mark-up code that sets headers
	Choosing an URL that reflects content and search behaviour
	Ensuring that page content has satisfactory word count and image use
	Managing content so duplicate (old) pages are removed and new content has appropriate links to other sections
System-based	Checking that links function and are not broken
	Ensuring that the download speed is acceptable
	Making the website accessible over a range of devices particularly mobile and also the new development of voice search, e.g. Siri.
	Using https:// pages to signal security

Off-page optimisation is achieved by linking your page to external websites and encouraging others websites to link into the site. Google assesses not only the number of links into a page but also the links that lead from that page. The term *expert* or *hub page* is used to denote such a website. This is a page that contains many quality links out of that page. It is good to link logically to pages that update their content frequently such as news sites.

Internal link structures decide how one webpage connects to another in the same website. Internal linking boosts the overall rank. Strategies include:

- Creating meaningful links containing words, e.g. instead of "click here" write "click here to learn about internal links".
- Ensuring that tabs at the top of the page and the buttons on the sidebar link together and contain key words.
- Placing links for keywords in body text as well as on images when a mouse hovers over it (image title.tag) or text placed within the image to describe it (alt text), to be read by spiders.
- Using links that that are useful to the website visitor

Behaviour signals from users communicate to search engines how much interaction occurs. If interaction is high then the search engine records this as a signal of a high quality website. There are various signals: including engagement with content, e.g. click-through; remaining on the page; book-marking in Favourites and social sharing. Enabling a page so that it can be shared on social media or bookmarked easily in a browser will optimise its search engine ranking.

Push media

When we formulate an advertising campaign we select a specific message (e.g. are giving 20% off all orders this week) and we select a channel mix (e.g a Facebook post, an advertisement on websites with related content, an email or text). In order to inform future advertising decision making we need to track the effectiveness of each message and channel. Advertising on other websites is called display or banner advertising and will incur a cost for either the number of users to whom the content is displayed (cost per thousand or CPM), the number of clicks on the advertisement (cost per click or CPC) or the number of people who click and then proceed to other website actions (cost per action or CPA).

Keywords are the foundation of PPC advertising. In PPC, keywords might be referred to as *adwords*. In PPC the organisation pays the search engine to be associated with certain adwords so that when that word is entered into the search engine, the organisation's website will listed first on the results page. Some adwords will be more popular and cost more per click. So PPC keywords need to be chosen carefully since synonyms, or words with a similar meaning might be cheaper, and keyword planners provide a tool that generates alternative words. For example it might be cheaper to use 'business school' rather than 'university'. Keywords can be used to filter out unwanted clicks by telling the search engine not to show the listing for certain terms. For example, in the UK the word 'school' is not usually applied to a university. An additional strategy to increase value gained from a campaign is to promote the use of a particular word in association with a product or offer. For example we can educate customers through an offline ad campaign to use a neologism (new word), e.g. Marmite invented the word 'marmariti'. Alternatively, we can teach customers to put two words together that are not readily associated, e.g. 'Lidl surprise'.

For PPC, keywords should deliver the best value, i.e. to minimise the cost paid per click whilst achieving the campaign conversion target. There are three interlinked approaches to selecting key search terms:

1 Demand-based which would select a keyword based on its popularity from historic search data and competition for that search term amongst from other brands;

2 Cost-based which would select a keyword based on the CPC;

3 Insight-based which would select a keyword based on the predicted search intent of the customers that the site wishes to attract (persona modelling).

Insight-based selection involves developing the personas (types) of people who could potentially visit the site, and doing this involves putting yourself in the shoes of the customers searching for your product (Aloha Ward, 2017). This can be done using a two-stage approach. First there is a research stage to build the persona profile using segmentation techniques from advertising and marketing research (Jackson, 2016). The data for this can be gathered from secondary sources on market trends, competitor analysis and primary organisational data including: sales data, interview data, survey data and digital analytics such as the most visited sections of the organisational website. The second stage is to determine the customer journey for each persona (Chaffey and Smith, 2013). Such development involves identifying the persona goals, which are the reason for them visiting the website, the tasks they will complete before taking action, the questions they may have, the pain points and the trigger terms (Jackson, 2016). Table 9.4 is an example of a possible persona for prospective MBA student.

Table 9.4: Example of an MBA Student Persona

Persona Profile	Mary is a 26 and a graduate in English. She has worked as a sales executive for 3 years and is now returning to work after her first child. She would like to work in business management.
Goals	Gain business management knowledge to be able to perform well in her new desired role
	Make connections with other industry leaders that might lead to finding a better job.
	Study flexibly to manage her personal commitments
Scenario	Mary is rethinking her professional goals. She'd like to advance her career faster after taking maternity leave. She has noticed how other colleagues with MBAs have been able to get promotions within the company, or in other organisations. She feels she needs more knowledge to work at a senior managerial level, and that's why she thought an MBA would be a good option.
Tasks prior to action	Information Search:
	Online search for options nearby that fit her current personal and professional commitments
	Ask family and friends for recommendations
	Evaluation of alternatives:
	Look at the different rankings from the lists of schools
	Look at online reviews from other students
	Look at the marketing material provided by each university.
Considerations and Questions	Which programme offers the best value for money?
	Which programme has been positively rated by previous students?
	Which programme is more flexible?
	Which programme is closer?
	Where are programme graduates working?
	How many of the students have a business background?
Pain points	Needing to have managerial experience do well in the programme.
	MBA programmes with many international trips
	Nearby programmes are not career-orientated
Trigger Terms	Flexible programme
	Suitable for non-specialist
	High employment rates

Keyword planning tools help demand-based and cost-based decision making by reporting the popularity of each search term. For example, Google's keyword planner provides the historical search volume, cost per click and estimated conversion. Table 9.5 shows the listing for the keyword for the postgraduate degree "Masters of Business Administration" which is shortened to "MBA".

Table 9.5: Demand analysis for MBA as a keyword

Keyword (by relevance)	Average monthly searches	Competition	Suggested bid
Masters	10k-100K	Low	£0.68
Postgraduate	1k-10k	Low	£0.28
MBA	1k-10k	Medium	£5.80

Advertising campaign analytics are concerned with the rate of response and conversion (Peterson, 2004). Response measures the number and characteristics of website visitors – typically through clicking on a link embedded in the message content. Conversion is the number of responders who go on to purchase or perform another requested activity when they visit the website.

Campaign evaluation requires the benchmarking of current brand performance. This involves measuring the current volume of visitor behaviours and conversion rates for the brand using the selected keywords, e.g. the average position in the organic and paid listings (if applicable). The next stage is gap analysis which involves identifying the shortfall between current performance and the desired level of future performance. This analysis should be followed by a campaign to achieve a digital marketing objective (e.g. engagement, conversion or traffic) using the different keyphrases that are relevant for the brand.

A campaign does not have to involve only one persona and one set of keyphrases. Adwords can be used to form a campaign that will target PPC results effectively to the right customers and provide analytics to assess advertising effectiveness. A campaign will focus upon achieving the best result for a product classification, location or target group. There should be no changes in campaign structure since alterations will be erase the metrics already collected. If a different approach is need then it is best to create a fresh campaign. Figure 9.4 shows a typical campaign structure.

Figure 9.4 shows that for university there may be several campaigns operating, those that focus upon product grouping and those that focus upon potential students. It is common to structure a campaign using the catego-

9

ries that are used to structure the website. Within each campaign there are different adgroups each adgroup reflects a particular theme that has been developed for the campaign. It is recommended that at least one of the PPC advertisements features one or more of the keywords in the title so that it clearly signals the relevance of the content to the person searching. Digital marketers test for the best PPC advertisement by putting several different ads within each ad group and rotating them using the "ad rotation" setting. Advertisements can be ranked according to whether they gained the most clicks or the most conversions, once the highest performing ad has been determined the software will automatically show it more often. Ideally each ad group should be distinct from the other groups and have a distinct landing page that clearly meets the information seeking needs of the individual user. Other settings which automate the process of serving the PPC advertisements are placing a restriction on how much should be spent per click and per conversion. In addition the locations and networks upon which the advertisements should be shown can be limited.

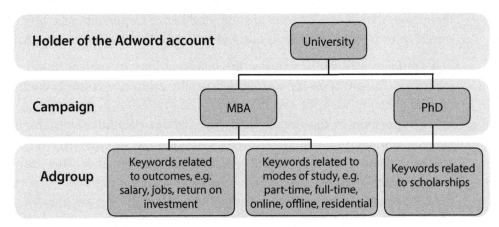

Figure 9.4: Example of an adgroup campaign

Exercise 9.1

Compile a range of hotel visitor personae, e.g. business woman, family with children. Design some ad groups to match the search intent for these personae. Test some of these key words by entering them into a search engine and analyse the PPC and organic search results. Click through and assess the suitability of the landing pages.

Combining SEO and PPC SEM

There is a key decision to be made on the role of SEO, PPC and paid placements within any digital marketing campaign. Table 9.6 compares each technique according traffic quality, flexibility, consumer attitude and technical skill required.

Table 9.6: Comparison of SEO and PPC

Criteria	SEO	PPC/ Paid Placement
Traffic quality	Inconsistent Takes time to see result	Fast Consistent Fake clicks can waste money
Flexibility	Tags can be changed easily at little cost to increase effectiveness	Adgroup rotation automatically finds the best combination Re-marketing can increase impact
Consumer attitude	Positive: tends to view as trustworthy	Negative: tends to view as untrustworthy
Technical skill required	Harder to implement Complexity in changes to search engine algorithms	Simpler to implement Complexity in bid management

Maybe the best route is to use both organic SEO and PPC. Such a hybrid approach involves thinking strategically about how each technique will contribute tactically to the attraction rate of the website. For example, a brand might produce specialist gardening decorations (e.g. www.plantsupports.co.uk), and knows that experienced gardeners will have knowledge of the key search terms. They will optimise the page to contain these terms, and as a result the page will rank highly in the SERPs for someone searching for "plant hoops". However the brand knows that at certain points of the year it is beneficial to run a PPC campaign for other customers who are not so experienced, for example at the times of major flower shows and gardening exhibitions or at Christmas. The brand would bid to be placed highly for keyphrases that a novice gardener might use such as "garden ideas" or "great garden gifts". SEO which focuses on keyword research, quality content writing and link building will deliver a long term return on investment but will take time to be successful. For a boost to returns, a Pay Per Click campaign can be used tactically, to boost display quickly for a limited and specific time period.

Acquisition

Acquisition is a measure of the online interaction that occurs after user awareness of digital content (Peterson, 2004). Interaction is defined as clicking on links and browsing digital content. Visitors can arrive at a digital site from following one of three routes: (1) search engine listing; (2) referral from other websites that feature links to the destination site; and (3) a pathway which results from direct input of the URL into the browser, e.g. a bookmark or clicking on a link in an e-mail message. Metrics measure the source of the traffic, e.g. which search engine, keywords, or referring site. Analytics examine the performance of page, content and visitor ratios (Table 9.7).

Table 9.7: Key analytics: acquisition

Percentage of new visitors	New visitors/ unique visitors
Ratio of new visitors	New visitors/ returning visitors
Interested visitor share	Visits of more than X minutes/ Total visits
Open rates	Audience impressions/Total e-mail addresses
Average no. of visits per visitor	Visits/ visitors
Average no. of pages views per visit	Page views/ number of visits
Average page views per visitor	Pages views/ number of visitors
Page stickiness	Duration of visit per page/ no. of visitors per page
Heavy user share	Number of visits/number of more pages/ total visits
Average views by content per visitor	Content page views/ content unique visitors
Content focus	Average views by content per visitor / Total number of content pages
Percentage of visits under 90 seconds	Visits under 90 seconds/ all visits
Average time spent on site	Time spent surfing all pages/ number of visitors in that time frame

Once visitors have entered the site we can gather metrics on when they visit, how long they stay and whether their interaction with content results in conversion (Chaffey and Ellis Chadwick, 2012:563). The page where a visitor enters the site is called the landing page. The landing page should accurately reflect the keyword or keyphrase that was used to generate the search results and/or the call to action that was present in any PPC or paid placement advertisement. Sometimes the landing page will be the same as the organisation's home page, but it might be that other pages are ranked more highly in SERPS, and metrics will inform digital marketing of the top pages and content requested. It can be particularly insightful to explore if there are any differences between new visitors and repeat visitors, and adjust content or promotional messages accordingly.

If a landing page is not a true reflection of the search results, then this may result in immediate exit or *bounce*. Metrics can be used to measure the bounce rate, which is are the number of visitors that access one page only and leave after a very short time. We infer from this that visitors were not satisfied with the website content that they saw and immediately left. To reduce bounce rate the digital content should match the search results and the channel should contain key features that form the core of the e-service offering. For example this might be key information, key products or being able to transact in the location or language of the user.

Metrics should be gathered on each page a visitor views, when he or she views it, and in what order. This allows us to construct a map of how each user moves through a website. This is called a click-path analysis. The progress of moving from the landing page to conversion has been imagined as a funnel (Figure 9.5). Acquisition involves two more funnel stages towards conversion, and at each point the visitor might exit. After bounce, the second stage is *browse*, which is where the visitor interacts with the online information in order to learn more about the product offering and the functionality of the digital channel, e.g. how easy it is to scroll or move around on the site, or how reliable is the content provision. Metrics can inform us of how many pages were examined from the initial landing page to purchase. This can allow a comparison of the length of the click-path from home page to purchase, from search engine to purchase and from any special offer in a PPC campaign to purchase. We can also judge a page 'stickiness', which is the time spent and frequency of page viewing and is seen as an indication of information quality.

9

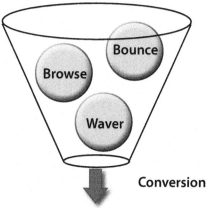

Figure 9.5: Customer funnel

The third stage is *waver*, this is where the customer evaluates the pros and cons of making a purchase, not only in terms of the goods on offer but also in terms of the digital transaction channel as opposed to alternatives such as offline stores. Wavering may involve repeated visits to the digital channel to compare different aspects which are important to making the final purchase, for example information on delivery costs, after-sales guarantees, security of personal details etc. (Court et al 2009). The result of waver might also be where the visitor departs after placing the goods in the online basket but does not proceed to payment. Shopping cart abandonment can be a signal that website processes such as check-out procedure are not working well or can signal that costs such as shipping costs are too high.

The final stage is *conversion*. A good online advertising campaign will have a clear conversion outcome as an end goal. This can be purchase, download, inputting of details or duration of interaction with specific online content. When we measure conversion we are concerned with at which point and how many responders abandon the site, for example we may find that by more finely targeting our message we reduce the number of responders but also decrease the proportion who abandon the website.

Hemann and Burbary (2014:103) explain that "real-time web analytics, give you the ability to do just what their name implies: watch what users are doing on your website live, literally as it happens". One way of testing how changes in process or content impact upon user click-paths to conversion is A/B testing. This means seeing if one type of page layout works better than an alternative. Website configuration tools allow brands to divert visitors to the original (A Page) and the revised page (B page). This allows an organisation to see if changes in message content or site layout increases conversion.

Conversion

Both response and conversion need measuring, since if we only measure response we gain knowledge of the size or quantity of the audience, but we do not get any insight into the value or quality of that response. In other words whilst we may have 4000 visitors, if only 100 of them purchase our goods then our campaign was not targeted at potential customers. Ahola Ward (2017:53) writes that search engine optimisation is not just about attracting the visitor: "search dominance rests upon understanding the search landscape well enough to snare the visitor successfully into your funnel. It's no longer good enough to bring raw traffic to a site (in most cases); today's marketer must bring converting traffic."

A specific goal is needed in order to measure conversion. Dedicating resources to simply bringing people to your website without a specific goal is wasteful (Peterson, 2004). It can be argued that broad exposure to website content will help to build brand awareness and establish a brand identity. However counter arguments would stress that such an unfocussed approach means that the brand loses the opportunity to connect meaningfully with customers. First, because no information is gathered on who responds, the opportunity to personalise messages and customise content is lost. Second, because there is no information on the attractiveness of specific offers or products, the opportunity to improve brand satisfaction is lost.

There ia a wide range of analytics related to conversion but there is a tendency to focus upon sales and orders rather than alternative goals (Table 9.8).

Table 9.8: Key analytics: Conversion

Analytics	Calculation
Conversion rate	Completions/ starts
Abandonment rates	One minus (number of visits at current step/ number of visits at previous step)
Cost per conversion	Cost of campaign to date/ conversion to date
Rolling campaign ROI	Profit to date/ cost to date
Total campaign ROI	Profit to date/ total costs
Segment conversion rates	Segment convertors/ visitors to lower value segment
Average order value	Total revenue/ total orders
AOV for new and returning visitors	Average order value/ New or Returning visitors
Percent of orders from new and repeat customers	New customer orders/ all orders Return customer order/ all orders
New and repeat customer conversion rates	New customer orders/ new visitors Return customer orders/ returning visitors
Sales per visitor	Gross sales/ visitors
Searches yielding results to search no results	Page views to results found page/ page views to no results found page.

9

Retention

Retention metrics measure the behaviour of users who return to digital content (Table 9.9). These are called repeat visitors and are distinguished from unique visitors. It is useful to measure the nature of the content that repeat visitors are accessing, the referring site and whether the user is purchasing for the second time. Repeat visitors are those who has been to the website before whereas a retained visitor is someone who has completed a conversion activity on your website and who continues to return (Peterson, 2004). The visitor retention rate indicates success at repeat business.

Table 9.9: Key analytics: retention

Analytic	Metrics
Ratio of returning visitors to new visitors	Returning visitors/ new visitors
Percentage of returning visitors	Number of returning visitors/ number of all visitors
Average number of returns in a month (can be performed for key segments).	Daily returning visitors/ Monthly returning visitors
Average frequency of visit	Days between visits/number of visits -1
Percentage of retained visitors conversions	Retained visitor conversions/retained visitors
Customer retention rate	Repeat customers/ all customers

Analytics track the activity of repeat visitors and retained visitors, and new visitors or unique visitors. Brands can use this information to segment visitors into different groups and compare differences in behaviour between converted and unconverted audiences. This information will also give insight into which products attract repeat visitors and which products give the best retention results in repeat sales. By comparing the conversion rate between new, repeat and retained customers we can select where best to direct marketing resources. Peterson (2004) writes that visitors may return for support information, additional research as well as repeat purchase. He argues that being able to group repeat visitors according to online behaviour allows the organisation to customise website content. It may be useful to consider what the 'average visitor' does on a website, for example the frequency of visit and the average number of pages viewed.

Peterson (2004) writes that it is hard to get visitors to be loyal to a particular website without a high degree of brand loyalty, however his focus is on repeat purchase rather than the retailing service provided by the website as a storefront. In the case of a sales or news site, repeat visits might be good but if it is to the 'help' and 'product support' pages, repeat visits might be bad.

There should be a clearly defined the period over which a return will be measured, e.g. day, week, month. For example, a news site might measure return over the span of a day, whilst a site selling holidays might measure return over a longer span. Retention can be measured automatically in terms of set time frames, e.g. daily returns, monthly returns. The standard way of measuring retention is to use cookies which are placed in the web browser.

A key analytic is the ratio of returning visitors to new visitors. Ideally we do not want to see all of the traffic from returning visitors, as this would mean that we had no new visitors and thus we were not extending the reach of the website. Equally we would not want to see all unique visitors, with none returning as this would indicate dissatisfaction with the website.

It can be helpful to analyse the ratio of returning to new visitors over particular time periods to see if there is a shift at certain times of the year. For example the number of return visitors might peak at New Year for an MBA website as people make New Year's resolutions. It is also useful to see if repeat visits are linked to any campaigns, e.g. retargeted advertising. Knowing the frequency of return visits helps with planning marketing activity and site changes, e.g. content planning cycles. Such insight can save money through preventing over-frequent content change, e.g. the organisation may plan to update daily, but the frequency of repeat visits are monthly.

Summary

Analytics and metrics provide insight into how a website is helping customers move from search towards a conversion goal. Conversion goals are important as they help an organisation achieve its overall marketing aim, for example to make a sale or to encourage interaction with particular content. The digital customer lifecycle details the stages through which a customer progresses. This chapter has introduced a range of metrics and analytics that are available at each stage.

9

Exemplar paper

Chaffey, D., and Patron, M., (2012), From web analytics to digital marketing optimization: increasing the commercial value of digital analytics, *Journal of Direct, Data and Digital Marketing Practice*, **14** (1), 30-45.

The paper provides a clear overview of how to apply web analytics to improve digital marketing performance. It shows the barriers preventing organisations from improving conversion rates as well as listing the variables that improve conversion rates, which are: perceived control, having a structured approach, having someone directly responsible and incentivising staff based on conversion rates.

■ Additional reading

Wedel, M. and Kannan, P.K. (2016), Marketing analytics for data-rich environments, *Journal of Marketing*, **80**(6), 97-121.

Xu, Z., Frankwick, G.L. and Ramirez, E. (2016), Effects of big data analytics and traditional marketing analytics on new product success: a knowledge fusion perspective, *Journal of Business Research*, **69**(5), 1562-1566.

References

Ahola Ward, A. (2017), *The SEO Battlefield*, O'Reilly Media Inc, Sebastopol.

Cabel, (2008), Japan: URL's are totally out, http://www.cabel.name/2008/03/japan-urls-are-totally-out.html [Accessed 19th October 2017]

Court, D., Elzinga, D., Mulder, S. and Vetvik, O.J. (2009), The consumer decision journey, *McKinsey Quarterly*, https://www.mckinsey.com/business-functions/marketing-and-sales/our-insights/the-consumer-decision-journey [Accessed 4th August 2017].

Chaffey, D. and Ellis-Chadwick, F. (2012), *Internet Marketing: Strategy, Implementation and Practice*, Pearson Education, Harlow.

Chaffey, D. and Smith, P.R. (2013), *eMarketing eXcellence: Planning and Optimizing your Digital Marketing*, Routledge, Abingdon.

Hemann, C. and Burbary, K. (2014), *Digital Marketing Analytics*, Que Publishing, Indianapolis.

Jackson, S. (2016), *Cult of Analytics: Data Analytics for Marketing*, Routledge, Abingdon.

Malaga, R. A. (2009), Web 2.0 techniques for search engine optimization: two case studies, *Review of Business Research*, **9**(1), 132–139.

Net Market Share (2017), Desktop search engine market share, https://www.netmarketshare.com/search-engine-market-share.aspx [Accessed 13th October 2017]

Nielsen, J. (2006), F-shaped pattern for reading web content, http://www.useit.com/alertbox/reading_pattern.html, [Accessed on January 18th 2007]

Peterson, E.T. (2004) *Web Analytics Demystified: A Marketer's Guide to Understanding How Your Website Affects Your Business*, Ingram.

Sen, R. (2005), Optimal search engine marketing strategy, *International Journal of Electronic Commerce*, **10**(1), 9-25.

9

10 Social Media Metrics and Analytics

The use of social metrics and analytics may be referred to as 'social listening' (Hemann and Burbary, 2014:32). Social listening provides a revolutionary new way by which to study consumer behaviour as social media channels enable real-time collection of data of customer responses using cost-effective and non-intrusive techniques (Canhoto and Padmanabhan, 2015). There are different tools that are used to gather data from the wide and growing range social media channels. For example, Facebook offers a free analytics platform that enables page owners to view metrics on community activity and content performance. The increase in brand-related social media activity has resulted in both start-ups and established media monitoring companies developing a bewildering array of specialist software (Hemann and Burbary, 2014).

Social media metrics and analytics assess the influence of social media activities on the relationship between the brand and the consumer (Barker et al., 2013). Online consumer engagement (OCE) refers to online behaviour that goes beyond purchase to result in involvement, interaction, intimacy and influence (Van Doorn et al., 2010; Haven and Vittal, 2008). Social Impact theory explains how interaction between individuals influences behaviour and states that the degree of impact of a message is associated with the number of sources exerting influence, the immediacy of the message and the strength of the source (status and other characteristics) (Perez-Vega et al., 2016). To aid clarity it is helpful to identify social metrics that measure involvement, interaction, intimacy and influence, and to consider the role of immediacy, strength and numbers.

Involvement

Involvement metrics measure the presence of the customer at the brand touch point, e.g. the social media fan page (Chan-Olmsted and Shay, 2015). Key metrics are: impressions, followers/subscribers and likes. Reach metrics quantify how many people have viewed (have been reached) by the social media content, and this measure is equivalent to the circulation statistics of printed media. Reach can be measured as being owned, paid or earned reach (Hemann and Burbray, 2014). *Owned* reach relates to the number of people who view the post on the brand page itself. *Paid* reach relates to the numbers who view the post as part of a sponsored story or as an advertisement placed within their social media feed. *Earned* reach refers to the number of people who view a post as a result of it being shared by a friend.

Impression metrics focus upon the content as unit of measurement to count the number of times a person has viewed content or had the opportunity to view content without liking, and is the simplest indicator of presence. Follower/subscribers and likes are metrics that focus upon the individual as a unit of measurement – you cannot double 'like' content. When an individual likes a social media page then they have viewed content; in contrast, following/subscribing is a page level metric that results in their ongoing presence at the brand touch point and content being posted into the individual's own online presence or them being alerted when new content arrives. A commercial survey undertaken by comScore and Facebook indicates that individuals who liked the "Starbuck's Facebook page or who had a Facebook friend who had liked the page spent 8% more and transacted 11% more frequently over the course of a month" (John et al., 2017:110). However, this may be a case of correlation not causation; those who like a page might already be positively disposed towards the brand which would explain why they would purchase more than non-followers.

Involvement metrics form the basis of conversation reach, and topic trend analytics (Table 10.1). Conversation reach identifies how many brand followers are participating in a specific brand conversation across one or more social media channels (Barker et al., 2012). Conversation reach is a useful measure of content effectiveness, which is known as *message resonance*. One challenge in calculating conversation metrics is how to identify and delimit the scope of the conversation. In some media it is relatively easy to delimit the conversation, e.g. the Twitter hashtag can be used. Topic trend analytics calculate the percentage contribution of an individual topic to the number of all topic mentions and thus contextualise a particular topic within the ongoing stream of topic mentions. For example, a digital marketing manager might track the Halloween ideas as a percentage of all mentions relating to brand use.

Involvement analytics should be evaluated longitudinally across time in order to have a benchmark against which to compare current statistics. This allows a brand to identify when a conversation is expanding and travelling beyond the normal audience, i.e. going viral. Once a trend is spotted then digital marketers can choose to allocate more or fewer resources to developing the conversation, for example by focusing on fostering dialogue within the more active channels and by ensuring that the sentiment within the conversation remains positive.

Table 10.1: Involvement analytics

Analytic	Calculation
Conversation reach	Total people participating/ total audience exposure
Topic trends	Number of specific topic mentions/ all topic mentions

Interaction

Interaction metrics measures how an individual read, likes or share content at each brand touch point (Chan-Olmsted and Shay, 2015) (Table 10.2). Interaction moves beyond passive liking or following and relates to metrics of comments, retweets, and replies. When an individual makes a comment they offer an opinion on the post that they are viewing. Comments can be directly on the post or replies to comments on that post. Channels such as Facebook, YouTube and Slideshare show the comments and replies in a common thread whereas others, e.g. Twitter, do not link comments in this way. Retweets are specific to Twitter and are when an individual shares content with their followers. Interaction metrics are used to calculate analytics such as audience engagement and share of voice, as well issue resolution time and response rates.

Table 10.2: Interaction analytics

Analytic	Calculation
Audience engagement	Total comments+ Shares+ Trackbacks/ Total views
Share of voice	Number of brand mentions/ Total mentions of competitors
Issue resolution time	Total no. of issues resolved satisfactorily/ Total no. of service issues
Issue response rate	Total issue response time/ Total no. of service issues

10

Social networking sites (SNS) are rapidly being adopted as a component of customer services (Causon, 2015). Using social media for customer support can be up to 87% more cost effective than traditional channels for organisations (Klimis, 2010). The cheap, convenient and public nature of SNS means that making a customer service enquiry is easy, enjoyable and effective for customers (Andreassen and Streukens, 2013). For example, Dell use social media mostly as a customer relationship management tool to deal with problems with customers. Complaining is a form of negative engagement with the brand. Resolving a complaint effectively and efficiently is important as other members of the community are able to view complaint content. However, survey evidence shows that only 11% of social media messages get a direct response from businesses and that expectations of customers of a 30 minutes time laps before response are unmet (Sproutsocial, 2016).

Issue resolution rate and issue resolution time are two key analytics to assess brand performance in addressing customer service issues. Issue resolution rate is the number of solved issues divided by the total number service issues. It is important to record accurately the number of solved issues by asking service personnel to log the result and also by following up enquiries with a simple online survey. An organisation has the option of comparing the issue resolution rate of social media with the issue resolution rate of the call centre. Low issue resolution rates can be addressed by staff training and more detailed investigation into frequently received issues.

Issue response time is the average time it takes for a human-generated response to a social media complaint and is calculated by dividing the total issue response time by the total number of service issues. The goal is to continually reduce the average time lapse between issue and response. Social media response times should try to equal that of other channels, e.g. call centres, online chat or e-mail. It is important to recognise that automated responses are not sufficient. Research shows that prompt and appropriate responses can form positive consumer attitudes (Lee and Song, 2010). However, if the customer service response creates dissatisfaction, then the resultant negativity will be amplified (Kim et al., 2016).

Audience engagement captures the ratio of passive views to active use of content which puts the performance of a particular post. A trackback is when a user puts a link (such as an URL) in a message that refers back to the original content. Identifying variation in audience engagement with content highlights the hot topics for a brand fan-page. Audience engagement should be measured over time and in comparison with other posts in order to understand if a particular post is doing better or worse compared to the average.

Share of voice shows how well brand content is performing in social media. Share of voice is calculated by dividing the total number of brand mentions by the total mentions of competitors. Measuring share of voice over competitors enables a brand to track how well it is developing its online presence. In addition to showing how the brand compares to its competitors, share of voice can also be calculated by channel, to identify which social media channels are having the greatest impact. Tracking over time also enables a brand to see when content is no longer performing. For example, share of voice may decline if the immediacy of content falls. In addition, if a competing brand grows its share of voice then the digital marketing managers should try to identify which competitor content is the cause. For example, a competitor might be operating a particularly successful viral campaign, or have increased the volume of content or gained a particularly influential content source. Gaining such competitive intelligence will inform future social media content planning.

Intimacy

Intimacy measures the depth and valence of the emotion that the individual holds for the brand (Chan-Olmsted and Shay, 2015). Social media data gives insight into consumer emotion or sentiment (Table 10.3). Emotion impacts upon consumer decision making for example if you are in a good mood then you are more inclined to take a risk (Johnson and Tversky, 1983) and be inclined towards making an impulsive snap decision (Forgas, 1991). In addition social media can capture consumers stated opinions, beliefs and attitudes towards a brand. Sentiment analysis or opinion mining is used to identify the presence of emotion in content, and the strength and nature of the emotion (Canhoto and Padmanabhan, 2015)

10

Table 10.3: Intimacy analytics

Analytic	Calculation
Sentiment ratio	Ratio between positive and negative brand mentions

The sentiment ratio calculates the proportion of positive to neutral to negative comments in social media. The proportion of each type of sentiment is calculated dividing positive, neutral and negative brand mentions by all brand mentions. The focus of the analytics can be the brand, a product or a campaign. The sentiment ratios should also be trended over time and across channels in order to measure the online brand profile. Automated analysis tools are used to score sentiment, but a weakness of these tools is that they are unable to discern tone of voice, e.g. the difference between sarcasm and authenticity (Hemann and Burbary, 2014). An alternative would be to use manual sentiment analysis, but this approach introduces issues of speed and accuracy given the volume and velocity of the data. A further complication is that the classification system of three categories of positive, neutral and negative is not very nuanced and limits interpretation. Hemann and Burbary (2014) recommend using a five point scale (Figure 10.1)

Figure 10.1: A five point sentiment scale (Adapted from Hemann and Burbary 2014).

Clearly all digital marketing managers would like to manage brands that have consistently positive sentiment but it is important to learn from all forms of sentiment, particularly when experimenting with innovation and new product formulations. Monitoring and tracking sentiment is important to both customer services (who want to know if negativity is related directly to product or service experience) and public relations departments (who want to know if the brand is being associated with a negative trend or story).

A digital marketing manager should use positive sentiment to identify individuals and online communities which are particularly favourable towards the brand and offer rewards and privileged information. Neutral sentiment offers the opportunity to increase dialogue to reinforce positive perceptions and address concerns. Strategies for dealing with negative sentiment need to be subtle in order to not provoke aggression. One approach is to use source strength to increase positive social impact. For example, the brand may ask a brand advocate to provide a counter argument or use a senior executive as the brand spokesperson.

Exercise 10.1

Select two celebrity Facebook pages. Select three posts and evaluate the conversation reach of each post and the sentiment ratio. Which celebrity is doing better?

Influence

Social media influencers are individuals who exert influence over others on social media due to their status and number of followers (an example would be a popular blogger). When a social media influencer talks about the brand, this would be within the influencer's owned channel and thus would be earned media for the brand. Within its owned media the brand will have brand advocates, who have a strong connection to the brand and are either brand employees or loyal customers (Table 10.4). Survey evidence shows that employees are perceived as a credible source of information by 52% of consumers and that sales leads gained by employee brand advocates are seven times more likely to convert compared to other leads (Hootsuite, 2017).

Table 10.4: Influence analytics

Analytic	Calculation
Satisfaction score	Community feedback (input a, b, c...)/ All community feedback
Net promoter score	Percentage of promoters minus the percentage of detractors
Active advocates	Unique advocates/ total advocate influencers
Active influence	Unique advocates influence/ total advocates influence
Advocacy impact	No. of advocacy driven conversions/ total volume of advocacy traffic

Brand advocates can be used in digital marketing strategy to develop an online community by interacting with content, resolving customer queries, addressing complaints and closing sales. An advocacy programme seeks to recruit and reward brand advocates who can communicate effectively, post regularly and are knowledgeable about the brand. Influence metrics and analytics (Table 10.4) measure the likelihood of the person to advocate to

10

others on behalf of the brand in order to inform digital marketing strategy (Chan-Olmsted and Shay, 2015).

The **active advocate** analytic calculates the number of active brand advocates as a proportion of all brand advocates and indicates the health of the advocacy programme (Barker et al., 2012). The percentage of active advocates should be specified within the digital marketing strategy and take into account the anticipated strategic role of advocates. An advocacy programme should be tracked and accompanied by evaluation of the impact of key campaign initiatives (e.g. rewards and events). Advocacy programmes require careful curating to ensure that resources are not wasted in boosting advocacy unnecessarily but that sufficient reward is given to ensure the required interest and enthusiasm.

Active influence calculates the influence of an individual advocate as a proportion of the influence of all the brand advocates, i.e. it helps the marketer identify 'star' advocates. Influence can be measured using internally set targets, e.g. number of re-tweets, shares, followers etc., or by external influence algorithms, e.g. Klout scores. Klout (www.klout.com) gives an individual a score between 1 and 100 in terms of their individual influence across social media, however there is uncertainty over way in which Klout computes the scores, which has caused some controversy (Hemann and Burbary, 2014). Active influence can be calculated over one or several social media channels. An individual's active influence score can be used to determine the characteristics of an active advocates. Digital marketing strategy might seek to diversify or intensify the active advocates, i.e. encourage advocates who differ or are similar to the existing top-ranked individuals.

Advocacy impact calculates the number of conversions as a proportion of all advocacy traffic within a stated period, e.g during an advocacy campaign. Conversion can be measured as sales, but also can include downloads and sign-ups to events. It is important to set clear parameters when determining the advocacy impact analytic since conversions may be the results of consumers gathering information and being influenced by several different owned, earned and paid communication sources. Parameters will include delimiting the time within which impact will be calculated, specifying the channel or channels within which the impact will be measured and also determining the attribution model.

An attribution model divides the credit for a conversion according to previous customer interaction with the media, and the example given assumes that the advocate is the final touch point before purchase is made (Figure

10.2). Attribution is used to incentivise and reward advocates and so choice of model is important. It is possible to assign each digital marketing campaign that involves advocacy with an identifier and also to provide identifiers for each individual advocate in order to track conversion i.e. a specific url to include in communications. If an advocate is also able to act as a sales person and take an order then the last interaction model would offer an incentive, if the advocate cannot place the sale but is able to refer the consumer to a transaction channel then the last non-direct interaction model is more appropriate. Finally if the advocacy programme is designed to stimulate interest then the first interaction model would be most suitable. Attribution models require skill and resources to implement with linear, time decay and position-based models being the most complex.

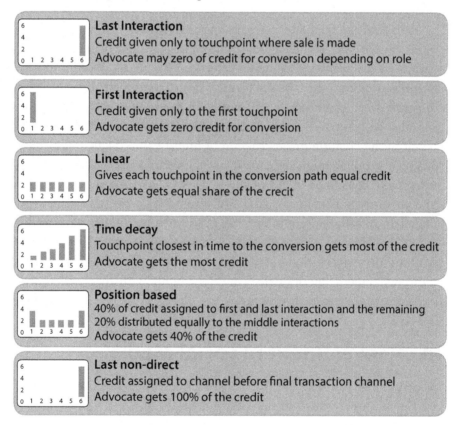

Last Interaction
Credit given only to touchpoint where sale is made
Advocate may zero of credit for conversion depending on role

First Interaction
Credit given only to the first touchpoint
Advocate gets zero credit for conversion

Linear
Gives each touchpoint in the conversion path equal credit
Advocate gets equal share of the crecit

Time decay
Touchpoint closest in time to the conversion gets most of the credit
Advocate gets the most credit

Position based
40% of credit assigned to first and last interaction and the remaining 20% distributed equally to the middle interactions
Advocate gets 40% of the credit

Last non-direct
Credit assigned to channel before final transaction channel
Advocate gets 100% of the credit

Figure 10.2: Range of attribution models

A **satisfaction score** calculates the ratio of positive to negative community feedback as a proportion of all brand community posts within social media channels. The **Net Promoter Score** (NPS) divides customers or posts into three groups:

- **Promoters**: satisfied customers who are loyal and share positive word of mouth and so help to build brand sales
- **Passives**: who are satisfied but who do not promote the brand
- **Detractors**: who are dissatisfied customers who will share negative word of mouth and damage sales (Barker et al., 2012).

Customers are allocated to each group according to either a survey questions or through classification of social media content. The first step is to calculate the percentage of positive, passive and negative customers as a proportion of all customers – this would be *sentiment analysis* if using posts. The second step is to subtract the percentage of detractors from the percentage of promoters. The NPS can either be negative or positive. A brand should aim for a positive NPS (Barker et al., 2012).

Analytics can facilitate comparison across different channels and between paid, earned and owned media campaigns to identify the contribution of each towards positive interaction between a brand and its community members. Feedback might take the form of direct comments, likes or the posting of content in response to a call out from the brand. Each type of feedback can also be compared using this analytic. Brand community feedback may result in the creation or destruction of brand value (Skalen et al., 2015). For example a brand might ask for a comments and ideas which results in an integrated, coordinated and positive series of interaction between the brand and consumers (Grönroos, 2011), or alternatively there may be a series of negative, misaligned comments revealing inconsistent goals (Brodie et al., 2013). Skålén et al. (2015) identify that a brand should align its procedures (community rules), understandings (appropriate and valued knowledge) and engagement (emotionally charged intent) with the brand community and correct any areas of misalignment.

Return on investment in social media

Return on investment (ROI) is a metric used to assess the financial return on the money invested in marketing activity. ROI is a financial measure of profitability that is expressed as a percentage, and is the net profit divided by cost. It is used by shareholders to determine if an organisation is worthy of investment. In terms of brand management, ROI is used to judge how brands contribute to the overall profitability of the organisation and to allocate budget. ROI is considered to be relatively objective and is easy to understand (Fisher, 2009).Thus ROI is a widely accepted indicator of performance.

However, the suitability of ROI as an assessment of advertising has been an area of longstanding debate (see White and Miles, 1996) and using ROI to measure social media output is equally contentious (Fisher, 2009). Fisher (2009:190) argues that "a customer is worth far more than their initial spend with your company: you need to factor in future purchases and the influence they have through social media". As a result brands are recommended to select appropriate and focused metrics that are aligned to strategic digital marketing goals (Fisher, 2009).

Whilst the ROI equation is easy to calculate, estimating the profitability of social media is much harder. Social media is not only used as a sales channel but also as a source of information and a forum within which to voice complaints. In both cases there may be some cost saving that can be measured, but is difficult to attribute the contribution of social media towards generating profits. Facebook has been seeking to strengthen the link between social media advertising and offline sales by encouraging brands to send data on sales after a campaign to Facebook where they will match the sales data to those who viewed the advertisement, thereby giving the campaign ROI.

Future directions in social listening

Two future directions of social listening are: 1) ability to gather and measure image data; and 2) the ability to provide visual representations of social media sentiment and use. Image analytics measure and analyse images (such as the brand logo), emojis, memes and other media formats to identify sentiment. A meme is a piece of online content which is copied and spread rapidly between individuals. Image analytics can help a brand spot when its logo is being used in a negative way. The use of images on social media is growing trend. The increase in the number of images being shared is partially driven by the launch of new channels that specialise in enabling the sharing of images, such as Instagram, and also with the rapid adoption of camera phones.

Visual representations of social media provide the digital marketing manager with an interactive display of social media data. Visualisation methods increase understanding and also provide an overview of large datasets (Xu et al., 2013). Advances in technology such as GPS-enabled mobile phones, enables analysts to overlay information on sentiment and activity onto maps of geographic locations. In 2012 the London Eye was illuminated with a social media light show, with the colour of the wheel being determined by the nature of the sentiment expressed in the tweets that day. An algorithm

10

was designed that converted the social emotions being expressed into colour and motion (Barnett, 2012).

Ethics of social listening

Digital platforms collect and analyse personal data to generate user profiles that contain information on personal characteristics, the connections in their network (including the characteristics of those connections, and the interaction between them). In the digital context there is considerable focus upon consumer awareness and ability to control the extent to which they are subjected to 'dataveillance', which refers to the surveillance of a person's activities using a data trail (Ashworth and Free, 2006). Privacy and surveillance are inherently linked, with surveillance being a "means for trying to derive and accumulate benefits for certain groups or individuals at the expense of others ...[as it]...tries to bring about or prevent certain behaviours" Fuchs (2014:158).

Privacy concerns can be divided into two areas: 1) uncertainty of how information is collected; and 2) how information will be used once it is collected (Sheehan and Hoy, 2000). Personal data can be split into two types: that which is input into digital channels by the consumer (explicit information), and that which is collected as a result of their digital consumption (implicit information) (Grant and Waite, 2013). Although individuals express privacy concerns, they do not always adjust settings to protect their privacy (Gross and Acquisti, 2005). This may be due to the high perceived ease of use of social media posting compared to the low ease of use in managing privacy settings (Lee et al., 2014). On one hand, whilst data-mining tools are growing in sophistication they are being matched by the growing sophistication of ad-blocking and anti-cookie programmes.

Privacy settings may not be used because the majority of users are unaware of the scale and complexity of data aggregation that underpin social media sites. Debatin et al. (2009:84) suggest that "for the average user, Facebook-based invasion of privacy and aggregation of data, as well as its potential commercial exploitation by third parties, tend to remain invisible". Social media is widely adopted; it deeply penetrates the everyday lives of consumers and is taken for granted by many.

Skeggs (2017) states that although "most people think they're using Facebook to communicate with friends", in reality they are revealing "how much they can be sold for, now and in the future, and how much their friends can be sold for" as channels seek to monetise the data they collect. Campbell and Carlson (2002:592) identify a shift towards the "commodification of privacy" when the individual sees privacy not as a right but rather as a commodity that is exchanged in return for perceived benefits, such as free access to a social media channel. As such, permitting the gathering of personal data is 'participatory surveillance', and is seen as a transaction cost. There are different levels of data sensitivity and that sensitivity of personal data varies according to different contexts: online shopping, social networking and information searching (Bateman et al., 2011; Ortlieb and Garner, 2016). They identify five different data categories (Table 10.5).

Table 10.5: Data categories. Adapted from Bateman et al., 2011; Ortlieb and Garner, 2016.

Data categories	Examples of data
Contact details	E-mail, phone number, address, state, country
Observable attributes	Age, gender, ethnicity
Individual attributes	Religious views, politics, sexuality, relationship status
Financial,	Debit/credit card, Paypal
Offline behaviours	Hobbies, education, favourite book, favourite film
Online behaviour	Search history, purchase history

The failure of regulation to keep pace with digital activity means that there are many ethical and legal challenges. A brand manager may face considerable pressure to gather and use digital information to ensure competitive advantage. Dahl (2015:230) writes that "much of the current marketing communication regulation has no effective means of dealing with social media-based marketing campaigns, and until very recently digital and social media were outside the remit of advertising regulators". There is a tension between society's demands for continued (information) privacy, a lack of regulation to govern activity and the desire to commercially exploit data (McCreary, 2008). Any course of action needs to consider not only the legality of the action but also the tolerance of the online community to the use of their information.

10

Exercise 10.2

Looking at the information listed in Table 10.5, think about how willing you would be to disclose this information when shopping online, when social networking and when searching for information online. Score your perceptions on a scale of 1= not willing to disclose to 5= Extremely willing to disclose. Now check the privacy settings of the digital channels you use and see if you are implicitly disclosing this information.

Questions of surveillance extend to marketing research practices. Research ethics state that when gathering data, participants should give informed consent. Informed consent is when "participants are made aware of the research and its benefits and implications, and they are given the opportunity to withdraw" (Tuten and Solomon, 2015:278). It is possible to gain informed consent for explicit information connection, however for researchers there are questions surrounding implicit data collection. For example, when gathering and analysing posts, there are challenges related to maintaining anonymity of participants, issues of consent and ownership of data when the content has been re-posted. Whilst the data for some channels, such as Twitter, are in the public domain and could be considered available for analysis, there is a still a duty to act ethically in the treatment of content (Todd, 2016).

Summary

Social media analytics provide a new way of studying consumer behaviour. Social media platforms provide a range of real-time data that shows the level of brand involvement, interaction, intimacy and the degree of influence of brand advocates. In order to track the performance of a social media marketing campaign, digital marketers need to select the analytics that are appropriate for the digital strategy. There are considerations of channel performance and attribution of influence. In addition it is important to consider issues of ethics and legality to ensure that the brand reputation is protected.

Exemplar paper

Canhoto, A.I. and Padmanabhan, Y. (2015). 'We (don't) know how you feel'–a comparative study of automated vs. manual analysis of social media conversations. *Journal of Marketing Management*, **31**(9-10), 1141-1157.

This paper examines Twitter conversations to reveal the levels of agreement between manual and automated analysis. They find significant differences between the automated and manual approaches to sentiment analysis. Overall the manual analysis was most likely to result in a score of positive sentiment, whereas the automated analysis tended towards neutral and negative scores. The results indicate that digital marketers should take time to familiarise themselves with the limitations of the analytical software.

■   ## Further reading

Fisher, T. (2009), ROI in social media: a look at the arguments, *Journal of Database Marketing and Customer Strategy Management*, **16**(3), 189-195.

Schweidel, D.A. and Moe, W.W. (2014), Listening in on social media: A joint model of sentiment and venue format choice, *Journal of Marketing Research*, **51**(4), 387-402.

Van Norel, N. D., Kommers, P.A.M., Van Hoof, J.J. and Verhoeven, J. W.M. (2014), Damaged corporate reputation: can celebrity tweets repair it?, *Computers in Human Behavior*, **36**, 308-315.

References

Andreassen, T. W., and Streukens, S. (2013), Online complaining: understanding the adoption process and the role of individual and situational characteristics, *Managing Service Quality: An International Journal*, **23**(1), 4-24.

Ashworth, L. and Free, C. (2006), Marketing dataveillance and digital privacy: using theories of justice to understand consumers' online privacy concerns, *Journal of Business Ethics*, **67**(2), 107-23.

Barker, M., Barker, D. I., Bormann, N. and Neher, K. (2012), *Social Media Marketing: A Strategic Approach*, Nelson Education.

Barnett, E. (2012), Happy Olympic tweeters light up London Eye, *The Telegraph*. http://www.telegraph.co.uk/technology/news/9408783/Happy-Olympic-tweeters-to-light-up-London-Eye.html, [Accessed 4th December 2017].

Bateman, P. J., Pike, J. C. and Butler, B. S. (2011), To disclose or not: publicness in social networking sites, *Information Technology and People*, **24**(1), 78-100.

Brodie, R.J., Ilic, A., Juric, B. and Hollebeek, L. (2013), Consumer engagement in a virtual brand community: an exploratory analysis, *Journal of Business Research*, **66**(1), 105-114.

Canhoto, A.I. and Padmanabhan, Y. (2015), We (don't) know how you feel–a comparative study of automated vs. manual analysis of social media conversations, *Journal of Marketing Management*, **31**(9-10), 1141-1157.

Campbell, J. E., and Carlson, M. (2002), Panopticon. com: online surveillance and the commodification of privacy, *Journal of Broadcasting and Electronic Media*, **46**(4), 586-606.

Causon, J. (2015), Customer complaints made via social media on the rise, *The Guardian*, https://www.theguardian.com/media-network/2015/may/21/customer-complaints-social-media-rise.

10

Chan-Olmsted, S.M. and Shay, R. (2015). Media branding 3.0: from media brands to branded entertainment and information. In *Handbook of Media Branding*, (11-32), Springer International Publishing.

Dahl, S.M. (2014), *Social Media Marketing: Theories and Applications*, Sage, Chicago.

Debatin, B., Lovejoy, J. P., Horn, A. K., and Hughes, B. N. (2009). Facebook and online privacy:Attitudes, behaviors, and unintended consequences, *Journal of Computer-Mediated Communication*, **15**(1), 83-108.

Fisher, T. (2009), ROI in social media: a look at the arguments, *Journal of Database Marketing and Customer Strategy Management*, **16**(3), 189-195.

Forgas, J. P. (1991), Affective influences on partner choice: role of mood in social decisions, *Journal of Personality and Social Psychology*, **61**(5), 708.

Fuchs, C. (2017), *Social Media: A Critical Introduction*, Sage, London.

Grant, I.G. and Waite, K. (2013), Online privacy: concepts, issues and research avenues for digital consumption, in Belk, R.W. and Llamas, R. (eds.), *The Routledge Companion to Digital Consumption*. Routledge. pp 333- 345

Grönroos, C. (2011), Value co-creation in service logic. a critical analysis, *Marketing Theory*,**11**(3), 279-302.

Gross, R. and Acquisti, A. (2005). Information revelation and privacy in online social networks. In *Proceedings of the 2005 ACM workshop on Privacy in the electronic society* (pp. 71-80). ACM.

Haven, B. and Vittal, S. (2008). Measuring engagement. *Forrester*. https://www.adobe.com/engagement/pdfs/measuring_engagement.pdf. [Accessed January 28, 2014].

Hemann, C. and Burbary, K. (2013), *Digital Marketing Analytics. Making Sense of Consumer Data in a Digital World*, Que Publishing, Indianapolis.

Hootsuite (2017), Social media advocacy: how to build a brand advocate program, Online at https://blog.hootsuite.com/social-media-advocacy-brand-advocate/ [Accessed 4th December 2017]

John, L.K., Mochon, D., Emrich, O. and Schwartz, J. (2017), What's the value of a like, *Harvard Business Review*, March-April,108-115.

Johnson, E. J. and Tversky, A. (1983), Affect, generalization, and the perception of risk, *Journal of Personality and Social Psychology*, **45**(1), 20-31.

Kim, S. J., Wang, R. J. H., Maslowska, E. and Malthouse, E. C. (2016), Understanding a fury in your words: the effects of posting and viewing electronic negative word-of-mouth on purchase behaviors, *Computers in Human Behavior*, **54**, 511-521.

Klimis, C. (2010), Digital marketing: the gradual integration in retail banking, *EFMA Journal*, **4**(226), 16-19.

Lee, L.L. and Song, S. (2010), An empirical investigation of electronic word-of-mouth: information and corporate response strategy, *Computers in Human Behavior*, **26**(5), 1073-1080.

Lee, Y. K., Chang, C. T., Lin, Y., and Cheng, Z. H., (2014), The dark side of smartphone usage: psychological traits, compulsive behavior and technostress, *Computers in Human Behavior*, **31**, 373-383.

McCreary, L. (2008) What was privacy?, *Harvard Business Review*, **86**(10), 123-30.

Ortlieb, M. and Garner, R. (2016), Sensitivity of personal data items in different online contexts, *it-Information Technology*, **58**(5), 217-228.

Perez-Vega, R., Waite, K. and O'Gorman, K. (2016), Social Impact Theory: an examination of how immediacy operates as an influence upon social media interaction in Facebook fan pages, *The Marketing Review*, **16**(3), 299-321.

Sheehan, K. B. and Hoy, M. G. (2000), Dimensions of privacy concerns among online consumers, *Journal of Public Policy and Marketing*, 19(1), 62-73.

Skålén, P., Pace, S. and Cova, B. (2015), Firm-brand community value co-creation as alignment of practices, *European Journal of Marketing*, **49**(3/4), 596-620.

Skeggs, B. (2017), Bev Skeggs on Social Media Siloing, http://socialsciencebites. libsyn.com/bev-skeggs-on-social-media-siloing [Accessed 1st December 2017].

Sproutsocial (2016), Customer Services, http://sproutsocial.com/ [Accessed 11TH December 2017].

Todd, M. (2016), Visualising social media analysis, https://www.socialsciencespace. com/2016/07/visualizing-social-media-analysis/ [Accessed 29th November 2017]

Tuten, T. and Solomon, M.R. (2012), *Social Media Marketing*, Pearson, London.

Van Doorn, J., Lemon, K. N., Mittal, V., Nass, S., Pick, D., Pirner, P. and Verhoef, P. C. (2010), Customer engagement behavior: theoretical foundations and research directions, *Journal of Service Research*, **13**(3), 253-266.

White, J.B. and Miles, M.P., (1996), The financial implications of advertising as an investment, *Journal of Advertising Research*, **36**, 43-54.

Xu, P., Wu, Y., Wei, E., Peng, T.Q., Liu, S., Zhu, J.J. and Qu, H. (2013), Visual analysis of topic competition on social media, *IEEE Transactions on Visualization and Computer Graphics*, **19**(12), 2012-21.

10

11 The Digital Marketing Skills Gap

Many students who are interested in a career in digital marketing may be discouraged from pursuing jobs in this sector because of the often incorrect assumption that a deep technical knowledge is needed to succeed as a digital marketer. This might be true for some roles that require different degrees of technical skill. However, there are many roles in this field that are suitable for those with skills in management, marketing, and creative arts. It is also the case that as digital technologies develop, there are several emerging roles that operate across different department functions. In these instances businesses are interested in the willingness and ability to learn, combined with an enthusiasm for digital activity. Finding the right person for the right role is important, however there is a gap between the skills that are required and the number of individuals who possess those skills.

The digital marketing skills gap

The digital marketing skills gap refers to the inability of employers to find qualified people to perform a digital marketing role. The UK government has found that in the labour market there is a shortage in suitable digital skills for digital jobs (Department for Business and Innovation Skills, 2016). A digital marketing skills gap has implications for a country. Not having the right people to perform the jobs that are needed will hinder economic growth at a micro (e.g. young graduates cannot find jobs as they don't have the skills that companies need), a meso (e.g. companies cannot grow as much as they could) and a macro level (e.g. the whole economy does not reach its full potential).

The contribution of digital skills to the performance of the economy is substantial, particularly in the United Kingdom. According to a report commissioned by the UK Parliament (2016), the UK digital industries grew two and a half times as fast as the whole economy between 2003 and 2013 and comprised 7.5%, or £113 billion, of the UK's gross value added (GVA) as of 2013. In addition, the estimated turnover of digital tech industries in 2014 was £161 billion, and there are 1.56 million jobs in the digital tech economy, of which 41% are in traditionally non-digital industries. In terms of remuneration, digital jobs also tend to be better paid than the average salary. In fact, the average advertised salary in digital jobs is just under £50,000, which is 36% higher than the national average (House of Commons, 2016).

There is considerable debate about whether such thing as a 'skills gap' exists, or whether employers are becoming so demanding that finding potential recruits is impossible (Cappelli, 2012). Nevertheless employers are keen to hire people with the right digital marketing skills, and several surveys indicate that they are struggling to find them (Department for Business and Innovation Skills, 2016).

The digital marketer model

A search for digital marketing roles using any recruitment website will show that several jobs require a combination of marketing management and technical skills (Figure 11.1). The depth of this knowledge will depend on the type of functions. Having sufficient technical skills has been identified as important in both academia and marketing practice (Schlee and Harich, 2010; Digital Hub, 2008). After all, professionals in digital marketing roles are expected to be able to implement the different strategies that they create.

Royle and Laing (2014) developed a *digital marketer model* to show that digital marketing roles can be placed on a spectrum with technical skills at one extreme and marketing management skills at the other. In addition to technical knowledge and the ability to strategically integrate digital tools into a wider marketing strategy, digital marketers are also expected to be proficient at other more 'generic' business managerial skills. These include the ability to conduct research to understand and react to changes in the environment, to deal with clients appropriately, and to have sufficient commercial awareness and communication skills. We are going to look at each of the different functional areas along this spectrum in more detail in each of the following sections.

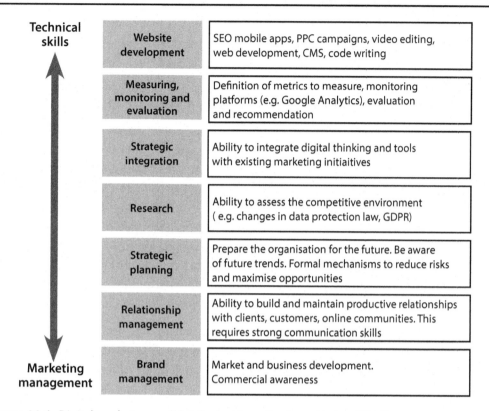

Figure 11.1: Digital marketer model. Adapted from Royle and Laing (2014).

■ Website development functions

Some basic understanding of how a website works is valuable. Such knowledge might include how to code and being able develop a website from scratch; however this kind of deep technical understanding is usually not required for all positions. Overall, some understanding of what is "under the hood" of a website is needed, so that digital marketers can communicate with other technical roles in a meaningful way, particularly when implementing digital strategy. For larger companies there may be a specialist department which are responsible for the technical operation of the website (Peterson, 2004). In the context of SMEs, there are several platforms that allow marketers to develop websites with little coding knowledge (e.g. wix.com, Wordpress).

Website development includes being able to implement search engine optimisation (SEO) and pay-per-click campaigns (PPC). SEO refers to the techniques aimed at ranking digital content at the top of search results when users conduct relevant searchers. PPC or keyword advertising campaigns involve bidding to appear at in the top results. SEO specialists would be

11

expected to understand on-and off-page SEO techniques such as keyword analysis, optimising the website to improve download speed and link building strategies.

■ Measurement, monitoring, and evaluation functions

Digital marketing tools facilitate the continuous measuring and monitoring of channel activity. Practitioners recognise evaluation, monitoring and measurement to be key challenges facing their implementation of digital communication solutions (Valos et al., 2010). The use of log files and page tags allows website owners to monitor the online behaviour of users. Several social media channels (i.e. Facebook, Twitter, and Linked In) have integrated measuring systems that marketers can use to monitor marketing performance. There is a wealth of diagnostic data available but utilising, combining and understanding the data that is available across the digital landscape is a distinct functional area (Hemann and Burbary, 20014).

Royle and Laing (2014) identify that determining the appropriate measurements to use and defining the evaluating mechanisms are desirable skills for marketing practitioners. Whilst there are a range of metrics that are available, there is still a lack of consensus over which one is the best approach to measure the effectiveness of digital marketing activities. For example, the ongoing debate on whether return on investment (ROI) should be used as a prevalent measure in channels such as social media, or if metrics (e.g. return on engagement, advocacy rates) are suitable for specific channels. Several practitioners argue that the absence of a best practice approach to digital metrics is problematic (Royle and Laing, 2014). Industry commentators repeatedly emphasise the challenge of developing accurate digital marketing metrics (Bughin et al., 2009; Fisher, 2009; Raab, 2011).

Exercise 11.1 Keeping up-to-date with digital metrics

Royle and Laing (2014) argue there is no consensus in the best metrics to be used to monitor and evaluate the effectiveness of digital marketing activities. In addition, with the rapid introduction of new tools and channels, new metrics can appear in a short period of time.

To keep on top of this, conduct an online search to find out what are the top digital marketing metrics from recent practitioners' publications. Make a list of those metrics that are similar, and those that are not. Try to explain why there are still different metrics recommended to be used in specific contexts.

■ Strategic integration functions

Strategic integration refers to the gradual combination and transformation of independent components of business organisations into cohesive and synergistic entities. In this context, it involves combining offline and digital approaches so that they complement each other to maximise the progress towards strategic objectives. Such a role involves having a working overview of digital technologies (without necessarily being a technical expert). In other words, marketers do not necessarily need to have the IT technical skills to code, but rather awareness and understanding of the different digital tools available and to be able to specify how those tools should be applied to achieve a strategic objective. For example, on-page SEO activity requires marketers to understand technical aspects such as alt descriptors and meta descriptors on web pages in order to be able to suggest keywords to maximise site traffic. However, the actual implementation of those would require the assistance of a webmaster with access to the back-end of the website.

■ Research functions

The ability to commission or undertake empirical research is a highly valued skill. Knowledge of how to utilise analytical management frameworks such as PESTEL analysis, and SWOT analysis is invaluable. The rapid growth of digital technology and capacities necessitates ongoing monitoring of macro-environment, especially in the legal and social aspect. For example, taking a legal perspective, many of the well-established platforms (e.g. Amazon, Google, Facebook, Uber) benefit from an unregulated environment, that allows them to grow (The Economist, 2016). A light touch regulatory stance was adopted partly in order to foster innovation across the technology sector, and also because many Internet platforms operate across national boundaries, making it harder to regulate.

However, as the market matures, regulation is being introduced to govern activity, and online companies need to be aware of the potential risks and opportunities associated with these changes. An example is the introduction of the EU General Data Protection Regulation (GDPR) which will be enforced from May 2018. GDPR was designed to harmonise data privacy laws across Europe, to protect and empower all EU citizens' data privacy and to reshape the way organisations across the region approach data privacy. International companies such as Google and Facebook have to comply with this regulation if they want to keep operating in the EU.

11

■   Strategic planning functions

Strategic planning is the ability to react to changes in the future (Royle and Laing, 2014). Good strategic planning will increase the level of ROI and foster innovation through the development of new products (Arend et al., 2017). There are three stages of strategic planning: futuregazing, foresighting and futureproofing (Royle and Laing 2014).

Futuregazing is speculation of what the future might bring, mainly based on current and past experiences. Futuregazing is an individual process. For example, a digital marketing manager notices that since the company has opened a Snapchat account there has been an increase of younger customers. During the planning process for next year's activities, the manager suggests to open an account in a new social media channel because of expectations that their target market (e.g. young customers) will use it, just as with Snapchat. This would be an example of a futuregazing approach.

The second stage, **foresighting**, is a more strategic approach to looking at the future in order to identify opportunities. Foresighting involves a team and evidence-based analysis of the global market and innovation. Unlike futuregazing, a foresighting approach would not assume customers would use a new platform, and would instead collect evidence that the target audience was systematically adopting new channels before suggesting introducing a new social media channel. Evidence would be critically discussed within organisational decision making units (i.e. a brand team) with the aim of winning consensus on the future action plans. Finally, **futureproofing** involves the adoption of formalised strategic approaches to minimise the risk of future developments and to maximise new opportunities. As illustrated in Figure 11.2, the further you move toward the right in this continuum, there is an increase in the strategic approach and formal mechanisms used to prepare for the future.

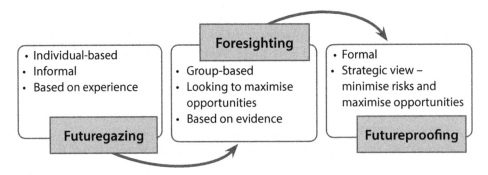

Figure 11.2: Strategic planning. Adapted from: Royle and Laing, 2014.

■ Relationship management functions

Several digital marketing roles require contact with customers. Being able to foster a collaborative and productive relationship through deep customer insight is a valued skill among employers in digital marketing. Relationship management can relate to company-to-company exchanges of business to business marketing (B2B) or the company-to-customer exchanges of customer marketing (B2C). In addition, growth in social media has resulted in posts that specialise in managing customer-to-customer relationships (C2C). For example, an online brand community manager will need to be aware of how certain posts or social signals (e.g. retweets or posts on Google+) influence rankings in search engines.

Relationship management functions require a more general ability to work in teams and to understand the needs and priorities of different stakeholders in a project. Supportive skills associated with good relationships with the customers are strong writing, communication, and presentation skills. Having a good relationship with customers and getting them to participate in the process of service delivery has many positive outcomes. Evidence suggests that this can generate positive word-of-mouth and more business referrals in the future (Maru File et al., 1992). Although many companies allocate training for developing the technical skills of their staff, little focus is given to relationship management initiatives (Maru File et al., 1992). From a student perspective, providing evidence of successful team work, and projects in collaboration with businesses, are good ways in which relationship management skills are developed and can be communicated to a potential employer.

■ Brand management functions

At the end of the continuum are brand management skills. It is important to note that digital marketing as a function does not operate independently to the brand and business (or at least it shouldn't). Thus digital marketing roles need to be thought of within the wider context of the business, and having a commercial awareness allows the marketer to devise and pursue initiatives that are commercially viable and beneficial for the organisation. One of the difficulties that marketers in digital roles face is that increasingly there is considerable overlap between functional skills areas. The following section discusses the implications of this trend in more detail.

11

The functional overlap in digital roles

Technology change affects all roles within an organisation, and for this reason almost every role has experienced a transformation in the tools that are used to perform that role and the activities that are associated with it (Quinn et al., 2016). Marketing roles have undergone a transformation resulting in an overlap in functions. For example, Figure 11.3 illustrates the overlap that exists between three key functions in an organisation: digital marketing, public relations, and customer service.

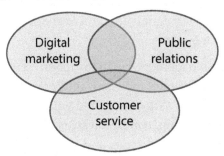

Figure 11.3: Functions overlap in digital roles. Adapted from Dalton (2010)

For example, a brand campaign placed within social media channels might originate within the digital marketing department as a result of insight gained from the customer service department. However, the originality of this campaign might require the skills of the public relations department to make sure that the dynamic of the campaign and message are aligned with the public image that the organisation is trying to portray. Working closely with the PR team can help anticipate any risks associated with the campaign, and define contingency plans if the campaign derails once it's live online. Finally, the positive and negative customer response to the campaign might require the skills of the customer service department. A close integration between the functions can deliver initiatives that improve the overall customer experience. For example, Starbucks developed the My Starbucks Idea initiative as a way to listen to customers. As a result customers submitted more than 210,000 unique ideas (Buffer Social, 2015).

There are numerous examples of social media campaigns that went wrong, and that illustrate the close collaboration that is needed between the digital marketing and PR teams. For example, Australian airline Qantas had a series of incidents that required this close collaboration. The airline ran into trouble in October of 2011, when more than 68,000 passenger were stranded worldwide due to a labour dispute with three company unions (Rourke,

2011). The Australian government intervened and held emergency court sessions. Qantas aircraft were back in the air after three days, with a ruling from the court to resolve the dispute within 21 days or face a binding arbitration decision (McGuirk, 2011).

With the matter with the unions still unresolved, Qantas launched on November 23rd of the same year another competition to win one of 50 pairs of Qantas first-class pyjamas and a luxury amenity kit (Miller, 2011). The company invited its followers to participate in this contest using the hashtag #QantasLuxury, yet the initiative backfired and the hashtag was used by Qantas' customers to express their frustrations with the airline. The initiative quickly became a means for consumers to complain about being stranded due to the labour dispute, as well as other unrelated complaints such as baggage loss and poor customer service. Within an hour of the hashtag being shared it reached over 500,000 users and resulted in 1.4 million impression (Social Media News, 2011).

Exercise 11.2

Place the responsibility for solving the reactions to the Qantas incidents within Figure 11.3. How easy it is to determine who should be the lead problem-solver in each instance?

Function skills and digital marketing management

Digital transformation extends beyond marketing departments. There is an overlap between offline and online functions, and this has created new roles and job titles within the marketing sector. In this section we will look at some examples of digital roles taken from job search database Indeed.com

■ Digital marketing manager

Digital marketing management is a broad role that requires being able to oversee, design and implement the digital marketing activities of an organisation. The more junior roles (i.e. assistant/officer) are usually in charge of the implementation, and sometimes involved in assisting the design of new strategies. More senior roles (director/head of digital marketing) require more experience, and usually focus on the strategic planning of a company's digital activities.

11

Figure 11.4 contains an example of an advertisement for a Digital Marketing manager role at a well-known skincare company based in London. Within the advertisement the different aspects of the digital marketing role discussed in this chapter are placed in bold type. The responsibilities section emphasises the ability to deliver the strategic integration of digital skills and knowledge in the marketing department. There is a clear focus on relationship management, as the role requires the person to be able to work "across brands and brand teams". The cores skills specify a mix of technical skills (e.g. SEM, eCRM), strategic integration (e.g. planning and implementation of campaigns), strategic planning (e.g. knowledge of new platforms, technologies and innovation in the digital landscape) as well as soft skills (e.g. communications skills and team player).

The role is responsible for working across brands to **implement the digital strategy** Travel Retail EMEA to target the travelling consumer. This will include **working alongside the brand teams** to manage digital media initiatives, including experiential digital campaigns in-store, media buys and pre-tail and social media campaigns to **increase consumer engagement**.

Core skills:

☐ A solid understanding of online marketing practices including **SEM, mobile marketing and e-CRM.**

☐ Expertise in **planning and managing digital media** including media buying, creative **planning** and **implementation**

☐ Knowledge of **social media** best practices and experience in planning and deploying multi-platform campaigns.

☐ A positive record in **planning and implementing Experiential Digital Campaigns in-store and online**.

☐ Possess a detailed **knowledge of new platform, technologies and innovation** within the digital landscape.

☐ Excellent **communication skills** and is a **team player**.

Average Salaries (Glassdoor, 2017)

Job title	National average	London
Digital Marketing Executive	£24,360	£35,375
Digital Marketing Manager	£35,525	£40,000
Senior Digital Marketing Manager	£54,000	£65,000
Digital Marketing Director	£98,333	£124,000

Figure 11.4: Digital marketing manager advertisement

■   SEO manager

SEO managers are specialists who possess good numerical skills and a very good grasp of analytical tools. Some knowledge on how websites are built and operate is also needed, but most of the heavy lifting in terms of coding is made by an IT specialist. However, SEO managers are required to communicate with other specialist departments such as IT, and to play an important role when working with other functional teams to make sure content is optimised to achieve the desired results in search engines.

Organic search is an important aspect of our **customer acquisition** and as part of our rapidly expanding team we are looking for a Head of SEO to join the marketing team. This role will cover **all the countries we operate in (currently UK and Germany, with more coming in 2018)**. This role will involve close **collaboration with our Editorial team**; advising them on best practices, analysing organic performance and highlighting opportunities for them. This role covers **working on YouTube SEO, for our large YouTube channel**. It will involve **working closely with our Product team (Product Managers, Designers, Analysts and Developers); advising the Product Director** on the best product SEO strategy, monitoring performance across the site and suggesting opportunities.

Core skills:

- ☐ **Setting and executing the SEO strategy** across all our domains
- ☐ **Analysing and reporting on SEO performance** to the C-level team
- ☐ Analysing and reporting on **YouTube SEO performance** to the C-level team
- ☐ **Working closely with the product team** and development team to advise and oversee site changes and technical SEO requirements
- ☐ **Link-building** planning creation and execution
- ☐ **Advising the Editorial team** on optimising content titles, descriptions etc.. for Google and YouTube
- ☐ **Competitor analysis**
- ☐ **Technical audits** & recommendations
- ☐ **Working closely with our experienced PPC team** to identify organic opportunities

Average Salaries (Glassdoor, 2017)

Job title	National average
SEO Executive	£24,180
SEO Manager	£30,450
Senior SEO Manager	£44,000
Head of SEO	Large corporations: £88K-£96K; SMEs: £29K-£31K

Figure 11.5: SEO manager advertisement

11

Figure 11.5 illustrates the responsibilities and job skills needed for a position as Head of SEO in an international company based in London. It is clear that the SEO management role goes beyond the technical aspects (website development) and the measuring, monitoring and evaluation of metrics. The position requires strong research skills in order to address the trends within the various international markets in which this company is operating. The ability to conduct competitor analysis was highlighted earlier in the discussion of the research function. Soft skills are also needed as the SEO manager will need work with other teams within the organisation, namely the product, PPC, and editorial team to integrate SEO best practices in each team.

■ Advertising manager

The advertising manager role requires using advertising platforms (e.g. Google, Bing, Yahoo) to plan and execute paid media campaigns. Frequently this role is focused upon search engine marketing, but some roles would also require to know how to run effective paid campaigns on display networks, and social networking sites (e.g. Facebook, Twitter, LinkedIn offer advertising opportunities), as well as the ability to execute re-marketing campaigns. Re-marketing campaigns show ads on the Internet to people that have previously visited a website or used a mobile app. Since several platforms offer their own certifications (e.g. Google AdWords), it is not uncommon for employers to seek specialists that have gained these qualifications.

Figure 11.6 contains an advertisement for a PPC manager role. A similar trend can be observed as with the Head of SEO in that a certain degree of specialisation is required, and in this case the technical aspect relates to creating and executing SEM campaigns in a wide range of platforms. For this particular position, a certificate is required plus a broader range of management skills, e.g. relationship management skills. In addition to technical skills, creative skills are required, e.g. copywriting experience. Finally the role also requires basic experience in terms of coding. In many cases, this is because it is the PPC manager who needs to retrieve the code from the platform running the ads (e.g. Google and Facebook have their own scripts). The retrieved code would be added to the website for analytics and to measure performance of the ads, as well as to inform remarketing. This is a good example of a demanding employer that is looking for a combination of technical, managerial, and creative capabilities to fit in one role.

PPC Manager

You'll be working with the Digital Marketing Team as the sole paid media expert, and will be responsible for **driving and executing the paid strategy across relevant channels**. We are looking for someone with a solid background in SEM who is willing to roll their sleeves up and do the 'doing' as well as the 'thinking'.

This is a **client-facing role** and you'll be **working with a broad range of clients**, looking to **build effective long-lasting relationships** to sustain and grow accounts.

Core skills:

☐ Experience in a paid search specialist position

☐ Proven PPC skills, **optimisation techniques and bid management**

☐ Must be **Google Certified**

☐ Ideally **experience with Bing & Yahoo** paid search

☐ Experienced in **display and remarketing**

☐ Experience of **paid social campaigns**

☐ Strong **Google Analytics and SEO knowledge**

☐ **Copywriting experience** is a must for writing ad-copy, client reports and landing pages

☐ Agency experience advantageous

☐ **Basic coding** knowledge (HTML, Javascript)

☐ Shopping / Ecommerce experience

Average Salaries (Glassdoor, 2017)

Job title	National average
PPC Executive	£22,330
PPC Manager	£34,762
Senior PPC Manager	£46,250
Head of PPC	Large corporations: £67K-£73K; SMEs: £38K-£41K

Figure 11.6: PPC manager advertisement

■ Community manager

11

Community management is a new role that appeared when brands moved to an active presence on social media. A community manager is responsible for developing and maintaining an online brand community. Sometimes, the community management is attached to a general digital marketing role and it is not uncommon to have a digital marketing manager or executive, who is also in charge of managing all forms of digital presence of the brand, including brand communities. However, in larger organisations, and in agencies, the role of the community manager usually exists as a standalone role. This blurred line in terms of responsibilities stems from an early unclear understanding of how online brand community management can be used to benefit brands (Ang, 2011). However, more recent evidence suggests that a cumulative usage of social media, including online brand communities, is positively associated to shopping activity (Zhang et al., 2017), and therefore we could expect that as more brands are aware of the positive impact of community management on their bottom line, the role will be outlined as a standalone one.

Community Manager

We are looking for an enthusiastic, personable, Community Manager to join our team in London. Our new Community Manager will **connect with our users and actively engage potential customers** to **create a community of advocates** for the **success of our products**. We need someone who can **gather information** from stakeholders and **nurture customers and prospects**. A Community Manager with strengths in **social media, forum moderation, email, telephone and in-person presentations;** someone who can **write and deliver engaging content**. A people-person and a fast-learner, this is a role for someone who loves bringing groups together and building relationships.

Core skills:

☐ A university degree in Communications, Business, Marketing or related field

☐ You have proven **work experience** as a Community Manager including:

☐ Experience launching community initiatives (e.g. **building an online forum**, launching an **ambassador or referral programme**, creating an event series or **managing an email newsletter**).

☐ Hands on **experience with social media management** for brands.

☐ **A love of people**. You're the life of the party and love connecting with people and understanding what makes them tick. You're the sort of person who knows everyone, or you're going to know them soon. You love when you can connect people who are able to benefit from your network

☐ The **technical knowledge**. You have hands-on **experience with online marketing and online community management tools**. Ideally you have exposure to **market research** techniques.

☐ You have outstanding **written and verbal skills**. You are detail-oriented, self-motivated and have the ability to prioritize and multitask.

Average Salaries (Glassdoor, 2017)

Community Manager: National average: £29,718

Figure 11.7: Community manager advertisement

Figure 11.7 contains a community manager advertisement. In this role there is an emphasis on creative skills, particularly being able to create relevant and engaging content to nurture and grow a brand community. There is some element of technical knowledge required, but this is focused upon being able to use the community management tools currently available, and specific channel features (e.g. scheduling posts, replying across platforms). We can conclude from the advertisement that an individual with a strategic planning and research skills would stand out from the crowd of applicants. It maybe that the organisation is seeking someone who is able to not only nurture the online brand community, but also that has the business awareness to make the connection to how this acts as part of a wider marketing strategy.

■ Social media manager

A social media manager is responsible for the social media presence of a brand. Many of the activities within the role are similar to those of the community manager, however, as illustrated in Figure 11.8, the scope of action of the social media manager tends to be broader and linked to continuing collaboration with other departments. Figure 11.8 also shows that the role involves budget management. We can also see how functional skills related to measurement, research, strategic planning, relationship management and brand management are strongly linked with the responsibilities outlined in this advert. One of the key responsibilities of the social media manager is to maintain a calendar of the content to be disseminated in the different social media channels of the brand. Due to the innovative nature of social media, where new platforms and social media management tools are constantly made available, the social media manager needs to be able to stay up to date with these changes, trying the new platforms and determining if they should be included as part of the communication channels of the brand. This is strongly related to the strategic planning skill discussed in the digital marketing model (Royle and Laing, 2014).

11

Social Media Manager

Your role, as Social Media Manager, will be to **maintain the brand's official social media handles** for platforms including Facebook, Twitter, Instagram and LinkedIn. You will be responsible for working with and **managing budgets** to **promote the brand's content** produced by the content strategists on behalf of their clients, and **liaising with editors** where appropriate to ensure maximum promotion for content. In addition, this role requires **innovative and appealing solutions** across social content types, and the successful candidate will frequently update the team on **latest trends** and their new ideas.

Responsibilities:

☐ To **maintain a calendar and plan across all social media platforms** including Facebook, Twitter, Instagram and LinkedIn as appropriate on a campaign-by-campaign basis for all live campaigns.

☐ Regular, clear and constructive **communication with key teams including Marketing, Editorial, Sales and PR** as well as the brand's team

☐ **Remaining ahead of social media trends**, updating the team in regular meetings

☐ **Working with the content strategists** at the brief and pitch stage to ensure social elements are fully integrated into the overall campaigns

☐ **Working with the project managers** at campaign stage to ensure social promotion and distribution is effectively coordinated with our distribution outlets, and that campaigns are achieving their desired efficacy

☐ **Using social analytics tools** to report on the effectiveness of campaigns and constantly developing better effectiveness for future campaigns

☐ Collating **competitor activity** on social media for comparison analysis

☐ **Managing asset creation** for content promotion (acquiring relevant images, selecting appropriate and engaging wording and producing short video gifs etc.)

☐ **Supporting regional digital producers** in any social campaign activity they are undertaking

☐ Proactively **supporting the Digital Content team** with admin and other tasks

Average Salaries (Glassdoor, 2017)

Job title	National average
Social Media Executive	£22,000
Social Media Manager	£28,500
Senior Social Media Manager	Large corporations: £47K-£68K; SMEs: £39K-£42K
Head of Social Media	Large corporations: £91K-£98K; SMEs: £48K-£52K

Figure 11.8: Social media manager advertisement

Summary

This chapter provides an overview of the digital marketing skills that are required in order to become a digital marketing practitioner. As illustrated by the examples of digital marketing roles in this chapter, the skills go beyond the scope of digital marketing related knowledge and include both technical and soft skills. Digital marketers are expected to develop a wider managerial skill set in order to face the current challenges and to anticipate future threats and opportunities in the future.

Exemplar paper

Quinn, L., Dibb, S., Simkin, L., Canhoto, A. and Analogbei, M. (2016), Troubled waters: the transformation of marketing in a digital world, *European Journal of Marketing*, **50**(12), 2103-2133.

Examines the influences upon target-market selection and critically discusses the implications for digital marketing jobs and the role of the marketing department within the organisation. They find that the rapidly changing digital landscape has resulted in several significant challenges and particularly highlight the marketing skills gap.

■ Additional reading

Wymbs, C., 2011. Digital marketing: The time for a new "academic major" has arrived. *Journal of Marketing Education*, **33**(1), 93-106.

Staton, M.G., 2016. Improving student job placement and assessment through the use of digital marketing certification programs. *Marketing Education Review*, **26**(1), 20-24.

References

Ang, L., (2011), Community relationship management and social media, *Journal of Database Marketing and Customer Strategy Management*, **18**(1), 31-38.

Arend, R. J., Zhao, Y. L., Song, M. and Im, S. (2017), Strategic planning as a complex and enabling managerial tool, *Strategic Management Journal*, **38**(8), 1741–1752.

Buffer Social (2015), 14 amazing social media customer service examples (and what you can learn from them), https://blog.bufferapp.com/social-media-customer-service [Accessed 10 December 2017].

11

Bughin,J., Shenkan,A.G. and Singer, M. (2009), How poor metrics undermine digital marketing, *The McKinsey Quarterly*, 3, 1-5.

Cappelli, P. (2012), *Why Good People Can't Get Jobs: The Skills Gap and What Companies Can Do About It.* Wharton Digital Press.

Dalton, B. (2010), Venn does social CRM become business as usual?, http://www.barrydalton.com/2010/04/13/venn-does-social-crm-become-business-as-usual/ [Accessed 10 December 2017].

Department for Business and Innovation Skills (2016), Digital Skills for the UK economy. http://www.legco.gov.hk/general/english/library/stay_informed_overseas_policy_updates/digital_skills.pdf [Accessed 10 December 2017].

Digital Hub (2008), The Digital Hub Enterprise Survey 2007, http://uploads.thedigitalhub.com/EnterpriseSurvey/DigitalHubEnterpriseSurvey2007.pdf [Accessed 09 February 2012].

Fisher, T. (2009), ROI in social media: a look at the arguments, *Journal of Database Marketing and Customer Strategy Management*, **16**(3), 189-195.

Glassdoor (2017), Search salaries and compensation, https://www.glassdoor.co.uk/Salaries/index.htm [Accessed 10 December 2017].

Hemann, C. and Burbary, K. (2014), *Digital Marketing Analytics: Making Sense of Customer Data in a Digital World*, Indianapolis: Que Publishing.

House of Commons (2016), Digital Skills Crisis, https://publications.parliament.uk/pa/cm201617/cmselect/cmsctech/270/270.pdf [Accessed 10 December 2017].

Maru File, K., Judd, B. B. and Prince, R. A. (1992), Interactive marketing: the influence of participation on positive word-of-mouth and referrals, *Journal of Services Marketing*, **6**(4), 5-14.

McGuirk, R., (2011), Qantas Airways grounds global fleet due to strikes, http://archive.boston.com/business/articles/2011/10/29/qantas_airways_grounds_its_entire_fleet/ [Accessed 10 December 2017].

Miller, D. (2011), Qantas Twitter campaign takes nosedive, http://www.abc.net.au/news/2011-11-22/qantas-twitter-hashtag-backfires/3686940 [Accessed 10 December 2017].

Peterson, E.T. (2004) *Web Analytics Demystified: A Marketer's Guide to Understanding How Your Website Affects Your Business*, Ingram.

Quinn, L., Dibb, S., Simkin, L., Canhoto, A. and Analogbei, M. (2016), Troubled waters: the transformation of marketing in a digital world, *European Journal of Marketing*, **50**(12), 2103-2133.

Raab, D.M. (2011), New metrics for social media, *Information Management*, **21**(6), 24-25.

Rourke, A. (2011), Qantas grounds entire worldwide fleet, https://www.theguardian.com/business/2011/oct/29/qantas-grounds-fleet-industrial-action [Accessed 10 December 2017].

Royle, J. and Laing, A. (2014), The digital marketing skills gap: developing a digital marketer model for the communication industries, *International Journal of Information Management*, 34(2), 65-73.

Schlee, R. and Harich, P.K.R. (2010), Knowledge and skill requirements for marketing jobs in the 21st century, *Journal of Marketing Education*, **32**(3), 341-352.

Social Media News (2011), The #QantasLuxury Fail, https://www.socialmedianews.com.au/the-qantasluxury-fail/ [Accessed 10 December 2017].

The Economist, (2016), Online platforms: nostrums for rostrums. https://www.economist.com/news/leaders/21699447-growing-power-online-platforms-worrisome-regulators-should-tread [Accessed 10 December 2017].

Valos, M.J. , Ewing, M.T. and Powell, I.H. (2010), Practitioner prognostications on the future of online marketing, *Journal of Marketing Management*, **26** (3-4), 361-376.

Zhang, Y., Trusov, M., Stephen, A. T. and Jamal, Z. (2017), Online shopping and social media: friends or foes? *Journal of Marketing*, **81**(6), 24-41.

12 Developing an Online Profile

Developing an online profile is a growing trend (Chen, 2013). The concept of personal branding suggests that, like brands, individuals can strategically select and highlight those attributes that will advance them towards their goals (Peters, 1997). Individuals should identify their unique value proposition and then translate this into a compelling personal brand statement (Chen, 2013). Personal branding can differentiate an individual within a competitive job market. The availability, low-costs and ease of use of a range of online tools enables individuals to effectively communicate across a range of digital channels. In the UK, a professional social networking site (PSNS) is LinkedIn. Other countries might have their equivalent site (e.g. Viadeo in France, Xing in Germany), and sometimes, depending on the profession there are niche PSNS as it is the case of Behance for those in creative industries. Weblogs or blogs are form of personal, easy-to-manage web site with content presented in reverse chronological order (Schiano et al., 2004). There are several free platforms that allow users to create a blog easily (e.g. WordPress, blogger). For students seeking to become digital marketers such tools offer a way to demonstrate digital skills and gain valuable experience. In addition there is enjoyment in engaging with the online audience and joining a growing community of online communicators.

Blogging

Blogs can be published independently or as part of a job role within an organisation. Blog content creators are called bloggers, and tend to be younger, better educated, more likely to be urban dwellers, and avid online shoppers

(Guadagno et al., 2008). Reading blogs is a popular online activity among certain segments of Internet users. Statistics provided by Wordpress, a blog host, indicate that over 409 million people read 23.7 billion blog pages in their platforms each month (Wordpress, 2017).

A brand may decide to create a blog to increase its ranking in search engine results pages, since blog content will be scored highly for recency and authenticity by the search engine algorithm (HubSpot, 2017). Due to the popularity and the amount of views and traffic that blogs generate world-wide, blogs are an important media channel for marketers. Alghawi et al. (2014) examine audience response to four types of company blogs written by their CEOs: expert, friend, diary and textbook. They find that consumers prefer CEOs who adopt the expert blogging style. Blogs are a central part of a content marketing strategy, and in fact a survey conducted by HubSpot (2017) found that 53% of marketers are using blogs to disseminate content. Blogging, although traditionally done in the form of long pieces of text, has evolved into other types of media. Blogging can be image-based, as in the case or Instagram or Pinterest. There is also microblogging, which involves shorter posts (e.g. Twitter only allows 280 characters).

■   Blog revenue models

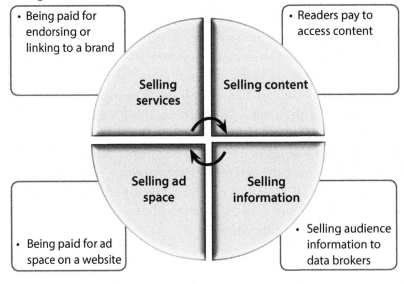

Figure 12.1: Four online revenue models

A revenue model describes the process by which money can be earned from the blog. Choosing a business model will help with decisions regarding how much resource to invest in content generation and promotion of the blog.

For example, if the blog is expected to generate the equivalent of a salary in terms of advertising revenue, then considerable time and effort will be needed to generate content to attract and retain a sizable and loyal target audience. It may be wise to pay to be listed highly in search engine results in order to grow this audience. There are four main revenue models: selling content, selling information, selling advertisement space and selling services (Figure 12.1)

Selling content

Selling content online generates revenue. Pricing methods in digital environments allow for greater flexibility, either by paying a subscription (e.g. a monthly Spotify subscription to have access to an extensive number of artists) or through licensing (e.g. Microsoft Office 365). Selling content online can be challenging, as users are used to accessing content for free (Lambrecht and Misra, 2016). A survey conducted in 2002 by Pew Research Centre asked if users would be willing to pay for access to a site that was previously free, with only 12% of interviewees saying they would, while 50% would try to find a free alternative, and 36% would simply stop accessing the online information or service altogether (Crosbie, 2002). Since then, attitudes towards online purchasing have become more positive, with a more recent survey finding that nearly two-thirds of Internet users (65%) have paid to download or access some kind of content from the Internet (Pew Research Center, 2010).

Some industries have been more affected by resistance to payment than others. For example, media companies are facing increasing competition from other sources that create content for free (e.g. Huffington Post for news, YouTube for videos and music). One selling option that has been adopted by established media companies is to offer a combination of free and subscription-based content, a hybrid business model. Typically older or more general or limited content is free, while the most valuable content or the full article is available only to paying members (Wang et al., 2005). Examples of the hybrid revenue model have been adopted by established names such as *The New York Times* and *The Economist*.

Selling information

Selling information is sending information about consumers' identities, habits, needs and online behaviours to specialist companies who use this data for activities such as programmatic advertising. Programmatic advertising is a digital advertising innovation where advertisements are placed before the user based on their previous online activity. Audience data is sold to third

12

parties so that they can develop and resell services to other companies. Data Management Platforms like Adobe Audience Manager allow marketers to store and house information (usually in the form of cookie IDs) and to generate audience segments to target specific users with online ads (Elmeleegy et al., 2013).

Selling information is a revenue stream for blogs or channels with significant audience numbers. For example, Google and Facebook, both leaders in their field as a search engine and social networking site, have developed alternative platforms that use data that they collect from their users. Ad serving solutions such a DoubleClick (owned by Google) and Atlas (owned by Facebook) are tools that run programmatic advertising campaigns and develop advanced attribution models. There are significant costs benefits that makes such data valuable. For example, programmatic advertising automates what previously was a skilled and time-consuming planning process. The speed of programmatic advertising enables real-time bidding exchanges (RTB) and demand-side platforms (DSP) (Elmeleegy et al., 2013) resulting in a process that takes less than 250 milliseconds and which is optimised to bring in the best results.

Selling advertising space

Selling advertising space is a common online revenue model. Websites like Google and Facebook obtain the majority of their income by selling advertising to businesses. According to Statista (2016), Google's revenue from selling advertising was worth US$79.3 billion in 2016. During the same year, Facebook's ad revenue was US$26.9 billion (Statista, 2016). Advertisements can be placed in content directly by the blog owner, but more commonly are placed by an advertisement broker. The most well-known broker of advertising is Google Ad Sense. The blogger can decide the spaces to allocate space to advertisers, and can also prevent certain advertisers from appearing. Google pays the blogger a percentage of what the advertisers paid. Bloggers are usually able to collect their money once they have reached an earning threshold of £60 (Google, 2017). The advantage of using a broker is that the blogger can focus on generating content and bringing traffic to the site, rather than spending time finding advertisers.

However, for blogs with low levels of traffic, selling advertising space directly would get higher fees. Twitter is a tool that is used by bloggers to attract brands who want to advertise. (Search the hashtag #PRrequest and you will find thousands of bloggers looking to connect with companies for advertising and sponsored posts.) There also specialised websites that connect bloggers with companies (e.g. http://beafreelanceblogger.com or http://www.hirebloggers.co.uk/ among others).

There are three main online advertisement revenue models: 1) cost per thousand impressions (CPM); 2) cost per click (CPC); and 3) cost per action (CPA). For display ads (e.g. banners on a website, or on your Facebook newsfeed), the most common payment method is the cost per thousand impressions, i.e. every 1,000 times that an ad is displayed on a user's screen. Generally CPM rates are the lowest since the brand does not know where or when the ads will be placed and rates rise the closer the links between the advert and the content. (Chaffey and Smith, 2013)

Selling services

Selling services is also referred to affiliate marketing. Affiliate marketing is activity that generates revenue through promoting products or services resulting in commission. An affiliate is a website owner (e.g. a blogger, or a website aggregator like Skyscanner) who promotes links that once clicked upon by the user directs them to the brand. If a sale is made, then the affiliate will receive a commission. Payment is either a set fee or a proportion of the profit from each sale that can be attributed to the blog content (also known as Cost per Acquisition or CPA). Brands seek to become linked to blogs because consumers are more prone to trust and believe in the opinion of a blogger as being independent to the brand (Sepp et al., 2011).

Some bloggers allow for sponsorships, usually for a fixed price for a period time, of specific sections on their blog. For example, many vloggers sell space within their YouTube channels to brands. Sponsorship arrangements can also be made as part of an exchange agreement, where neither of the parties pays anything, but offer space on each other websites for mutual benefit and promotion.

Unlike advertising space, the company is not paying for appearing but only if a sale or conversion is achieved. In terms of the legal aspects of selling content in a blog, the Advertising Standards Agency (ASA), the regulator of advertising in the UK, indicates in their advertising code that any form of advertisement must be clearly identifiable as such (Advertising Standards Agency, 2016). Therefore bloggers need to clearly identify sponsored content.

Commonly a blogger will sell sponsored content to brands. In practice, a brand would pay a blogger to write an unbiased review (a form of electronic word-of-mouth) and to publish it in the blog. Charges for sponsored post can

12

range from £30 per post at the lower end of the scale to thousands of pounds in blogs with high levels of traffic and readership (i.e. hundreds of thousands and more).

Attribution models

An attribution model can be defined as "the set of rules that determine how credit for sales and conversions is assigned to touchpoints in conversion paths" (Google, 2017b). From a blogger's perspective it is important to understand attribution when making a contract with a brand. From a brand's perspective it is important to understand attribution in order to evaluate the return of online advertising expenditure (Ghose and Todri-Adamopoulos, 2015). Metrics (i.e. click through rate and cost per acquisition) can suffer from a fundamental problem of attribution, when they give credit to the last click and ignore the impact of other marketing activities on sales (Google, 2017b). To solve this problem Google Analytics allows marketers to select the attribution model that they prefer to use. Table 12.1 illustrates a range of attribution models that are on platform, which are as follows:

- **Last interaction** attribution model takes into account the last touch point before a conversion, which might be the website url. Therefore the last interaction attribution model ignores any other paid or unpaid communications activities.

- The **last non-direct click** attribution model attributes the sale to the last channel from which the customer clicked through before converting. Under this mode, all direct traffic is ignored, and 100% of the credit for the sale goes to the last channel that the customer clicked through from before converting.

- The **linear** attribution model gives each touchpoint in the conversion path equal credit for the sale and divides sales revenue equally.

- The **time decay** attribution model gives the most credit to the touchpoints closest in time to the sale or conversion.

- The **position based** attribution model, 40% credit is assigned to each the first and last interaction, and the remaining 20% credit is distributed evenly to the middle interactions.

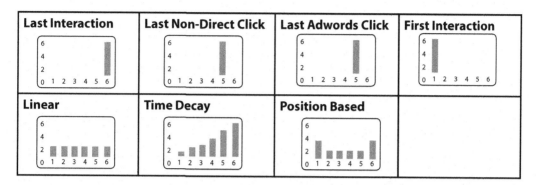

Table 12.1: Attribution models in Google Analytics. Adapted from (Google, 2017)

Exercise 12.1: Finding sponsors for your blog

Imagine that you own a blog about the student lifestyle. Visit Twitter search (https://twitter.com/search-home) to look for the latest PR opportunities using the hashtag #PRrequest. Make a list of potential brands that could sponsor a post that you have written, or a future post.

If you have a Twitter account, contact one of the brands, and find out what kind of elements they are interested in when it comes to bloggers they want to collaborate with. Are they looking for high traffic blogs? Or do they prefer niche and specialised ones?

■   Building a successful blog

A successful blog has the potential to deliver a strong online revenue stream. There are four factors that determine blog success: post frequency, range of media usage, search engine optimisation (SEO) and level of traffic (Rizky and Pardamean 2016). These factors combine as shown in Figure 12.2.

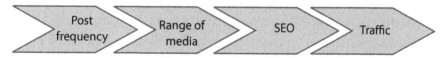

Figure 12.2: Blog success factors

Post frequency and relates to time between blog posts, e.g. a week, a day, two weeks. Bloggers may decide to blog on a weekly basis, usually on the same day of the week. Regular posting keeps the audience used to a specific day on which to expect new content. A good level of post frequency makes a blog attractive to brands who are looking to sponsor or pay money for advertising. (Fisher, 2009).

12

Media usage relates to the use of other forms of media (e.g. video, pictures) in addition to text. Certain blogs are mainly picture driven (e.g. Tumblr features mainly pictures and users can add short texts and hashtags to it) while other support large amount of text, pictures, and videos (e.g. blogger, WordPress).

SEO activities are those that the blogger is implementing to rank higher in search engine result pages (SERPs). SEO seeks to boost the ranking of a blog without making payment through ensuring that the content is rated highly by the search engine algorithm. Tactics will focus upon on-page optimisation of content to ensure that it connects with popular search terms and also using off-page optimisation by building links to other highly ranked sites. For example, a blogger writing about films might ensure that the names of popular actors and directors feature in the blog regularly and also that the blog links to the websites of the local cinema.

The preceding factors should increase the blog traffic which will determine the amount of online revenue that a blog can generate. From all the factors described in this section, Rizky and Pardamean's (2016) findings suggest that the implementation of Search Engine Optimisation strategies is the one that more positively impacts blog revenue. If we consider that there are over a billion websites currently online (Internet Live Stats, 2017), making sure that a blog can be found by those looking for its content could indeed be the source of more quality traffic and therefore potentially more revenue.

Developing a LinkedIn presence

Evidence suggests that HR practitioners conduct checks online of shortlisted candidates before meeting with them (Career Builder, 2016). So the likelihood that the HR manager finds your online presence is rather high. An advantage of having a presence in channels such as LinkedIn is that these popular sites are usually well ranked in SERPs. Therefore, this allows some level of control of what potential employers will see when they search for you (statistics show that not many people go to the second page in Google). The process of building a LinkedIn presence is set out in Figure 12.3.

Figure 12.3: The process of building an LinkedIn Presence

■ Research the market

The first stage is to determine the job roles for which you would like to be considered. Research can be a mixture of online and offline techniques. One option is to visit the website of your University Careers service and see the roles which other graduates with your degree background have gained. You can also search online for organisations that match graduates to jobs (for example a leading website in the UK is www.prospect.ac.uk). Once a role has been identified, the next stage is to analyse the information available by conducting a content analysis that captures the words and phrases used to define the roles. One option will be to search LinkedIn for people in those roles and make a note of how they position themselves and the words that they use to describe themselves.

It is important to research the organisational culture of the employers in the sector. This will help you to determine the visual tone and the type of language you will use in your profile. For example, some tech companies are more relaxed in terms of business clothing (i.e see how Mark Zuckerberg dresses) but are very sensitive to accuracy in expression (no typos allowed in computer code).

12

Exercise 12.2 Researching the Market

Identify the roles for which you would like to apply. Search online to identify a list of the frequently mentioned knowledge, skills and experience required for these roles.

Use the list as a score sheet for your own personal brand. Grade each keyword as either being 3= good experience, 2= some experience or 1= no experience. Think about all sources of experience both paid work internships, volunteering or academic projects.

■ Define communication objectives

This research enables the identification of areas of strength and weakness. Where possible identify how future training or job roles might close some of the gaps in skills, knowledge and experience. It is important identify how to communicate clearly the areas of strength (those which score 3 and 2). It is best not to dwell on the gaps by remembering that a job candidate rarely ticks all the boxes on a job description. Individuals will be at different ability levels for any role being advertised and sometimes a junior role might be offered to those who clearly show potential but are not quite at the level of the advertised post. Transferrable skills are those which an individual can use in a range of employment settings; examples would be communication, research, leadership, team working and project management abilities. Examples of communication objectives are listed in Table 12.2

Table 12.2: Example communication objectives for a digital marketing manager role.

Good experience	Communication skills Team player New platform knowledge SEM experience Knowledge of customer engagement theory
Some experience	Offline experiential campaigns E-CRM Social media best practice
No experience	Online experiential campaigns Mobile marketing
Communication objectives	Highlight transferrable skills, identify innovation and evaluation skills, emphasise ability to embrace new areas (mobile/experiential marketing).

■ Designing positioning information

Positioning information includes both visual and text that gives a succinct overview of the individual. When a brand transfers to social media, key elements such as the brand logo, the brand tone-of-voice and the brand proposition are maintained. Similarly in personal branding, your name, your photograph, your professional tone, your current experience and skill set need to be selected to meet the communication objectives.

Your name should be the name by which you wish to be known in the workplace by your boss, i.e. no nicknames. It is helpful if you use the name which is consistent with your identity documentation. Your profile photograph is important – LinkedIn profiles with photographs get more views (up to 14 times more!) than profiles without a picture (Abbot, 2014). A good photograph is up to date and accurately reflects your appearance. The profile photograph should communicate your professional tone (formal vs informal). For example you may be communicating that you are a confident business communicator or you may which to demonstrate that you have creative skills. Some universities provide professional photographers for CVs in careers fair, which provides a great opportunity to acquire a professional photograph. Whilst it may be possible to call on the expertise of friends or family you might also consider paying for a professional photograph. Freelance websites like bark.com can make this process affordable.

In the photograph, it is important that your face is clearly presented. Abbot (2014) recommends that your face should take up about 60% of the frame and features the top of your shoulders to just above the top of your head, it should be only you in the frame (no friends, partners or pets). The expression on your face should be a friendly smile so the person viewing the photograph can imagine having an informative conversation with you. Clothing should be that which you would wear to work, and generally solid colours photograph better than patterns. Finally it is important to choose a background that is not distracting and which is neutral, i.e. not in a bar unless you want to work in the brewing industry, and not at the beach unless you are applying to travel agents.

The headline is the third element that is always displayed in your LinkedIn profile. The headline appears under your name and relates to your current role. Graduates need to formulate a headline that not only accurately gives their current status but also differentiates them from the crowd. It is important to indicate that whilst you are a student in X degree you also have a range of

12

appropriate knowledge and abilities to position you favourably in relation to your target roles. You should research how your university markets your degree and also look at how other students are presenting themselves. Most importantly as soon as you get a full-time role it is important to update your LinkedIn profile so it no longer states you are a student.

Start to formulate your headline by identifying the keywords related to the jobs which you are targeting (include here keywords relating to transferable skills). Here are a series of questions which you can use to help shape your headline, the results of which are in Table 12.3.

- What is the job title I am aiming for? (e.g. digital marketing executive)
- Who do you want to employ you? (e.g. advertising agencies).
- What can you bring to this role? Use verbs and action words. Mapping out the activities required in each role can also help you building this section (e.g.team-player)

Table 12.3: Comparison of headline content

Before	After
Student in Business Management (currently looking for new opportunities in digital marketing)	Recently-qualified digital marketing executive seeking agency experience. Good knowledge of customer engagement, SEM and new innovations, experienced team player with excellent communication skills.

It is important to remember that your headline statement will be used by search engines, so try to include important search terms that a recruitment agency might use to locate potential job applicants (based on this consideration you might like to amend the headline content on the right to read "recently-graduated").

By default LinkedIn draws on your current role to compile your headline statement. This is helpful if your current role is part of your career progression. When you complete your profile for the first time, LinkedIn uses your current role as your default headline. However you may wish to change this if you are in a transitional role, e.g. working in retail whilst you complete your degree. Signalling that you're a recent graduate instead of just a student can help recruiters know that you're ready to start on a new permanent position. If you're doing internships, you can also put that role in this section.

The summary statement should communicate your biggest achievements and try to hook the reader into your story. It is common to see empty summary statements on individual profiles, which is a wasted opportunity.

Taking advantage of this space enables you to clearly communicate the promise of your personal brand to the reader. You can add media files in this section, which would be a good way of indicating your skills at using different digital media. The summary statement should be considered in the same way as a cover letter or candidate statement that accompanies a CV. It will provide evidence of your knowledge and commitment to the post which you are seeking and highlight the most relevant achievements and strengths that make you a good candidate for the role.

■ Selecting evidence

LinkedIn requires you to provide an employment history. This section provides evidence to support the claims you made in the preceding sections. For example in Table 12.3 the claims were recent qualifications, good knowledge of customer engagement, SEM and new innovation and team player experienced with excellent communication skills. It is important to remember that it is not vital to list every single job and role that are relevant to your career path. This becomes easier over time, but at the start of a career completing this section can be challenging. There are two strategies, depending on whether you are a recent graduate with limited industry experience or a graduate with some industry experience (Table 12.4). Where possible include graphics, videos and other multi-media.

Table 12.4: Two employment history strategies.

Some industry exposure (internships)	Limited industry exposure
List job titles but describe skills that you gained in the job and how you used them in your responsibilities.	Focus upon transferrable skills and case study knowledge of particular sectors gained from coursework.
Give an indication of the scale and scope of the business and your contribution in terms of problem solving or innovation.	Provide evidence of your work in pdfs and other formats, e.g. slides of presentations. E-portfolios illustrate your digital skills.
Focus on how internships build upon each other if you have done more than one.	Highlight any outstanding achievements, e.g. gaining an A grade, being involved in a student society or contributing to university initiatives such as open days.
	There is a special section on LinkedIn where you can list your accomplishment and add links to other media.

12

The education section also provides important evidence to support your claims and you can apply content marketing strategies to differentiate your profile from other candidates. Search LinkedIn to see how other recent graduates use this section to demonstrate the range of skills and knowledge that they have. A good approach is to move beyond lists of qualifications and courses that have been taken and focus more upon communicating the content of those courses. One technique to communicate your knowledge is to draw on the aims and objectives of each course that are relevant to the positions for which you are applying. Attach multi-media files of your work and focus also upon the managerial skills that you gained, such as researching both online and offline sources, analysing data, written and verbal presentation skills and working within a team under pressure. Evidence of broader managerial skills is valued by employers. Therefore, it is important to signal clearly how your university courses prepared you for professional practice.

Networking

LinkedIn is a social network that can help you maintain and develop connections that will help you progress your career. Your network can act as a powerful indicator of your key strengths. Word of mouth information is very influential. Social influence principles shape online behaviour, with reviews affecting the perception of consumers in the products and services that they purchase. If we translate these principles into the context of LinkedIn, the featured skills and endorsement section will signal to employers the areas where others recognise your abilities and are prepared to publicly give you a good review. Consider asking for endorsements not only from previous employers but also fellow students who were in group teams with you as well as your lecturers. According to social impact theory, the strength (who's endorsing you), immediacy (when they did it) and number of endorsements can positively affect the perception of your profile to those reading it. LinkedIn has a facility which you can use to invite an endorsement statement or you can select skills to appear which others can click on to provide endorsement. Make sure you select these skill sets based on your communication objectives. Recommendation content is important, so make sure that you ask people that are willing to spend enough time writing a meaningful recommendation instead of just a couple of lines, or alternatively provide a prepared suggested statement and invite them to edit and then post.

It is also possible to enlarge your network by following companies and special interest groups. These follows will appear in the interest section on

LinkedIn. There are a number of online communities related to specific professions and different topics of interest. It is possible to locate such groups by using the search feature at the top of the page and then filtering based on Groups. There are two important things to consider. First, the groups you belong to are displayed on your profile under the interest section and serve as a signal to HR managers of the topics that you are actively looking for and with which you are engaging. Second, engaging in a positive way with the wider community of practitioners can help you not only to make connections with possible future colleagues, but also to establish your voice in the field and join the dialogue around your practice. Thus this may open up future job opportunities.

Keeping your digital knowledge up-to-date

Digital marketing is a rapidly changing field of practice and it is important to continue learning about new developments. New platforms are launched continuously throughout the year, and while many of them will fail, some others will gain traction with consumers. Similarly, tools that are commonly used by digital marketers such as Google Adwords or Twitter regularly change features. Keeping up-to-date with all these changes is critical to a successful career in digital marketing and forms part of continuing professional development (CPD).

CPD is a process of tracking and documenting the skills, knowledge and experience that are gained both formally through additional qualifications and informally through attending events and networking with others. Evidence of CPD is highly regarded by future employers and also can be used to make a case for promotion. Research shows that individuals with professional qualifications and memberships might earn up to an additional £152,000 throughout their career (IDM, 2017). There are several organisations that provide opportunities for CPD and a selection of these are identified in Figure 12.4.

Please note that this list is not exhaustive and there may be a range of other organisations available. In addition to these organisations there are also a range of Massive Open Online Courses (also known as MOOCs) in digital marketing. MOOCs allow students and practitioners from around the world to have access in a convenient and affordable way to knowledge from experts in different locations. Some well-known MOOCs offering digital marketing

12

related content are Coursera, and Lynda, which incidentally was purchased by LinkedIn in 2015 and it is now offered for free if you subscribe with them.

Figure 12.4: Opportunities to update knowledge

The Chartered Institute of Marketing, The Marketing Society and the Institute of Direct and Digital Marketing offer marketing qualifications, marketing courses, regional events and webinars. The IDM has a specific focus that is closely aligned with digital marketing. Membership of these organisations requires a fee but includes access to online resources including specialist publications. Google provides several training sites for professionals and students. Many of them provide certification upon completion for a small fee and are recognised by employers. Some roles (PPC specialists) usually require a Google Adwords certification. The Google Partner Programme provides training for agency staff and consultants, leading to certifications in Google Adwords, Google Analytics, Mobile Site, and Digital Sales. The Google Digital Garage is a learning environment that is geared to students and provides a comprehensive view of digital techniques, including social media and e-mail marketing. Finally, The HubSpot Academy is a CRM platform used by many organisations which has developed a series of certifications in a wide range of topics including inbound marketing, content marketing, and e-mail marketing. Many of the certificates are either free or are available after purchase of HubSpot products.

Summary

Developing an online profile provides the individual with the opportunity to demonstrate digital skills and promote a personal brand message. Both blogs and LinkedIn require the strategic selection of content in order to develop a compelling narrative and connect with the audience. An awareness of online revenue models enables the digital marketer to select the correct approach for their blog and being mindful of the blog success factors will help in building traffic. LinkedIn caters directly to the need for professional self-promotion and by asking critical questions related to self-presentation the individual can maximise the impact and efficacy of personal information. Finally, it is important to be aware of the various organisations that provide a route to maintain and enhancing digital marketing knowledge.

Exemplar paper

Rangarajan, D., Gelb, B. D., and Vandaveer, A., (2017), Strategic Personal Branding—and How it Pays Off, Business Horizons, 60(5), 657-666.

Based on a series of interviews with US and European sales-based professionals the authors offer a process of strategic personal branding. They find that it is important to base the personal brand on individual personal values and competencies and be open to updating and changing these criteria to reflect career progression.

■ Additional reading

Vallas, S.P. and Cummins, E.R., (2015), Personal Branding and Identity Norms in the Popular Business Press: Enterprise Culture in an Age of Precarity, Organization Studies, 36(3), 293-319.

Van Dijck, J., (2013), You Have One Identity': Performing the Self on Facebook and LinkedIn, Media, Culture and Society, 35(2), 199-215.

12

References

Abbot, L. (2014), 5 tips for picking the right LinkedIn profile picture, https://business.linkedin.com/talent-solutions/blog/2014/12/5-tips-for-picking-the-right-linkedin-profile-picture. [Accessed 1 November 2016].

Advertising Standards Agency (2016), Recognising ads: Blogs and Vlogs, http://www.asa.org.uk/advice-online/recognising-ads-blogs-and-vlogs.html, [Accessed on 21 June 2017].

Alghawi, I. A., Yan, J. and Wei, C. (2014), Professional or interactive: CEOs' image strategies in the microblogging context, *Computers in Human Behavior*, **41**, 184-189.

Career Builder (2016), Number of employers using social media to screen candidates has increased 500 percent over the last decade, https://www.careerbuilder.co.uk/share/aboutus/pressreleasesdetail.aspx?sd=4%2F28%2F2016&id=pr945&ed=12%2F31%2F2016 [Accessed 11 December 2017].

Chaffey, D. and Smith, P.R. (2013), *eMarketing eXcellence: Planning and Optimizing your Digital Marketing*, Routledge, Abingdon.

Chen, C.P. (2013), Exploring personal branding on YouTube, *Journal of Internet Commerce*, **12**(4), 332-347.

Crosbie, V. (2002), Online Content: The 2002 Report, https://www.clickz.com/online-content-the-2002-report/76405/ [Accessed 11 December 2017].

Elmeleegy, H., Li, Y., Qi, Y., Wilmot, P., Wu, M., Kolay, S. and Dasdan, A. (2013), Overview of turn data management platform for digital advertising, *Proceedings of the VLDB Endowment*, **6**(11), 1138-1149.

Fisher, T. (2009), ROI in social media: a look at the arguments, *Journal of Database Marketing and Customer Strategy Management*, **16**(3), 189–195.

Ghose, A. and Todri-Adamopoulos, V. (2015). Towards digital attribution: measuring the impact of display advertising on online search behavior, *MIS Quarterly*, **40**(4), 889-910.

Google. (2017). Payment Thresholds - AdSense Help, https://support.google.com/adsense/answer/1709871 [Accessed on 6 July 2017].

Google, (2017b), Attribution modelling overview, https://support.google.com/analytics/answer/1662518?hl=en [Accessed 03-01-2018].

Guadagno, R. E., Okdie, B. M., and Eno, C. A. (2008), Who blogs? Personality predictors of blogging, *Computers in Human Behavior*, **24**(5), 1993–2004.

HubSpot (2017), 2017 Marketing statistics, trends and data - the ultimate list of marketing Stats, https://www.hubspot.com/marketing-statistics, [Accessed 21 June 2017].

IDM (2017) https://www.theidm.com/become-a-member

Internet Live Stats (2017), Total number of websites - Internet Live Stats, http://www.internetlivestats.com/total-number-of-websites, [Accessed 10 July 2017]

Lambrecht, A. and Misra, K. (2016) Fee or free: when should firms charge for online content?, *Management Science*, **63**(4), 1150-1165.

Peters, T. (1997), The brand called You, *Fast Company*, **10**(10), 83-90.

Pew Research Centre (2010), 65% of Internet users have paid for online content, http://www.pewinternet.org/files/old-media//Files/Reports/2010/PIP-Paying-for-Online-Content_final.pdf [Accessed 11 December 2017].

Rizky, A. and Pardamean, B. (2016). Critical success factor in monetizing blogs, *TELKOMNIKA*, **14**(2), 757–761.

Schiano, D. J., Nardi, B. A., Gumbrecht, M. and Swartz, L. (2004), Blogging by the Rest of Us. In *CHI'04 extended abstracts on Human Factors in Computing Systems*, 1143-1146.

Sepp, M., Liljander, V. and Gummerus, J. (2011), Private bloggers' motivations to produce content–a gratifications theory perspective, *Journal of Marketing Management*, **27**(13-14), 1479-503.

Statista, (2016), Google's ad revenue from 2001 to 2016 (in billion U.S. dollars), https://www.statista.com/statistics/266249/advertising-revenue-of-google/ [Accessed 11 December 2017].

Wang, C.L., Zhang, Y., Ye, L.R. and Nguyen, D.D. (2005), Subscription to fee-based online services: what makes consumer pay for online content?, *Journal of Electronic Commerce Research*, **6**(4), 304-311.

Wordpress (2017). Stats, https://wordpress.com/activity/, [Accessed 21 June 2017]

12

Index

Printed in the United States
By Bookmasters